Between Two Armies
       At Fredericksburg

BETWEEN TWO ARMIES AT FREDERICKSBURG

THE CAPTAIN BENJAMIN FRANKLIN WELLS FAMILY PAPERS

Edited and Annotated by
Rebecca Campbell Light

The American History Company
Fredericksburg, Virginia

Copyright 2010 by Rebecca Campbell Light
All rights reserved, no part of this book may be reproduced in any form or by any method without permission in writing.

Published by
The American History Company
Fredericksburg, Virginia 22401

Cover design by Amanda Guyton

Printed in the United States of America

First Edition

Library of Congress Cataloging-in-Publication Data
ISBN 2-370000-016669

Light, Rebecca Campbell
    Between Two Armies at Fredericksburg:
    The Benjamin Franklin Wells Family Papers
    Edited and Annotated by Rebecca Campbell Light--1st Ed.
    Includes bibliographical references and index.

Contents

Dedication	vii
Illustrations	ix
Preface	xvii
Acknowledgements	xxi
Chapter I – Fredericksburg on the Brink of War	1
Chapter II – Sping 1861: The Captain Wells Family	7
Chapter III – Civil War!	24
Chapter IV – Fredericksburg 'a Captured Town'	45
Chapter V – A Northern Spy Boards at the Wells' House	67
Chapter VI – Running the Blockade	108
Chapter VII – The Northern Invaders Arrive	114
Chapter VIII – McLaws' Mississippians Defend the Town	120
Chapter IX – Between two Armies: The Bombardment	133
Chapter X – Between two Armies: The Battle	148
Chapter XI – 1863: Living in a Ruined Town	161
Chapter XII – Running the Blockade: Again	169
Chapter XIII – Trials and Disappointments	183

Chapter XIV – More Disappointments	195
Chapter XV – Release from Prison: A Family Reunited	207
Chapter XVI – Picking Up and Moving On	214
Chapter XVII – The Boy Spy Returns to Town of 'Lost Love'	220
Epilogue:	
Part I – A Family's Final Goodbyes	240
Part II – More Adventures for the 'Boy Spy'	245
Part III – Photo Gallery of the Wells House	255
Bibliography	260
Endnotes	267
Index	295

This book is dedicated to the real heroine in the Wells' family, Mary A. (Mamie) Wells Lorigan (1842-1875), for her unwavering faith and nobility of purpose. A daughter of Capt. Benjamin Franklin Wells, who was then held prisoner at Fort Henry, Maryland, she traveled the blockade between Virginia and Washington, D.C. At the White House, she gained two separate audiences with President Abraham Lincoln to plead her case on behalf of her father. A Presidential pardon for Captain Wells' release was finally signed by Lincoln just weeks before his assassination.

Illustrations

1856 Birdseye View of Fredericksburg, Virginia 1

Advertisement for Baltimore & Fredericksburg Steamboat *Patuxent* 4

Alexander Keene Phillips, owner of first dayboat service on the Rappahannock River 5

Captain Benjamin Franklin Wells' sketch of steamboat *Eureka* 7

Edward L. Henry watercolor, *Packet Boat on the Erie Canal* c.1830 9

1852 Advertisement for B. F. Wells packet boat *Northumberland* 9

1856 Daguerreotype of B. F. Wells packet boat *Antelope* 10

1856 Detail of Fredericksburg Harbor and Wharves 12

1881 Stereopticon image showing location of Benson's boarding house 14

Benson's boarding house (Wells House) on Sophia (Water) Street 15

1861 Advertisement announcing steamboat *Eureka's* schedule 16

Rev. Archibald A. Hodge, Fredericksburg Presbyterian Church 21

1881 Stereopticon image, Fredericksburg Presbyterian Church 22

Montgomery Slaughter, the 'War Mayor' of Fredericksburg 23

Brig. General Daniel Ruggles, First Commander of Virginia Forces on the Rappahannock in the Civil War 24

Virginia Governor John Letcher 26

Sketch of attack of Confederate Batteries at Aquia Creek by U.S. Vessels 30

Rose O'Neal Greenhow, Confederate spy in Old Capitol Prison 32

Richardetta (Hooe) Ruggles, wife of Gen. Ruggles with son in 1897 33

Residence of Brig. General Ruggles sacked and pillaged during Battle of Fredericksburg 34

Fredericksburg residence of Commander Matthew Fontaine Maury and Family during the Civil War 35

Betty Herndon (Maury) Maury, Civil War diarist 37

Sketch from Steamboat Schedule during the Civil War 39

1861 Harper's Weekly sketch of The *French Lady* 40

Lt. Richard Launcelot Maury and Commander Matthew Fontaine Maury 41

Captain George N. Hollins, Confederate States Navy 42

Edwin Forbes May 15, 1862 sketch of *Fredericksburg Court House occupied by Federal troops as a barracks and by the Signal Corps* 45

Edwin Forbes May 11, 1862 sketch *Remains of Burnt Steamers and Sailing Vessels on the Rappahannock* 49

1881 Stereopticon image looking East-Southeast across Caroline Street in direction of town wharf 50

Captain B. F. Wells signature certifying sketch of *Eureka* 52

General Marsena Rudolph Patrick, USA, Provost Marshal of

Fredericksburg 57

The Farmers Bank of Virginia, General Patrick's Headquarters 58

Edwin Forbes May 6, 1862 sketch *Rebuilding the railroad bridge across the Rappahannock to Fredericksburg, Va.* 59

John Lawrence "Jack" Marye Jr. of "Brompton" 60

Sketch of *Explosion of a Confederate Magazine near Fredericksburg, Va. caused by a torpedo, May 25th, 1862* 61

1881 Stereopticon image, Fredericksburg Court House 63

Ann Eliza (Pleasants) Gordon, wife of Douglas H. Gordon Esq. 64

Provost Marshal General Patrick, mounted up 65

Joseph Andrew (Orton) Kerbey, Northern Spy 67

Brig. General USV Theophilus F. Rodenbough, USA 70

Honorable John Covode of Pennsylvania 72

Colonel Herman Haupt, USA, Chief of Military Construction and Transportation 72

Colonel Henry C. Hoffman, USA, Commander 23rd N.Y. Vol. 82

1671 Tombstone of Capt. Wells' ancestor William Wells the 1st of Southold, Long Island, N.Y. 83

Colonel Henry C. Hoffman, USA, in camp 84

Wartime view of Mary Ball Washington tomb and monument 85

9th New York Infantry, "Hawkins Zouaves" on parade 86

Colonel Lafayette C. Baker, USA, U. S. War Department Chief of Detectives 88

Wells House, interior center stairway 90

Colonel Daniel C. McCallum, USA, Superintendent of U.S. Military Railroads 98

Thomas T. Eckert, Chief of U.S. War Department Telegraph Office 101

Edwin M. Stanton, U.S. Secretary of War 102

1881 Stereopticon image of Fredericksburg looking Northeast across Chatham Bridge 112

Brig. General William Barksdale's Mississippi Brigade pickets, on burned railroad bridge in Fredericksburg 120

Major General Lafayette McLaws, CSA 122

Alfred R. Waud sketch, *Harper's Weekly* of Dec. 13, 1862: *Union and Rebel Soldiers on Opposite Sides of the Burned Railway Bridge* 123

The Peel Brothers of Mississippi (c.1860 photo) 125

Page from letter written by Dr. Robert Hunter Peel, 19th Mississippi Infantry Surgeon 127

Dr. Robert H. Peel and brother, Adjutant Albert Peel, CSA 128

Captain Silvanus J. Quinn, CSA, Barksdale's Brigade, 13th Rgt. I (in later life) 130

Pvt. Rufus Bainbridge Merchant, Cobbs Georgia Legion, Cavalry, xiii

Cobbs Brigade (in later life) 131

Masthead of *Fredericksburg Star,* Rufus B. Merchant, Editor and Owner 132

Map of the 1862 Battle of Fredericksburg 133

D. E. Henderson painting of Fredericksburg refugees in woods 135

Henri Lovie sketch: *Bombardment of Fredericksburg by the Army of The Potomac, Dec. 11, 1862* 137

The Wells House cellar fireplace, Fredericksburg, Virginia (1966) 138

The Wells House cellar fireplace, Fredericksburg, Virginia (2003) 139

Henri Lovie sketch: *Volunteer Storming Parties Crossing the Rappahannock* 141

Henri Lovie sketch: *Burnside's Army Crossing the Rappahannock* 142

Front Entrance of Wells House 143

Alfred R. Waud sketch, *Harper's Weekly* of Jan. 3, 1863: *Our Soldiers in the Streets of Fredericksburg* 144

Arthur Lumley sketch: *Union Troops Pillaging the Wallace House* 145

Henri Lovie sketch: *Destruction of Fredericksburg by Union Bombardment and Looting* 146

Chapter of Mamie Wells *Reminiscences: The Battle,* on front page of *Fredericksburg Star, July 18,* 1888 147

Brig. General James Nagle, USA, Cdr. 9th Army Corp., 2nd Div., lst Brigade and Colonel Joshua K. Sigfried, USA, Cdr., 48th Pennsylvania Infantry 149

Captain James Wren, USA, Co. B, 48th Pennsylvania Infantry 150

Henri Lovie sketch: *Grand Army Recrossing the Rappahannock, Dec. 15, 1862* 152

Extract of Mamie Wells letter published in Richmond paper, Jan. 2, 1863 155

1887 Redwood sketch: "Barksdale's Mississippians opposing the laying of pontoon bridge" 157

Fredericksburg Houses Destroyed in Battle 160

Selling of rats 161

Timothy H. O'Sullivan photo: *View of town from East Bank of the Rappahannock, Feb. 1863* 162

Small boat on river bank and Timothy H. O'Sullivan photo of pontoon boat 163

Rappahanock River landings map: route of Mrs. Wells and children to Lancaster County, Va. in October 1863 165

Old Capitol Prison, Washington, D.C. 169

U.S.S. Louisiana from *Frank Leslie's Illustrated* 182

Chapter of Mamie Wells *Reminiscences: Trials and Disappointments* on front page of *Fredericksburg Star,* Aug. 1, 1888 182

Fort McHenry Prison where Captain Wells was held prisoner 186

Exterior of the White House c.1860 187

Anthony Berger photo of Abraham Lincoln, Feb. 9, 1864 190

Mathew Brady photo of Henry J. Raymond, founder and Editor of the *New York Times,* during the Civil War 198

Wartime View of Northwest façade of the White House 201

Alexander Gardner photo of Abraham Lincoln, Feb. 5, 1865 208

U.S. War Department Pardon of *Franklin Wells* and release from prison, dated Feb. 18, 1865 213

Mattituck House Hotel, Long Island, N.Y., managed by Capt. Wells postwar 214

1882 Advertisement in Long Island, N.Y. paper for Capt. Wells packet steamer *Jane Teed,* named in honor of his wife 216

1888 U.S. House of Representatives, A BILL for relief of Benjamin F. Wells Sr. 218

1887 Review of Kerbey's book *The Boy Spy* in Long Island paper 219

The Exchange Hotel and Museum, Postwar Fredericksburg, Va. 223

1888 News article reporting donation of 12-lb. cannonball fired into Wells House on Dec. 11, 1862 224

Front porch of Wells House 227

Juliet Annie Downs, inherited Wells House postwar 228

Juliet Annie Downs 1897 wedding invitation addressed to Major J. O. Kirby (sic) 229

Martha Stephens' House on Sunken Road c. 1865 236

Martha Stephens' monument: "Friend of the Confederate Soldier" 236

The Gunnery Spring: "Whoever partakes is fated to return again" 238

Tombstone of S. Eugenia "Geno" Wells 240

Tombstone of Jane Teed Wells 241

1889 Obituary of Mrs. Jane Teed Wells 242

Tombstone of Capt. Benjamin F. Wells 243

Photo of Major Kerbey c.1911 245

1900 U.S. Senate, A BILL for the relief of Joseph Orton Kerby 249

1906 Book Review of Kerbey's *Land of To-Morrow* 251

Portrait of Kerbey, c.1905 252

Ilustration from Kerbey book *The Boy Spy,* showing gravestone epitaph inscription: "The Boy Spy" 254

Photographs of the Wells House 255

Preface

One of the most unusual stories to come out of my years of research into the experiences of civilians during the Civil War years in the Fredericksburg, Virginia area is that of the Captain Benjamin Franklin "Frank" Wells' family.

Just prior to the outbreak of the war, Captain Wells moved his family and his steamer *Eureka* from Georgetown, D.C. to Fredericksburg, Virginia, with the belief that there would be no war between the states. Beginning in 1861, his passenger and freight steamer operation on the Rappahannock River was initially a financial success, with few inconvenient "impressments" by Confederate forces. Leading up to the first Union army occupation of Fredericksburg in the spring of 1862 however, the *Eureka* was seized by the Potomac Flotilla as a "prize of war." Armed with a light 12-pounder artillery piece, the *Eureka* served as a Union gunboat for the duration of the conflict.

Repairs to the destroyed railroad line between Aquia Creek and Union army-occupied Fredericksburg and the rail bridge over the Rappahannock were finally completed in May 1862. Carrying his letter of introduction from Washington, D.C., a youthful and adventurous spy (later known as "The Boy Spy") named Joseph Orton Kerbey rolled in to work undercover as a civilian employee of the U.S. military railroad. Joining a Union army officer and a northern salesman as boarders in Captain Wells' house, Kerbey soon became enamored with the young Wells' daughter, Geno Wells.

Caught between the two armies leading up to the December 1862 Battle of Fredericksburg, the Wells family sought refuge in the basement of their house where they remained for five days and nights. In a letter published in a Richmond, Virginia newspaper in January 1863, Mamie Wells described in detail their ordeal during the bombardment and battle.

Charged with running the blockade twice and carrying supplies to the Confederate government, Captain Wells was imprisoned the second time with a three-year sentence of hard labor at Fort McHenry, Maryland. Mamie Wells crossed Union lines to gather necessary signatures for a petition to present to the president to secure her father's freedom. She twice gained an audience with Abraham Lincoln before finally receiving a presidential pardon for her father's release on February 18, 1865 – less than two months before the president was assassinated.

With the help of Kerbey, Captain Wells in 1887 petitioned the U.S. Congress for reimbursement for his loss of the *Eureka* during the war. In 1889, the Fredericksburg *Star* reported that the two were seen back together on the streets of Fredericksburg:

Revisit of a Former Old and Honored Citizen
The patriarchal old gentleman seen on our streets with Major J. O. Kerbey the last few days is Capt. B. Frank Wells, of Long Island, N.Y. The older citizens all recognize in this silvered, but active and vigorous old gentleman the figure of a well and favorably known citizen of the town, during the 'days that tried men's souls.'

The generation that has grown up here since the war would find the true history of this former citizen of our town as interesting, perhaps, as any of the stories of modern fiction. His life has, indeed, been wondrous wonderful.

The readers of the Star *will recall the deeply interesting story of Mamie Wells, that we published last summer, which details one eventful part of the Captain's family history. More recently we have had the pleasure of reviewing a romance of "Secret Service and Secret Love," the scene of which is located in Fredericksburg during the war, the male characters being well known officers of both Federal and Confederate armies, and the charming lady residents of town. The title is "Geno"– not an ideal name nor an ideal character—but a true and* *thrilling story of the war. The bitter and the sweet of realism, with the bark on. The father of Geno is Captain Wells, but the <u>Star</u> hopes soon to publish some of the advance sheets of Major Kerbey's interesting and true story.*

Aside from the desire to revisit old scenes, sadly and sorrowfully familiar to Captain Wells, and to meet once more with those who shared the privations and hardships of the war, he comes here to look up from among the survivors some testimony in regard to the seizure of his boat by the U.S. Government in May 1862.

Before the war, Captain Wells brought to the Rappahannock River a new steamer, the "Eureka," and ran her with financial success to himself, and satisfaction to the people of the town and along the river country below…

Left in war-torn Fredericksburg in the fall of 1863 with her husband still in prison, Jane Wells and her eight children gathered up what they could fit into a pontoon boat. Towed by a canoe, they set out on a harrowing six days' and five nights' trip down the Rappahannock to "Monaskon," a steamboat landing in Lancaster County, Virginia. Upon their arrival, they were taken in by a black family then residing in the mansion house.

Sadly, within a few years after the close of the war, Captain and Mrs. Wells buried seven of their children, lost to the effects of exposure during the December 1862 shelling of Fredericksburg and subsequent deprivations during the war.

Where they relate to the Wells' family, the post-war writings of Major J. O. Kerbey (the Northern spy) are woven into this book's narrative. Kerbey wrote of his wartime romance with Geno Wells while a boarder in the Wells' home in *The Boy Spy* (1889), and his part in causing the near arrest of Captain Wells in the summer of 1862. In a second book, *On the Warpath: A Journey Over the Historic Grounds of the Late Civil War* (1890), Kerbey details his return to the town of 'lost love' after the war, and his visits with the family then living in the old Wells' House.

Soon after Kerbey's book *The Boy Spy* came out, a Fredericksburg hotel and museum began receiving visitor inquiries about the Wells' family and where they had lived during the late war. A newcomer and not being familiar with the Wells name, the Exchange Hotel's proprietor began making inquiries of the town's older citizens. Wartime Mayor Montgomery Slaughter observed to him *Oh yes, I knew them very well – they were very sweet girls.* The proprietor, doubling as a tour guide, soon added to his published list of local attractions: *The Wells House, home of 'Geno,' the war heroine of the Boy Spy narrative.*

Papers of the Captain Benjamin Franklin Wells family survive today, leaving a record of the many challenges they faced during the Civil War. The National Archives in Washington, D.C. houses the 1865 "Petition of Mary [Mamie] Wells to Abraham Lincoln" and the 1887 "Petition of B. F. Wells to Congress" in which he was seeking reimbursement for Federal seizure of his steamer the *Eureka* in 1862. Mamie Wells' *Reminiscences of the Late War,* published posthumously as a weekly series in the Fredericksburg *Star* in 1888, further document the trials and hardships the family endured.

Lastly, the Wells House stands today in silent testimony, bearing witness to "the days that tried men's souls."

Acknowledgements

Much gratitude goes to my friend Lee Brady, former owner of the Wells' House, for making her home available for our research and allowing Robert A. Martin to take the photographs found in this book.

I am deeply indebted to John J. Hennessy, Chief Historian of the Fredericksburg and Spotsylvania National Military Park, for reviewing the manuscript and for his very helpful suggestions. Also providing expert advice were noted author/historians Donald C. Pfanz and Frank O'Reilly, who helped identify Union officers in the neighborhood of the Wells' House during the 1862 Battle of Fredericksburg.

A debt of gratitude also goes to Barbara Pratt Willis, Chief Librarian of the Virginiana Room of The Central Rappahannock Regional Library for her review of the manuscript, providing knowledgeable fine-tuning on local history.

When I was contacted by Fredericksburg native Judith (Hawkins) Barton, a descendant of Juliet Anne Perry, purchaser of the Wells' House in 1863, I was elated with her news: Passed down and in her possession was a photograph of her Great Aunt Juliet Annie Downs who inherited the Wells' House, and Juliet's 1897 wedding invitation addressed to Major J. O. Kerbey (the Northern spy), both shared for use in this book.

I was equally happy to receive a call from the late Virginia Lindlay Goolrick Hinkle, a descendant of Brig. General Daniel Ruggles, CSA, a Fredericksburg resident named Commander of Virginia State Forces on the Rappahannock at the beginning of the Civil War. Hanging on her wall was a handsome portrait of General Ruggles, which she graciously allowed to have photographed for use this book.

Much appreciation also goes to the Lucerne County Historical Society, Wilkes-Barre, Pennsylvania, and in particular F. Charles Petrillo Esq., who sent a photograph of the 1856 daguerreotype of Captain Wells' packet boat *Antelope* in Wilkes-Barre, in addition to an advertisement for his packet boat *Northumberland.*

Helpful also was Mrs. Roberta M. Hoffman of Elmira, N.Y., widow of Allyn W. Hoffman, a descendant of Colonel Henry C. Hoffman, USA, Commander of the 23rd N.Y. Infantry, who boarded at his old friend Captain Wells' house during the Union Army occupation of Fredericksburg in the summer of 1862. Mrs. Hoffman put me in touch with Richard S. Buchanan, present owner of Colonel Hoffman's former home in Elmira, who was kind enough to research the Colonel's personal letters written from Virginia during the war.

Jeffrey M. Walden of the Mattituck-Laurel Library in Mattituck, Long Island, New York, located a newspaper obituary of Captain Wells in the Southold N.Y. Library. Mr. Walden was kind enough to take gravestone photographs. He also found a Long Island newspaper critique of Kerbey's book *The Boy* Spy, mentioning "its heroine Geno Wells," and making reference to when Captain Wells conducted the Mattituck House there after the war.

Finally, I wish to thank my husband, Otis T. Light, the "light of my life," for bearing with me while I indulge in my passion for local history, and for his encouragement and support throughout the duration of this project.

Rebecca Campbell Light
Fredericksburg, Virginia
March, 2011

Chapter I – Fredericksburg on the Brink of War
✢

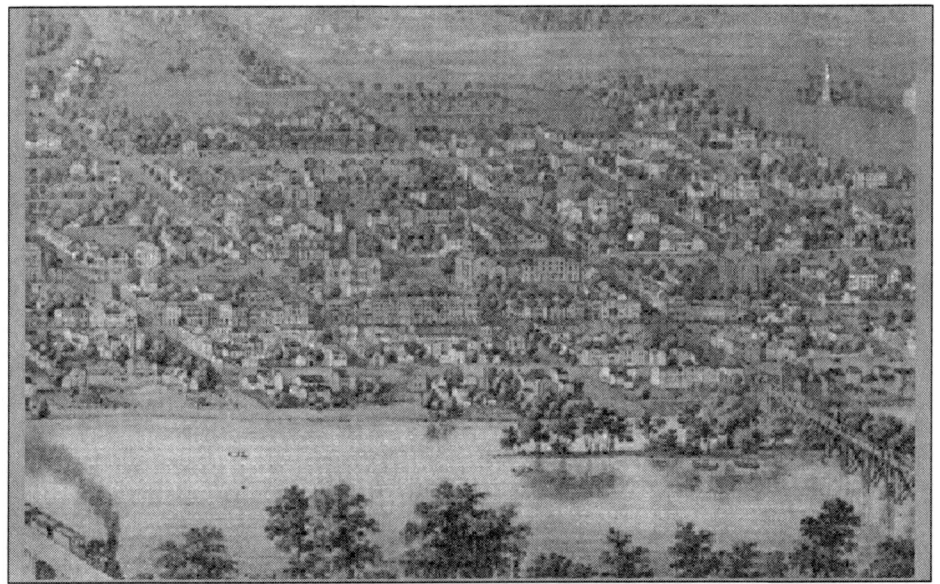

The Wells House faces the Rappahannock River at the southern tip of Scott's Island
Birdseye View of Fredericksburg, Virginia, 1856

(E. Sachse & Co., Baltimore, Md.)

Upon returning from a 4th of July steamboat excursion on the Rappahannock River in 1859, a Fredericksburg resident wrote a letter to the local paper describing a trip down river:

…The steamer Virginia[1] left her wharf and glided beautifully down the river 'like a thing of life,' at every turn of which scenery, enchanting and lovely, was revealed to view – fields laden with harvested wheat, flourishing corn, meadows newly mown, forests of living green waving us a welcome as we passed beneath their fragrant shade – enlivened with feathered songsters pouring forth their grateful praise, in rich melody, or gaily skipping from branch to branch displaying their rich plumage amid the dark foliage – beautiful residences here and there dotting the winding shores of our own Rappahannock -- all conspired to present a picture as beautiful as it

was varied…we reached Tappahannock about 4 o'clock, where we were saluted by several rounds of cannon and welcomed by the citizens…[2]

Five months before Abraham Lincoln was elected President of the United States, journalist George Fitzhugh[3], a resident of Port Royal on the Rappahannock River in nearby Caroline County, Virginia, visited Fredericksburg. His impressions of the town in June 1860 were published in *DeBow's Review*, a journal of agricultural, commercial and industrial progress in the Southern states, and in a Fredericksburg newspaper the following month:

Our Visit to Fredericksburg. – We have just returned from a visit of two weeks to Fredericksburg. It has been six or seven years since we have been there…we find the town continues slowly to grow and improve. Fredericksburg has 'seen the elephant' without damage to her nerves, and may now look confidently forward to better days. The removal, or rather abolition of the old chancery court, it was predicted, would ruin her. – She withstood it, and continued in a slow but steady course of improvement. Then the railroad passing through her from Richmond to Acquia Creek, was portentous of evil; yet it harmed her not. Next the Central and Alexandria and Orange roads, cut off almost every inch of her back country, and now her ruin seemed inevitable.

But she is still alive and growing; houses to rent can scarcely be had; new houses are going up and manufactures starting into life. They have at a heavy outlay, brought excellent water-power to the town, and we observed a very large manufactory nearly completed, which will be worked by this power. At another point a large shoe factory will soon be in operation. Her iron foundries have already acquired quite an extensive Southern reputation. Fredericksburg has a population equal in all respects to any of the same number in the Union. Despite of the let-alone policy of Virginia, hitherto, through the great energy and public spirit of her people she has been able to hold her own. Now that the policy is changed, and that State protection to state interests has become the order of the day, she may look forward with certainty to happier days.

...The situation of the town is beautiful and healthful, and its society the most polished and attractive with which we are acquainted, because it is thoroughly Virginian. It is her attractiveness, growing out of the high character of her population, that is the secret of her wonderful vitality. People go there to live on their incomes, to educate their families, and to enjoy intellectual, moral, and religious social intercourse. This sustains the town. The family stocks in Fredericksburg are, in talent, genius, and morality, far above the average, and their natural good qualities are carefully cultivated by excellent educations, in which morality and religion are equally attended to with Greek and Latin. The grandparents of most of the citizens probably lived and died in this town. A majority of the people are of English descent, but in no place with which we are acquainted is there so large an infusion of Scottish blood. A few families are of Irish and French Huguenot extract. Recently a considerable number of Germans have settled in the town. Society is, however, made up chiefly of persons whose ancestors for many generations were native born Virginians. The citizens are much connected and inter-related, and one is welcomed with a sort of family, familiar, and affectionate address, which, coming from a people habitually refined, is extremely winning. In some of the less frequented parts of town, we were particularly struck by the tabby-cat appearance of the shop men. They sunned themselves in front of their stores, where we are sure we saw them sunning themselves thirty years ago...a customer seemed to embarrass and disturb them; yet, with a sort of lofty Castilian politeness, they waited on him, and then returned to sunning themselves...Nowhere in town are they a busy, fussy people...Business is looked upon as decidedly ungenteel and to be disengaged the height of respectability.[4]

Up until this time, mostly Baltimore-based steamboats monopolized the Rappahannock River trade.[5] Only within the past decade had sporadic dayboat service appeared on the Rappahannock River. Inheriting his late father's shipping business acumen,

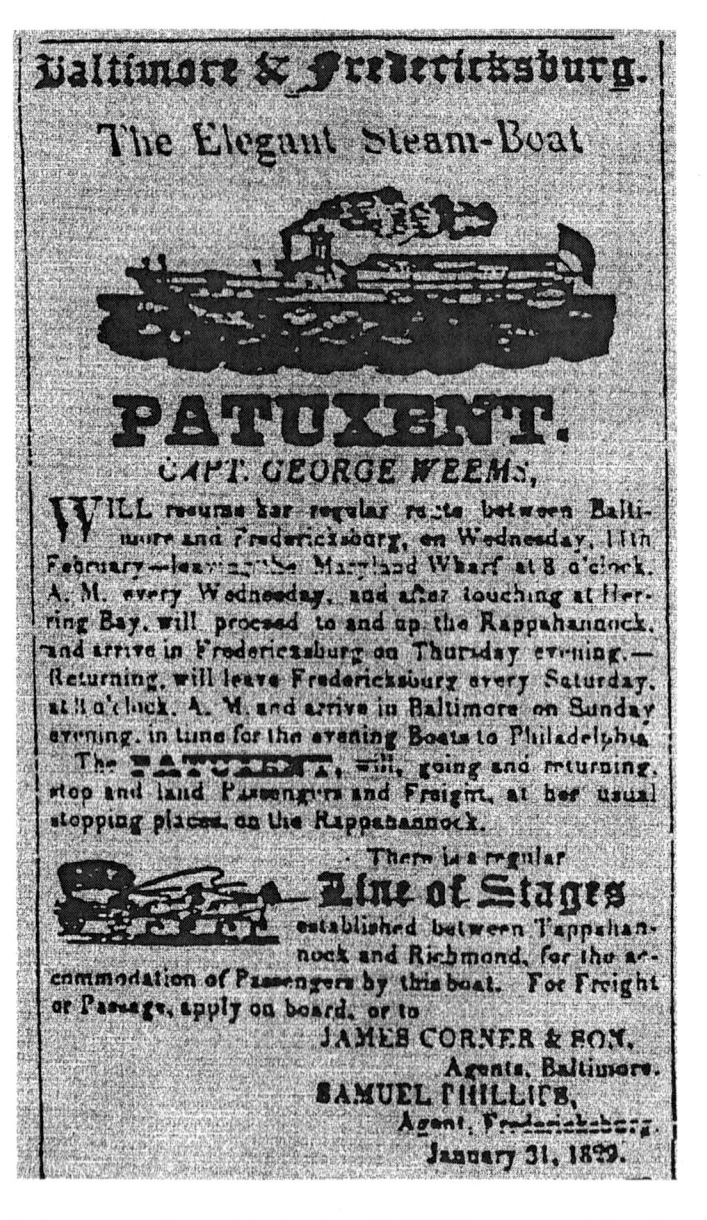

> **Baltimore & Fredericksburg.**
>
> The Elegant Steam-Boat
>
> **PATUXENT.**
>
> **CAPT. GEORGE WEEMS,**
>
> WILL resume her regular route between Baltimore and Fredericksburg, on Wednesday, 11th February—leaving the Maryland Wharf at 8 o'clock. A. M. every Wednesday, and after touching at Herring Bay, will proceed to and up the Rappahannock, and arrive in Fredericksburg on Thursday evening.— Returning, will leave Fredericksburg every Saturday, at 8 o'clock, A. M. and arrive in Baltimore on Sunday evening, in time for the evening Boats to Philadelphia.
>
> The PATUXENT, will, going and returning, stop and land Passengers and Freight, at her usual stopping places on the Rappahannock.
>
> There is a regular Line of Stages established between Tappahannock and Richmond, for the accommodation of Passengers by this boat. For Freight or Passage, apply on board, or to
>
> JAMES CORNER & SON,
> Agents, Baltimore.
> SAMUEL PHILLIPS,
> Agent, Fredericksburg.
> January 31, 1839.

Fredericksburg merchant Alexander K. Phillips owned the first dayboat service on the Rappahannock River. Purchasing the 103-foot sidewheeler *FOX* in August 1853, Phillips established a river route between Fredericksburg and the mouth of the Rappahannock.[6] Tragedy soon struck the next month when the *FOX* was discovered on fire at the Fredericksburg wharf, finally sinking to the waterline.[7]

ALEXANDER K. PHILLIPS

Prosperous Fredericksburg merchant Alexander K. Phillips owned the first dayboat service on the Rappahannock River. He became first President of The National Bank of Fredericksburg in 1865.

(Photo courtesy Lemuel W. Houston, "A Bank for Fredericksburg," 1989)

The following year, the Norfolk-based Old Dominion Steamship Company offered their steamer *William Selden* to operate twice weekly between Fredericksburg and the mouth of the Rappahannock, in addition to weekly service between Norfolk and Fredericksburg. Proving too large for the intended service, they replaced her with the *Joseph E. Coffee,* a smaller sidewheel river steamer. The *Coffee's* twice-a-week service initially made a profit, but lack of trade between Rappahannock river towns and Norfolk caused Old Dominion Steamship Company to withdraw her from the route.[8]

Captain Benjamin Franklin Wells of Georgetown, D.C. was the third to offer a *long sought after* riverboat on the Rappahannock. Wells had been engaged in a not so lucrative packet boat operation on the C&O Canal. Into his third year at Georgetown and still not showing enough profit to support his large family, Wells packed up his steamboat *Eureka* and headed south to Fredericksburg in the spring of 1861.

Sadly, Fitzhugh's prediction that the town could *confidently... look forward with certainty to happier days* did not survive the year.

Chapter II – Spring 1861: The Wells Family Arrives in Fredericksburg

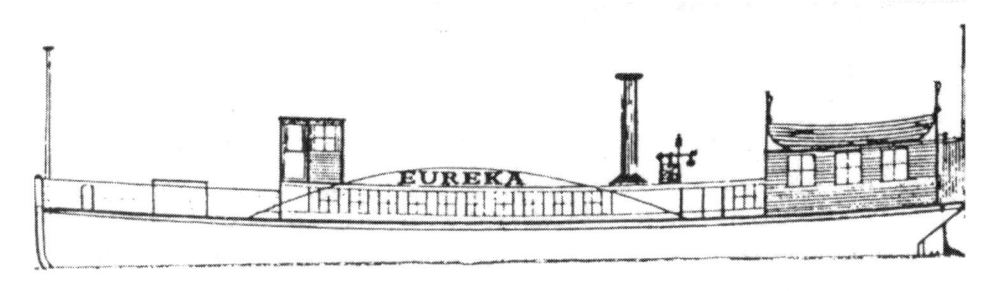

Steamer *Eureka* built by Capt. Wells the winter of 1860-61.

Captain Wells Sketch included in his 1887 Petition to Congress. (National Archives)

>   *...In the Spring of 1861 about the 1st of March I took my steamboat the Eureka (then new) to the Rappahannock River in Virginia...I went to the Rappahannock solely for the purpose of making a living for myself and family...In common with a large number of the citizens of Virginia I was to believe that the State would not secede, and on these presentations decided to remain in Virginia with my boat...As the best portion of Virginians were for Union we got along very well and believed there would be no War, but everybody knows what followed. The 75 thousand men were called for and the State ceded. I was looked upon by a portion of the Virginians as a damned Yankee...*
>   Captain Benjamin Franklin Wells in 1887 Petition to Congress

Back in Georgetown, D.C., in the fall and winter of 1860-1861, Captain "Frank" Wells built the *Eureka,* a sleek passenger and freight steamer. Complete with elegant cabins and a ladies' saloon, he put the finishing touches on the steamer in early February 1861. During this same time, the Peace Convention called for by Virginia was held in Washington, D.C., and the convention of seceded states was meeting in Montgomery, Alabama.

Just days before Abraham Lincoln would give his inaugural address, Captain Wells and his *Eureka* crew, with sixteen-year-old Ben Wells Jr. as its engineer, steamed down the Potomac River out of Washington, D.C. and up the Rappahannock River to Fredericksburg, Virginia. This move would be the beginning of an initially successful twice-a-week day-boat line between Fredericksburg and Tappahannock, Virginia.

Of Puritan stock descending from William Wells I (1638-1671) of Southold, Long Island, N.Y., Benjamin Franklin Wells was born on November 27, 1814, in the village of Southold in Mattituck, New Suffolk County, at the eastern end of Long Island, N.Y.[9] At its settlement in 1640, the churches were of the New England Puritans, many of whom were Presbyterian.[10]

In 1836, Benjamin F. Wells married seventeen-year-old Jane Teed in Somers, New York. The couple moved first to New Jersey and then Wilkes-Barre, Pennsylvania, where most of their children were born. There, Wells operated a packet-boat in the Susquehanna River and Wyoming Valley area. As described in 1842, Wells' canal boat was a popular attraction in Wilkes-Barre featuring sumptuous meals:
> *...The canal then raged and the canal horn quickened the heartbeats of the people as the flying packet-boat, Capt. Wells commanding, would proudly come into port. A distinguished mark of a heavy man about town then was to be able to rush on board, shake familiarly the captain's hand and indulge in one of the boat's gorgeous meals for the sum of 25 cents.*[11]

E. L. Henry watercolor c. 1830 (From the Collection of the Rochester City Hall Photo Lab)

GRAND EXCURSIONS!

TWICE A WEEK,

Between Wilkes-Barre and Northumberland,

During the months of September and October, 1852.

THE Packet Boat NORTHUMBERLAND, Capt. G. Tred, will leave Wilkes-Barre on Monday and Thursday of each week, commencing on Thursday Sept 9th, as follows:

Leave Wilkes-Barre at   4 o'clock A. M.
"   Berwick,   10   "   "
"   Bloomsburg,   12½ "   "
"   Danville,   3½ "   P. M.
Arrive at Northumberland, 6   "   "
Leave Northumberland at 4 o'clock A. M.
"   Danville,   6½ "   "
"   Bloomsburg,   9½ "   "
"   Berwick,   12½ "   M.
Arrive at Wilkes-Barre,   8   "   P. M.

Fare through each way, Two Dollars---Way fare in Proportion.

Ladies and Gentlemen of Northumberland, Danville, Cattawissa, Bloomsburg, Berwick, and all the intermediate places, will find this a rare chance to visit the Wyoming Valley, with its beautiful scenery and extensive coal fields, and citizens of the valley will also find it a beautiful excursion to traverse the entire length of the North Branch to Northumberland.

The above arrangements make a perfect connection with Packets running from Northumberland to Harrisburg, and those running up the West Branch to Williamsport; also, at Wilkes-Barre with the Packet and Stage running to Scranton three times each day, connecting with the Lackawanna and Western Railroad running into western New York, and making only ten miles staging between Harrisburg and the Great Erie Railroad.

N. B.--There will be an Omnibus run between Wilkes-Barre and Pittston, in place of the Packet, on Mondays, Tuesdays, Thursdays and Fridays, and the Packet will run as before, on Wednesday and Saturday.

B. F. WELLS,
Proprietor.

Wilkes-Barre, Sept. 8, 1852--tf.

Proprietor B. F. Wells' advertisement in *Luzerne Union* newspaper, Wilkes-Barre, Pa., Sept. 8, 1852. (Courtesy   F. Charles Petrillo Esq.)

By the fall of 1852, Proprietor B. F. Wells was advertising *Grand Excursions! --on his Packet Boat* **Northumberland**, with his brother-in-law, Captain Gilbert G. Teed,[12] as ship's captain. The fall excursions on Wells' packet boat *Northumberland* offered a rare chance to visit Pennsylvania's Wyoming Valley with its beautiful views.

1856 Inaugural run of Capt. Wells packet boat *Antelope*, Wilkes-Barre, Pennsylvania

(Daguerreotype by Charles F. Cook, courtesy Luzerne County Historical Society, Wilkes-Barre, Pennsylvania.)

Wells began operating a stagecoach line over the mountains in 1848 and for about ten years continued staging and packet-boating in that section of Pennsylvania. In the 1850 Wilkes-Barre census Wells listed his occupation as "Innkeeper," housing a bartender, two hostlers (stablemen), three stage drivers, and seven guests.

Wilkes-Barre daguerreotyper Charles F. Cook was on hand on April 28, 1856 to photograph the inaugural run of Captain Wells' newly built passenger canal boat ***Antelope*** (see above), with the local paper reporting events:

*New Packet boat – Increased Speed!! On and after Monday, April 28, 1856 the new packet boat **Antelope** will commence her regular trips between Wilkes-Barre and Rupert....* In addition, reporting one week later: *The Packet made its first regular trip on Monday crowded with passengers. The German Band was on board and added to the liveliness of the scene as the **Antelope** left the wharf...*[13]

Captain Wells was awarded the mail run between Northumberland and Wilkes-Barre, Pa., but when the Lackawanna & Bloomsburg Railroad was completed in late 1857, his contract was revoked and given to the railroad. He then sold his horses and stagecoaches and took the *Antelope* to Philadelphia where he had it converted to steam power.

The family then moved to Georgetown, D.C. in 1858, where the Captain ran his packet-boat on the Chesapeake & Ohio Canal. In June 1858, he placed an advertisement for steamer *Antelope* to operate on the C&O Canal out of Washington, D.C.[14] Originating from the Rock Creek basin in Georgetown, the steamer's destination was Harpers Ferry, Va., a distance of sixty miles and back. The schedule was three trips a week for three seasons (1858-1860). His contract[15] for the 1860 season was eight hundred dollars -- from which he realized no profit.

The Captain's next move in early 1861 was south to Virginia to try his hand at operating his new steamboat the *Eureka* on the Rappahannock River.

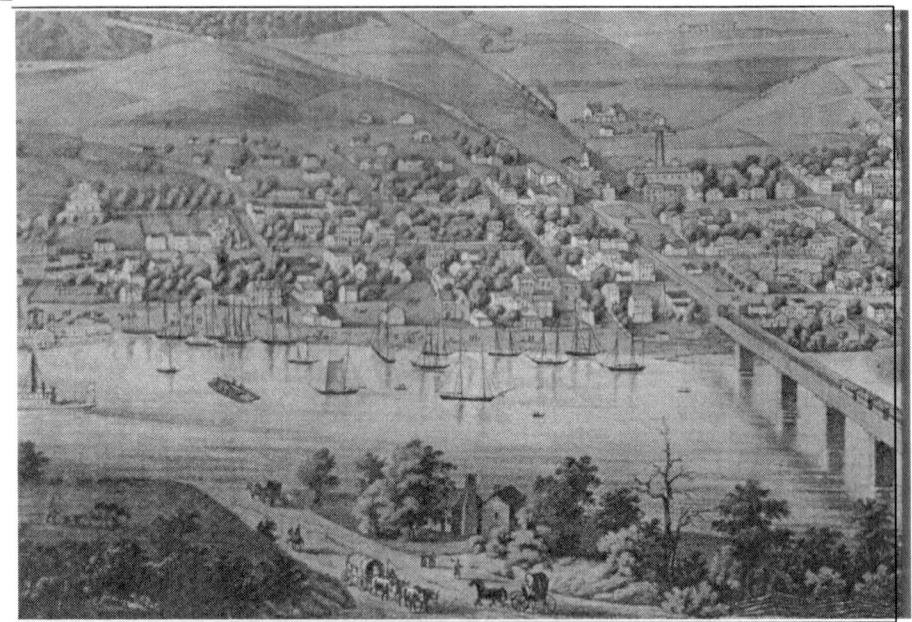

Detail of Fredericksburg Harbor and Wharves from an 1856 panoramic illustration

(E. Sachse & Co., Baltimore, Md.)

...In the spring of 1861 about the 1st of March I took my steamboat the *Eureka* (then new) to the Rappahannock River in Virginia. Her dimensions were as follows. Length – 88 ft., Depth of hold 4 ft., Width 13 ft., Size of cylinder 8x10 inches, Diameter of propeller 3 ft. 6 inches. The cost of the *Eureka* with life boat, life preservers, pump hose and furniture, etc. etc. was about $5,000. I went to the Rappahannock solely for the purpose of making a living for myself and family. And after running my boat a short time I was satisfied that I could make it profitable to locate there and run the *Eureka* on the Rappahannock. (Benjamin Franklin Wells, 1887)

Capt. Wells was issued his Certification of Inspection on the *Eureka* at the Port of Georgetown, D.C. on February 28, 1861. It was constructed of white oak, fastened with side keelsons and an iron hogging brace on each side. The machinery and boiler were built by Reany, Neafie & Co. of Philadelphia, Pa. The inventory included 1 Metal life boat; 1 force pump and 60' of hose; 2 pinchers with cables, 1 steering wheel, 1 compass; lanterns, sidelights and life preservers; funnel, steam exhaust pipe; Pilot House. Haircloth cushions were throughout the two Lounges. In the Ladies' Cabin, the cabin floors were carpeted; furnished with three stoves, tables, crockery ware, and cutlery. The *Eureka's* speed with 75 lb. of steam was 12 m.p.h.[16]

A Fredericksburg newspaper described the *Eureka* as ...*an attractive and substantial little steamer that did the accommodation business in an accommodating way all along the river. She was a neat, trim, passenger craft, with cabins elegantly upholstered and carpeted; the ladies' saloon furnished with cushioned sofas, and quite able to cope with the 'big fish' in point of speed.*[17]

Wells wrote:
In common with a large number of the citizens of Virginia, I was led to believe that the State would not secede, and on these representations decided to remain in Virginia with my boat.[18] *...When I went to Fredericksburg in March 1861 (about the first) I had the Certificate of Inspection on my Boat*[19] *and I had the Stars & Stripes also. I had a Washington man for Pilot*[20] *and he and myself were as good Union men as could be found. As the best portion of Virginians were for Union we got along very well and believed there would be no War, but everybody knows what followed. The 75 thousand men were called for and the State ceded. I was looked upon by a portion of the Virginians as a damned Yankee...*[21]

After running the *Eureka* a short time, and satisfied that he could make a profit, Wells began the search for housing for his family. As DeBows' reported the previous summer, rental houses in Fredericksburg were scarce. That same year the maiden Benson sisters, Isabella ("Miss Bella") and Mary Jane ("Miss Mary") Benson, had three boarders at their Sophia Street riverfront residence. Their boarding house advertisement ran:

To the Traveling Public—*the Misses BENSON having recently fitted up their residence at the corner of Sophia and George Streets, are now prepared to accommodate TRANSIENT BOARDERS. Their table will be furnished with the best the market will afford.*[22]

14

Above: Arrow pointing to location of the Benson sisters' boarding house (later known as the Wells House) at the corner of Sophia (Water) and George Streets.

(Detail of 1881 stereopticon image, courtesy HFFI)

The Benson sisters' boarding house rented by Capt. Wells in March 1861.

(Photo of Wells House courtesy *The Free Lance Star*, Feb. 18, 1966)

    In January 1861 however Mary Jane Benson was forced to put up her personal property as security for debts.[23] By March, the sisters had given up on transient boarders and turned the Sophia Street house and boarding operation over to Captain Wells. He was fortunate to find the ideal house to suit his family's needs. As an experienced innkeeper, he saw it sufficient to accommodate several boarders in addition to his own family of ten.

> A RIVER BOAT.—The Steamboat Eureka is announced to run regularly between Fredericksburg and Tappahannock, as a river boat, commencing on Thursday the 11th of April, To leave Fredericksburg, Mondays and Thursdays at 7, A. M. To leave Tappahannock Tuesdays and Saturdays. Let the merchants and public bestir themselves in behalf of the river boat. It is a desideratum long sought after and now offered without any capital on their part.—

Steamboat *Eureka* schedule announced in the *Fredericksburg News,* April 16, 1861.

The very week of the Eureka's planned inaugural run, the area was deluged by a heavy storm:

> *On Monday evening [April 8, 1861], the Rappahannock began to rise, and continued steadily to overflow its banks till Wednesday, at noon when it reached its highest point – some thirty feet higher than the high-water mark. Many families along the riverbank were compelled to vacate; in some cases rising to the second floor of their dwelling houses …some 12" higher than the great freshet of 1814 and some two feet higher than that of 1847. (*Nearly all of the Falmouth Bridge and several sections of the Chatham Bridge were carried downriver as was the lower level of Marye's Mill torn up by the rush of the water. Havoc struck John L. Marye's millrace at Alum Springs, which was destroyed as was his corn house containing some one-hundred barrels of corn. Marye also lost a servant by the name of Seaton, who died of fright when his house became surrounded by water. On Tuesday night, the gas house at the lower end of town overflowed and cut off the supply of gas throughout the town at once. Flood damage was also great down river with wharves at

Tappahannock and Port Royal, both over 200 feet long extending into the river, washed away and carried off.) [24]

Fortunately, Captain Wells found shelter for the *Eureka* during the storm and was soon back on the river, providing timely service to those in need of transportation and provisions. On April 16, 1861, the *Fredericksburg News* ran a belated announcement of Wells twice-a-week day-boat route between Fredericksburg and Tappahannock on the Rappahannock River.[25]

In 1861, the Wells family consisted of:

- 47-year old Captain "Frank" Wells (Benjamin Franklin Wells), *a man of deepest integrity and honor, though of quick, passionate temper; he was always ready to see and do the right thing by his fellow men.* One contemporary recalled that he was highly regarded, and another that his sympathies were openly with the South; that he had been engaged on the regular underground line between Richmond and Washington and the Potomac River during the first year of the war.

- 42-year old Mrs. Jane Teed Wells was an *estimable woman* and *truly one of God's noblest Christian women,* according to her obituary. The mother of twelve children in all, she was described in 1862 *as youthful in her happy manner as her young daughters.*

- 21-year old "Sue" (Susan Frances Wells), the eldest daughter at home, had been a *belle* in Georgetown, D.C. before the war. She was described as *a born coquette, and flirting was natural to her,* fond of tormenting the Union officers *just for fun, you know.* To Union officers she insisted that she was a *Rebel,* but according to the family, when the Confederates first had possession of Fredericksburg, she was a *Union girl* to them.

- 19-year old "Mamie" (Mary A. Wells) was described as the *good girl in the family,* known for her sweet disposition. A contemporary recalled that she was *a remarkable young lady,* that *during the bombardment and battle* of Fredericksburg, *a Florence Nightengale to both sides* in ministering to the wounded. When her father was imprisoned, she ran the blockade to the north and led an effort to gain his freedom, twice visiting President Lincoln in person. Before her early death in 1875, Mamie wrote *Reminiscences of the Late War,* published posthumously in 1888.

- 17-year old "Ben" (Benjamin F. Wells Jr.), eldest son, was an engineer on the *Eureka.*

- 14-year old "Geno" (Sarah Eugenia Wells) was described in manner quite as easy and winning as her elder sisters. Captivated by her charms, an enamored boarder (Northern spy J. O. Kerbey) wrote…*Her face was sweetly intelligent and while not lacking in resolution it was marked by that shyness which belongs to young girls who are well-born and bred in comparative seclusion…Her eyes, beautiful large dark expressive, that were in themselves a soul.*

- 12-year old George T. Wells

- 10-year old Emma Wells

- 6-year old "Nellie" (Ella Augusta Wells) and

- 4-year old Nelson Thomas Wells

Within a month of the family's move to Fredericksburg, war between the north and south broke out. On April 12, 1861, Confederate batteries bombarded the Federal garrison at Fort Sumter in Charleston, S.C., the fort officially surrendering two days later.

President Lincoln on April 15, 1861, issued a Proclamation for 75,000 militiamen from all states that had not declared a secession, including Virginia. Secretary of War Simon Cameron followed the Proclamation with a telegram to Virginia Governor John Letcher to "…cause to be immediately detached from the militia of your State the quota designated in the table below…"[26].

Counseling of the recently reconvened Virginia Secession Convention, Gov. Letcher replied to Cameron: "Sir: I have received your telegram of the 15th, the genuineness of which I doubted. Since that time I have received your communication mailed the same day…I have only to say that the militia of Virginia will not be furnished to the powers at Washington for any such use or purpose as they have in view. Your object is to subjugate the Southern States, and a requisition made upon me for such an object…will not be complied with. You have chosen to inaugurate civil war, and, having done so, we will meet it in a spirit as determined as the administration has exhibited toward the South."

As the Northern states were raising militia and volunteers, the Virginia State Convention went into a two-day secret session. Formerly "conditional Unionists" like Delegate John L. Marye Sr. of Fredericksburg,[27] were now left with no neutral ground. On April 17, 1861, the second day of the secret session, Delegate Marye took the floor:

Sir, with what views did I enter this body? What interest had I to serve? What was the Virginia sentiment that directed my action? <u>The preservation of the Union</u>… *I did not realize it as an insurmountable difficulty for this body to carve out such measures of compromise as would result in furnishing efficient guarantees…I anticipated that the trouble with regard to the acceptance of the guarantees we might propose would be with the South, not with the North; and what was the basis of my calculation? In the absence of any personal knowledge of the extent of that fanaticism and folly at the North which have wrought results so disastrous to the country, I conclude that the magnitude of* *her interest in preserving her connection with the South was too controlling to yield to the dominion of prejudice… All my fond and sanguine calculations of reconstruction have failed, and the conclusion has been forced upon me that a difficulty…has become insuperable…<u>To my mind, the necessity of severing Virginia's connection to the Union is manifest. She has no middle ground to occupy.</u>* [28]

Later that day, Delegate Marye joined in with the majority vote, and the State Convention adopted the Ordinance of Secession of Virginia by a vote of 88 to 55, subject to voter referendum May 23rd.[29]

Responding to a citizens' meeting in Fredericksburg held the day following the secession vote, the Common Council of the town on April 19th appropriated $5,000 to fund a Home Guard, leaving …*the peace and quiet of the town to be preserved by the citizens, not subject to militia duty.*[30] On that same day, President Lincoln issued a Proclamation of Blockade against ports of the Confederate coastline.

As Presbyterians seeking strength through their faith, the Wells family would attend the Fredericksburg Presbyterian Church, with Rev. Archibald A. Hodge as pastor. Time with Hodge was short lived however, for within a month of their arrival, he announced that he would be leaving the post due to the imminent dissolution of the Union; that in his judgment, war was inevitable, that his ties bound him to the North, and for this reason, he must resign.[31] Initially, he went to pastor the Presbyterian Church at Wilkes-Barre, Pennsylvania, the Wells' former place of residence, and the Wells family would have the opportunity to pass on their regards to old acquaintances.

Fredericksburg Presbyterian pastor, the Rev. Archibald Alexander Hodge

(Presbyterian Historical Foundation)

By the end of April 1861, Rev. Hodge had relinquished charge of the church and was gone.[32]

    Among Fredericksburg's Presbyterian congregation was the family of John G. Hurkamp, a successful businessman. One of his daughters, Alice, was a schoolmate to the Wells children. In later years, she "remembered the Wells' girls very well, how attractive they were and popular." She also recalled that Captain Wells himself was "highly regarded in Fredericksburg."[33]

The Fredericksburg Presbyterian Church

(1881 Stereopticon image courtesy HFFI)

    Just elected for a second term in March 1861, Mayor Montgomery Slaughter would become Fredericksburg's "War Mayor." When asked in later years if he remembered the daughters of Captain Wells, the former mayor replied, "Oh yes, I knew them very well – they were very sweet girls."[34]

Mayor Montgomery Slaughter, the "War Mayor" of Fredericksburg

(Courtesy Fredericksburg Area Museum and Cultural Center)

Chapter III – CIVIL WAR!

Brig. Gen. Daniel Ruggles, First Commander of Virginia State Forces
on the Rappahannock in the Civil War
Shown in an early image as Lt. in the U.S. Army.

(Portrait photo courtesy of the late Virginia Lindlay Goolrick Hinkle)

    U.S. Army Brevet Lt. Colonel Daniel Ruggles, West Point class of 1833, and wife Richardetta were residing in Fredericksburg at the opening of hostilities. After the Mexican-American War, and up until 1858, Massachusetts native Ruggles served in Texas and participated in the Utah Expedition of 1858-59. On a leave of absence in 1859, he returned to Fredericksburg, where his wife Richardetta "Etta" Hooe Ruggles, a King George County, Va. native and great granddaughter of George Mason, had purchased a house on Charles Street.[35]

On April 17, 1861, the same day that the Virginia State Convention adopted the ordinance of secession, 51-year old Ruggles, offered his services to the state.[36] Resigning his commission as brevet lieutenant colonel, USA, Ruggles presented his credentials to Virginia's Governor John Letcher in person. Effective April 19, 1861, the governor commissioned Ruggles as Brigadier General of Virginia Volunteers and Militia. Ruggles made his headquarters in Fredericksburg, and from there he issued his first official orders:

Headquarters,
Fredericksburg, Va., April 22, 1861
GENERAL ORDERS,
No. 1.
By the authority of the governor of the State of Virginia I assume command of the volunteers and militia along the line of the Potomac River, extending from Mount Vernon south to the mouth of the Rappahannock River. Headquarters are established at this place until further orders.
DANIEL RUGGLES,
Brigadier-General Virginia Volunteers, Commanding Forces.[37]

Although opposed to Virginia's secession, Gov. Letcher was meanwhile involved in the creation of a Washington D.C. spy network by the time Virginia seceded from the Union -- an organization that continued in operation after Virginia joined the Confederacy in May, 1861.[38] Ruggles' interview with the Governor may well have included discussing Virginia's espionage capabilities and the necessity for a secret line to transport ciphered reports and other intelligence across the Potomac and Rappahannock Rivers.

Virginia Governor John Letcher

(National Archives)

Fredericksburg attorney Major William S. Barton of the Virginia Militia and soon to be Ruggles' assistant adjutant general, established the first wartime underground express between Maryland and Virginia. On April 20, 1861, Barton telegraphed Gov. Letcher: "A line of express may be established to Balta [Baltimore] from opposite Aquia Creek—a reliable man here will assist."[39] Gen. Ruggles followed with another telegraph on April 22, 1861: "Can I draw on you for one hundred dollars—Secret Service money to send a special messenger to Maryland immediately?" Gov. Letcher replied: "You are authorized to draw for the amount mentioned."[40]

As reported in a Richmond paper, the *Eureka* was impressed early in Ruggles' sweep of the Rappahannock River:

> **Fredericksburg.**
> --*This patriotic town is doing everything possible towards the defence of the State. There are three well organized and efficient companies in the place, and more forming...On Saturday night [April 20, 1861], Lieut. [Carter M.] Braxton of the Artillery, was detailed for the purpose of proceeding in steamship* **Eureka** *down the river and capturing one or more vessels which were lying in the stream between this and Port Royal. This service was promptly performed, and the vessels*

brought up yesterday morning [April 24, 1861] *just before day.*[41]

James McClure Scott, a member of Braxton's artillery company, recorded that shortly after the war broke out about two dozen soldiers from his newly formed outfit, under command of one of the battery's lieutenants, embarked on a naval mission: Impressing the steamer ***Eureka*** into service, they boarded her at the Fredericksburg wharf and headed down the Rappahannock with orders to gather in any shipping with questionable credentials. Downriver at Tappahannock, they rounded up several Northern trading vessels, and returned in triumph with their prizes to Fredericksburg.[42]

By Captain Wells' account, Lt. Braxton and his artillery company were carrying out an order by General Ruggles:

When the War broke out she [the Eureka] *was boarded by some man with an order from the General*[43] *then in command of Fredericksburg and they ordered me and my crew ashore. I did not go ashore as they agreed to have me stay onboard as long as I did not interfere with them. At the end of six days and nights I got rid of them by seeing a man (Capt. Lewis)*[44] *and got an order of release and ran my Boat as far down the river as I was allowed by the Confederates at Fort Lowery. I ran most of the season of 1861 entirely as a private Boat for my own advantage with the exception of three or four times I was impressed for a day or so to my disadvantage.*[45]

Ruggles and Lewis would have benefited from the order *of release,* allowing the *Eureka* access beyond Tappahannock, its twice-a-week port-of-call. With Wells' knowledge of the inlets and outlets of the Potomac and Rappahannock River, he could prove to be a valuable ally.

President Lincoln issued a second blockade Proclamation on April 27, 1861, extending the blockade (General Winfield Scott's "Anaconda Plan") to the ports of Virginia and North Carolina. On April 30th, the blockade of Virginia ports was in full operation.[46] By this time, local Unionists suspected Wells of blockade running, and it was the general feeling in town that Captain Well's sympathies lay openly with the South.[47]

In August 1861, ammunition bound for the lower Rappahannock was being loaded and unloaded by free blacks from Fredericksburg and Spotsylvania.[48] To support such activity, the *Eureka* was impressed to carry military supplies, munitions, and troops along the Rappahannock River in addition to towing sailing vessels and barges.[49]

The local paper described the martial atmosphere of the town:

TROOPS IN FREDERICKSBURG
On Wednesday our old town was alive with military. Six hundred soldiers in the Burg at one time changed the usually peaceful, quiet aspect of the place to martial enthusiasm and animation of the liveliest description. Company F from Richmond, the Caroline Grays, the Mercer Cavalry, the Mt. Pleasant Riflemen, our own Gray Guards, Artillery, etc., were among the number. The Armory Building presented a most warlike appearance; groups of soldiers in front and around it, and bristling bayonets stacked in true soldier style. Every other man on the street was in grey, red, or blue uniform, pistols shone and swords jingled, and war, defiant war seemed the order of the day. The citizens opened houses and hearts to welcome and entertain their brave comrades and cheered them on in defense of our country's rights and honor. Fredericksburg has not had such an awakening for years. Hurrah for the Old Dominion! 'The cry is still they come!' The Richmond Light Inf. Blues, under command of Capt. O. J. Wise, arrived yesterday, and other companies are daily expected. The Blues and Company F were drilled in the evening in the streets, before their quarters, the Court House and the Presbyterian Church. They are fine soldiers and their martial exercises excite wonder and admiration in the throngging crowds who witness them. It is intended that the Fairgrounds shall be used as their encampment for the present. The Caroline Troop, a fine looking set of men, about 80 strong, arrived yesterday and paraded today.[50]

With the order of release from the commander of the Rappahannock River, Captain Lewis, Wells was able to make a living running the *Eureka* as a private boat throughout the 1861 season. Wells details his trials during this time:

Some time in April 1861, after I had been running my boat on the river a few weeks, I was boarded by some Secessionists who ordered myself and crew all to go ashore for they had an order from the Commanding General[51] to take my boat. I protested and refused to go ashore with which I was forced to do so and after a consultation they decided that as their Pilot did not understand a steam boat, I was allowed to stay on my boat with my Crew. But the Secessionists had full charge and I could do nothing while they ran up and down the river for six days and nights and burnt up all my coal so that I was obliged to stop and lay up at Fredericksburg for there was no coal to be bought – and the Secessionists gave up my boat. After many inquiries, I found that there was wood on the wharves along the river below the city and I bought a buck and saw and employed a man who sawed the wood on deck while the boat was running – but the boat moved slow as the boiler was small and not made for wood.

I was pressed into the service of the Confederates on several occasions and I lost my trips by so doing and got no pay. On one occasion I was hailed and told to tow a raft up the river to Fredericksburg. I refused, but the man followed me on land to Fredericksburg and threatened me by saying he would send me to Richmond a prisoner and I was obliged to go down the river and tow the raft to Fredericksburg.[52]

By order of Maj. Gen. Robert E. Lee, Ruggles stationed troops at points along the Richmond, Fredericksburg and Potomac Railroad, which terminated at Aquia Creek in Stafford County, Virginia.

Ruggles' defenses at Aquia Creek faced their first challenge the evening of May 29, 1861, when two small Federal steamers fired shells at Confederate battery there. Fearing a Federal landing at that place, Ruggles, with seven hundred men from the 2nd Tennessee Regiment and a battalion of volunteers, set off by train from Fredericksburg, but the engagement had ended by the time the train arrived. Two days later the Federal gunboats were back.

On the morning of May 31st, the USS *Thomas Freeborn*, the USS *Anacostia*, and the USS *Resolute* arrived at Aquia Creek to challenge Ruggles' shore battery, prompting an engagement lasting almost three hours.

The Attack of Confederate Batteries at Aquia Creek by U.S. Vessels
(Library of Congress)

On the morning of the third day, June 1st, the same three enemy vessels returned to resume the fight, led this time by the heavily armed USS *Pawnee*. This engagement lasted five hours.

The Confederate shots hit the *Freeborn* causing her to leak badly and crippling her port wheel. The Confederate side received damage to the battery earthworks, the wharf was burned and buildings behind the battery were destroyed by fire, but no one was injured. Neither side claimed victory.[53]

At the direction of President Jefferson Davis, Ruggles' command ended on June 5, 1861, when he was superseded by Brig. Gen. Theophilus H. Holmes of N.C.[54] Ruggles however remained in the Department of Fredericksburg, and took over command for a short time during July 1861 when Holmes was with Gen. P.G.T. Beauregard's forces at Manassas.[55]

Rose O'Neal Greenhow, and her eight-year-old daughter 'little Rose' in Old Capitol Prison.

(Photo by Matthew Brady, Library of Congress)

Just prior to the Manassas battle the widow Rose O'Neal Greenhow, a Confederate spy in Washington, sent an urgent ciphered message to Gen. Beauregard, at Manassas in the care of Ruggles. The cover letter of the sealed package read:

To Col. Dan'l Ruggles near Mathias Point, Commanding Confederate Forces.

On the other side:
Let this go thro by 11 or 12 a.m. [sic] on the 16th inst. This must go thro' by a <u>lightening express</u> to Beauregard. Incur any expense

upon authority of my instructions and I'll certify to the bills when I return. G. Donnellan.

To Col. Dan'l Ruggles[56]

At 8 p.m. on July 16, 1861, the sealed communication was received at Beauregard's headquarters, dispatched by relays from Gen. Holmes' picket line below Alexandria, Virginia.[57]

Richardetta Hooe Ruggles (Mrs. General Ruggles) and son Major Mortimer B. Ruggles at the death of Gen. Ruggles in 1897.

(Courtesy William Brush Ruggles, Dallas, Texas)

Gen. Ruggles' house on Charles Street (still standing) was targeted for sacking and pillaging during the Battle of Fredericksburg.

(1937 VA Historical Inventory Photo, WPA, Library of Virginia)

As part of the new Federal flotilla, the *Pawnee* returned to cruise the Potomac River off Aquia Creek. While stationed at Aquia Landing in June, Capt. Lewis observed commercial steamers, including the *St. Nicholas,* freely plying the Potomac River without challenge by the Flotilla. Lewis soon became part of a secret plan hatched out of Gov. Letcher's office.

In on the plot was Naval Commander Matthew Fontaine Maury, a Fredericksburg native who in April 1861 resigned his position at Superintendent of the Naval Observatory in Washington, D.C. and offered his services to Governor Letcher.[58] A Washington letter published in a Boston newspaper after Maury's departure, considered his resignation *desertion of a post of duty…the meanest traitor…who stole away like a thief,* putting up a reward of *$3,000 for the Head of the traitor, Lieut. Maury.*[59]

Commander Maury's wife and younger children had meanwhile fled Washington, finding refuge at a cousin's home in Fredericksburg. Maury's married daughter, Betty Herndon (Maury) Maury and her three-year old daughter, Nannie Belle, soon joined them.[60]

Home of Cousin John Minor on Caroline Street, (still standing) where Matthew Fontaine Maury's family found refuge at the beginning of the Civil War.

(1927 photograph by Francis Benjamin Johnson, Library of Congress)

To help organize Virginia's military effort, Governor Letcher set up an Advisory Council consisting of Judge John J. Allen, Chief Justice of the Virginia Court of Appeals, Colonel Francis H. Smith, Superintendent of Virginia Military Institute, and Lt. Matthew Fontaine Maury, former Superintendent of the U.S. Naval Observatory in Washington.[61]

Replying to a letter from Gen. Robert E. Lee regarding a proposed raid on Federally held Newport News, Virginia, Governor Letcher seemed warm to the concept but had another plan in mind with Maury: *Oblige me by giving no orders to Company F, 1ˢᵗ Regiment of Virginia Volunteers, I have had a conversation today with Captain Maury, respecting some secret service, and if our plans shall be carried out, I will have need for this company.*[62] The attack on Newport News did not take place, but Letcher's and Maury's secret service plans may have been those implemented on June 28th when Captain George N. Hollins, Colonel Richard H. Thomas, and Captain Henry H. Lewis embarked upon an expedition with men from the 2nd Tennessee regiment.

Safely settled in with the rest of the Maury family at a cousin's house on lower Caroline Street[63] in Fredericksburg, Betty Herndon Maury resumed writing in her diary[64] on June 3, 1861. By the end of the month, she was recording her suspicions regarding Capt. Lewis' and her brother "Dick" Maury's involvement in a secret plot to seize Federal steamers.

Civil War diarist Betty Herndon (Maury) Maury
(Photo courtesy Virginia Historical Society)

Thursday, June 27, 1861...Dick [Maury], *Bob Minor, cousin Jack* [Maury] *and a number of sailors are here to report to Captain Lewis. No body knows <u>where</u> they are going, <u>when</u> they are going, or <u>what</u> they are to do, but I have a strong suspicion.*[65]

Friday, June 28, 1861. The secret party under Capt. [Henry H.] *Lewis started down the Rappahannock last night with five hundred of the Tennessee regiment who came from the Creek to join them. We heard today that the boat is aground on the bar and they will not be able to get off before one o'clock today when the tide rises. I hope their scheme will not be defeated by the delay.*

Monday, July 1, 1861. Well! Our secret expedition has returned. Yesterday afternoon we heard a steam whistle and knew that no boat was expected here for a week. In a few minutes all Fredericksburg was at the wharf. It was the **St. Nicholas!** *A prize! A Yankee steamer that runs between Baltimore and Washington.*

About two weeks ago Capt. [George N.] *Hollins and Col.* [Richard Henry] *Thomas (a man that dresses like a Japanese!) went over to Maryland and arranged with friends there to take the* **St. Nicholas** *by strategy. Col. Thomas went to Baltimore and with six or eight friends got on board the steamer as passengers. When they reached Point Lookout, Capt. Hollins with a few friends came on board as passengers also, and when the boat was fairly out in the stream they walked up to the Captain, told him that he was their prisoner and that the boat was in the hands of Confederate officers. He made some show of resistance at first, but soon saw that it was of no use and surrendered. The boat was then run into Coan Creek, on the Virginia shore opposite to Point Lookout, where Capt. Lewis's party, including the four hundred Tennesseans were awaiting them. They had left the* **Virginia**[66] *near the mouth of the Rappahannock and marched across the country to Coan Creek the night before.*

The plan was for the whole party to embark and under the Federal flag go up the Potomac, take the **Pawnee** *and* **Freeborn** *at*

Aquia Creek (they would never have suspected that she was in the hands of Confederate officers until they were boarded) and then come round to the mouth of the Rappahannock, take the blockading force there and come up with flying colors. But the Secretary of War would not allow the Tennesseans to embark. Said they might do any fighting that was necessary on shore, but not on board ship. The rest of the party, about a hundred officers and sailors together, would have attempted it but they had only a few hours of coal on board and the **Pawnee** *and* **Freeborn** *had left the Creek.*

As it was, all embarked except Capt. Lewis and a few others. Captain L. thought it was wrong to risk the lives of so many officers unnecessarily, and went out into the bay to see what they could find. The first vessel they met was a brig [the **Monticello***] laden with coffee. It made no resistance...They then met a schooner [the* **Mary Pierce***] and another [the* **Margaret***] with coal, both of which were taken in the same way.*

Col. Thomas went on board the **St. Nicholas** *dressed as a woman. The party on board did not know each other very well. Each one suspected the other and all suspected the 'woman.'*

Sketch from Steam-boat route schedule during the Civil War

(Cox, Brainard & Company, Mobile, Alabama)

THE "FRENCH LADY"

Cartoon of Col. Richard Henry Thomas, CSA, ("Zarvona") dressed as a French lady aboard the passenger steamer *St. Nicholas.*

(Sketch out of *Harper's Weekly,* July 27, 1861)

(Left) Lt. Richard Lancelot Maury (Courtesy Virginia Historical Society);

(Right) Matthew Fontaine Maury, "Pathfinder of the Seas." (Library of Congress)

It was Capt. Lewis's scheme. Papa only helped to carry it out. Capt. L was to have commanded the expedition. The President never fully approved of it. It had been 'hanging' in Richmond for more than a month. Cousin Jack and Dick are both army officers. I suppose Papa got them ordered on this expedition.[67]

There was no blockading vessel at the mouth of the Rappahannock when the prizes came in. Suppose she had gone for provisions.

With a dateline *Fredericksburg, June 30, 1861, Full Particulars,* the correspondent for a Richmond paper described Fredericksburg's reaction regarding *a most daring adventure which has been concocted at this place…Friday morning our town was thrown into a great commotion by a rumor being spread that a secret expedition was forming, whose object was unknown. Men were seen gathering in small groups at the corners of the streets, conversing on this all-absorbing topic. Some three or four days previously, a gentleman of the name of Thomas was seen about the streets with his head shaved very close and dressed in the Zouave style. He attracted upon himself universal observation, and was even suspected by some of being a spy. He was evidently affecting a character very adverse to his true one. ...*

Captain George N. Hollins, CSN, disguised himself wearing a white wig aboard the steamer *St. Nicholas.* (Library of Congress)

...Hollins...capturing the following prizes in addition to the St. Nicholas; a vessel laden with 3,500 bags of coffee, another laden with ice, and a third with coal. They have all been brought within the protection of our batteries. The St. Nicholas with one of the vessels is in sight of our wharf. This success has illuminated the countenances of our townsmen with exceeding joy. Their anxious and care-worn faces of yesterday are lit up with a luminous expression of joy and satisfaction. The crew of the St. Nicholas, consisting of twenty free negroes and nineteen white persons, are in our jail, and will, in all probability, be sent to Richmond.

The ladies generally are very zealous in administering to the wants of these noble young men...A good many of the sick are canteened out among the citizens, some houses taking as many as four or five.[68]

The raid led by Hollins and Thomas on the night of June 28, 1861 did not succeed in capturing their target, the *USS Pawnee*. However, the cargo vessels they seized as prizes near the mouth of the Rappahannock were laden with 3,500 bags of coffee, 270 tons of coal, and 200 tons of ice.[69] Hollins seized the schooner carrying the coal to refuel the *St. Nicholas,* and the ice and coffee were put to good use by Confederate hospitals in Richmond.

After the town turned out to greet the *St. Nicholas*,[70] so overjoyed were its citizens at the success of the daring raid that they hosted a ball in the raiding party's honor. To their delight, *the French Lady* appeared in hoops and skirts at the town celebration, then moving on down to Richmond, where *Zarvona* was also feted.[71]

Capt. Wells' involvement in the June 28, 1861 raid is unknown. However, during the Federal occupation of Fredericksburg during the summer of 1862, a rumor was circulated regarding Wells: According to information passed on by some unfriendly Unionist in town, the Captain was involved in a similar piratical scheme to capture commercial steamers out of Baltimore. Under the pilotage of Captain Wells, the rumored plan was to run the steamers into Confederate waters as prizes of war.[72]

Chapter IV – Fredericksburg: 'a Captured Town'

"Fredericksburg Court House occupied by Federal troops as a barracks and by the Signal Corps." Drawing by Edwin Forbes, May 15, 1862. (Library of Congress)

In the spring of 1862 I was not allowed to run my boat and she lay in Fredericksburg with part of a crew until the 18th day of April and I learned that the shipping was to be burned by the Confederates whenever the Union Army made its appearance.[73]

When Gen. George McClellan, President Lincoln's commander of the Army of the Potomac, announced that he finally had a definite plan of campaign for the spring of 1862 -- to advance to the Peninsula between the York and James rivers for his attempt on Richmond -- Lincoln was delighted.

Feeling vulnerable however, Lincoln detained McClellan's lst Corps of 30,000 men, headed by Gen Irvin McDowell. To protect the Capital, the president on 4 April 1862 reconstituted the 1st Corps into the new Department of the Rappahannock, to be headed by McDowell. While moving his army south toward Fredericksburg, McDowell was informed by the War Department that his troops could occupy

Fredericksburg, but not venture beyond. McDowell's approach compelled the small Confederate army to evacuate Fredericksburg.

Betty Maury wrote:
Sunday, April 13, 1862. All our forces have left except one Brigade commanded by Gen. [Charles W.] Field.[74] *They are here as out posts and scouts and expect to retire when ever the enemy come to take possession. We have piles of tarred lumber all along the bridges ready to burn them when ever occasion requires it. There were two forts on this river, but both have been dismantled...Most of our army stores have been removed from here.*

On the same day, April 13th, ships of the Federal Potomac Flotilla, under presidential orders, sailed for the Rappahannock River to assess Confederate forces in the area and neutralize any threat from that quarter.[75]

The following day, according to a report in the *New York Times,* the flotilla was proceeding up the Rappahannock toward Fredericksburg. At Urbanna, the gunboat *Jacob Bell,* encountering Confederate fire from rifle pits, opened fire, scattering the enemy in all directions.
Upriver, the whole fleet opened up on Confederate batteries at Lowry's Point, and two miles above at Tappahannock, the fleet fired a blank cartridge, hoisting a flag of truce. Some of the people of the little town responded by displaying white flags. Once landed, the American flag was raised over one of the largest houses and some of the townspeople responded that the flag would be torn down as soon as they left. If so, they were told, they would have six hours to leave the town before it was burned down.
Information provided the fleet by *contraband* at Tappahannock was that four large schooners and other obstructions had been placed in the narrow channel of the river five miles below Fredericksburg, to prevent approach to that town. Also, that the steamers *St. Nicholas, mounted with two guns, the Eureka and Logan,* were lying in the Fredericksburg harbor. The fleet remained off Tappahannock on April 15th.[76]

A Richmond newspaper reported a contrasting (Confederate) version of the above event. It stated that five Federal gunboats with about three-hundred men went up the Rappahannock as far as Fort Lowry.

Finding that the fort had been previously evacuated by Confederate forces, and after firing several rounds into the earthworks, they proceeded up to Tappahannock. Hoisting a Union flag over a fine residence, they... *perambulated about the town, stealing all the poultry and drinking all the liquor they could find, making the bars of the town contribute profusely to their appetite. ...Waiting upon the officer in command of this rabble, he was informed that the Union flag must be hauled down, and if he refused compliance with this demand, the ladies of the town would immediately dislodge this insignia of disgrace. The officer, perhaps akin in spirit to that King of France who 'Marched his men up the hill and marched them down again,' considering discretion the better part of valor, and not wishing to encounter the brave daughters of Virginia, prudently removed the obnoxious bunting which his own hands had helped elevate.*

They then went on board their boats, where some time was spent in drunken revelry; when another posse was sent ashore to arrest Captain Walker, an old river man who resides in the town. They endeavored to compel him to pilot them to Fredericksburg, which he declined doing, alleging that he was unacquainted with the stream in that direction. After finding it was impossible to obtain his services in the capacity of a pilot, he was released and permitted to return ashore.

Having satiated their poultry-stealing and liquor-thieving propensities at Tappahannock, they weighed anchor and moved off down the river to Fort Lowry...[77]

On April 19th, a Richmond paper[78] reported the latest war news from Fredericksburg:

> "*The enemy in Stafford – Probable Occupation of the Town of Fredericksburg.*

Information was received by the citizens of Fredericksburg, Va., at 4 o'clock on Thursday afternoon [April 17, 1862], *that the enemy was approaching through Stafford County, and the fact was at once communicated to our pickets and to Col.* [W. H. F.] *Lee's cavalry; but it seems that the latter previously had an intimation of the advance, and at once fell back, burning the three bridges across the Rappahannock, connecting Fredericksburg with Stafford, as they came into town. These bridges, as many of our readers are aware, were the railroad, Coalter's and Falmouth bridges.*

Yesterday morning [Friday, April 18, 1862], *at an early hour, the Yankees reached Falmouth, opposite Fredericksburg. One of our informants says that they threw a few shells across the river, but there being no response, the firing soon ceased. – (Of this, however, we are not positive.) – Meanwhile, the three steamers, the* **St. Nicholas,** *the* **Virginia,** *the* **Eureka,** *and some thirty sail vessels, lying at the wharf, loaded with grain, with a considerable quantity of cotton piled near the depot, were set on fire by our men and destroyed. The troops that were in and near the place, very few in number, and utterly inadequate to make a defence against a considerable force, evacuated Fredericksburg after having performed the duties required of them. Many of the citizens also left, abandoning their property to the 'tender mercies' of the enemy."*

Betty Maury wrote: *Good Friday, April 18, 1862. Last night we heard that the enemy were four miles from Falmouth. Did not know their strength. Our forces went across the river to meet them. I believe they had a short skirmish in the night.*

49

"Wrecks of Steamers burned by the Rebels," Fredericksburg 1862

"Remains of Burnt Steamers and Sailing Vessels on the Rappahannock"

Drawing by Edwin Forbes, May 11, 1862 (Library of Congress)

Above: looking downriver in the direction of the town wharf.

(1881 Stereopticon image looking East Southeast across 800 block of Caroline Street, HFFI.)

While we were dressing we saw great columns of smoke rising from the river, and soon learned that the enemy were in strong force, that our troops had retreated to this side of the river and fired the bridges.

I went down to the river and shall never forget the scene there. Above were our three bridges, all in a light blaze from one end to the other and every few minutes the beams and timbers would splash into the water with a great noise. Below were two large steam boats, the **Virginia** *and the* **St. Nicholas**, *and ten or twelve vessels all wrapt in flames. There were two or three rafts dodging in between the burning vessels containing families coming over to this side with their negros and horses.*[79]

As heavily outnumbered Confederate troops were busy with their bridge burning work and packing up to head out of town on April 18, 1862, the soldiers of Gen. Christopher C. Augur's brigade, Gen. Rufus King's division, were filing in along the Rappahannock River opposite Fredericksburg. Union artillery hastily positioned themselves on Stafford Heights to begin firing upon the retreating Confederate arsonists.

The Richmond newspaper[80] in the meanwhile corrected its previous report regarding the fate of the *Eureka:*

*From Fredericksburg...Only two steamers were burnt by our men before the town was evacuated – the **St. Nicholas** and the **Virginia**. We learn that the commander of the **Eureka** took his boat down the river, and she will probably be captured by the Yankees.*

In an effort to save his ship from both the Federals and the Confederate armies, Captain Wells, with his son Ben and boat pilot Peter B. Robinson, steamed downriver. Captain Wells described his harrowing experience:

*On the 18th of April 1862 when the Union Army arrived opposite Fredericksburg the rebels went to work and set fire to the bridges and were about to set fire to the shipping. In the confusion, with half a crew and great risk to my life by being shot by armed men on the rebel steamer **St. Nicholas**, I ran away from the rebels with the **Eureka** and went down the river. But having left my family at Fredericksburg, I was put ashore eight miles below Fredericksburg and walked back to my family, telling Mr. Robinson (the Pilot) to put the **Eureka** in a small creek near Port Royal on the North side of the river, as I was afraid the rebels would find her and burn her on the South side of the river where the rebels were.*

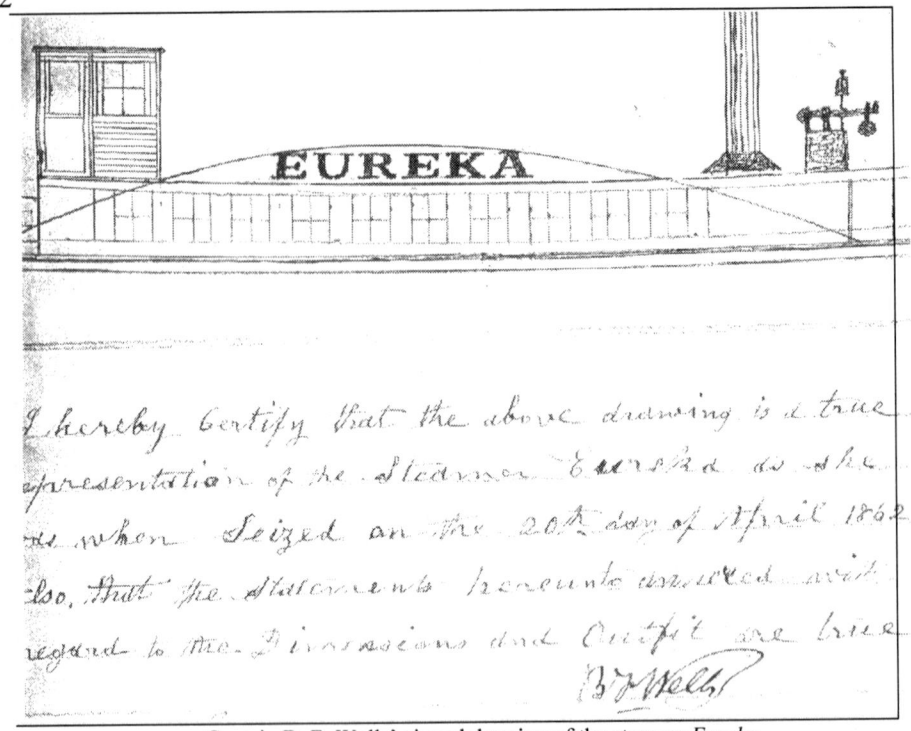

Captain B. F. Wells' signed drawing of the steamer *Eureka*

(Petition to Congress, Dec. 9, 1887, National Archives)

...On the 20th of April, ...Commander R. H. Wyman of the Steamer **Anacostia** of the Potomac Flotilla sent his barge into the small creek and seized my steamer, claiming her as a prize because found in so-called rebel waters.

...The first I heard from my boat was the arrival of my son about two weeks after the seizure. He was put ashore near the mouth of the river and walked home – For a long time I did not know what was done with my boat, nor did I wish to leave my family at such a time to look up my boat as my funds were very low.

Mr. Robinson ...said before he left the Rappahannock, the **Eureka** was manned by a crew from the **Anacostia** and sent up the Piankitank River in company with another small steamer, where there *was a rebel battery that riddled her and made a wreck of her. She had to be towed by the other small steamer back to the **Anacostia** and to Washington where she laid several months and then was sold in her crippled condition and bought by the U.S. Government...used in the Government service. The steamer **Eureka** was adjudicated in the United States Court for the District of Columbia as a prize and the prize proceeds of the forced sale distributed by the Auditor under an order of the Navy Department dated April 1862.*[81]

Captain Wells' son Ben also gave an account of the seizure of the *Eureka:*

...In the spring of 1862 the confederates put a stop to our running the steamer on the river and she lay in Fredericksburg and on the 18th day of April in the morning we were told that all the shipping was to be burnt as soon as the Union Army arrived. I went to work and got a little steam and soon the bridges were on fire and while the men were getting ready to fire the shipping and in the confusion the Capt. turned the boat's head down stream and let her go with very little steam to go with. We expected the Confederates would fire on us but they did not and we got away – the Capt. was put ashore about eight miles below the city and the boat left in charge of Mr. Robinson (the Pilot) with orders to put the boat into a small creek on the northern side of the Rappahannock river and it was done the same day.

After the Captain left the boat there were only three of us (the crew) and on the 20th two barges from the United States Steamer 'Anacostia' came into the creek where the 'Eureka' was and seized the 'Eureka.' Mr. Robinson protested and I went and got the United States Flag out from where it had been secreted for a long time and gave it to the Officer in Charge telling him the fact that it was the only flag the boat had ever carried. The colored man left the boat but Mr. Robinson and myself remained on board and were taken down the river with the 'Eureka' – We had a small lot of coal in the boat which we had kept for a long time as a reserve – enough to run a few miles, and the boat was started down the river after the 'Anacostia' and the 'Eureka' caught up but soon the coal gave out and the wood was used but her headway was so slow that the 'Anacostia' was obliged to take her in tow for her boiler was made for coal and wood could not be used to advantage – which I had learned long before.

I was taken to the mouth of the river and put ashore about 130 miles from home and I walked all the way and got home in about two weeks.

Benjamin F. Wells Jr.[82]

The USS *Anacostia* under Cdr. R. H. Wyman, a part of the Potomac Flotilla under the command of the U.S. Naval Blockading Squadron, discovered the hidden **Eureka** and claimed her as a prize of war. Escorting her return down the Rappahannock were the *Thomas Freeborn* and the *Island Bell*. These three vessels, while making a short expedition up the Piankatank River, were fired upon by a masked Confederate battery. Three balls tore into the **Eureka** – one through the smokestack, one through the pilothouse, and another through the deck, severing the steering chain. Disabled, she was towed back to Washington and purchased by the Navy Department.[83] A Fredericksburg paper reported that *she became one of the most useful steamers the government had during all the war, because of her speed and light draft. She was sort of a naval scout, being able to poke her nose on shore in shallow water and run into creeks that were inaccessible to the larger boats.*[84]

After repairs at the Washington Navy Yard, and with the addition of a light 12-pounder artillery piece, the **USS Eureka** was introduced to the Potomac Flotilla. In a dispatch to Secretary of the Navy, Gideon Welles, Potomac Flotilla Commander, Foxhall A. Parker described a "gallant affair" involving the **USS Eureka** on April 21, 1864:

Yesterday afternoon, as the **Eureka** *got within 30 yards of the shore just below Urbana, where I had sent her to capture two boats* *hauled up there, a large number of rebels, lying in ambush, most expectedly opened upon her with rifles and a piece of light artillery. Acting Ensign Hallock...returned the fire from his light 12-pounder and with small arms, and, although the little **Eureka** with officers and men has but sixteen souls on board, for some ten minutes (during which time the fight lasted), she was a sheet of flame, the 12-pounder being fired about as fast as a man would discharge a pocket pistol. The rebels were well thrashed, and I think must have suffered considerably. They fortunately fired too high, so that their shells and bullets passed over the **Eureka** without injury to the vessel or crew. It was quite a gallant affair and reflects a great deal of credit upon both the officers and men of the **Eureka**...* [85]

On April 19, 1862, Gen. Augur met with Mayor Montgomery Slaughter and a committee of townsmen. Agreeing to surrender the town, the committee assured Augur that Confederate troops were no longer harbored in the town and requested protection consistent with the rules of civilized warfare.

Widow Jane Howison Beale,[86] a resident of Lewis Street with sons in the army, also kept a personal journal. On April 27, 1861, she wrote:[87]

Fredericksburg is a captured town, the enemy took possession of the Stafford hills which command the town on Friday the 18th and their guns have frowned down upon us ever since, fortunately for us our troops were enabled to burn the bridges connecting our town with the Stafford shore and thus saves us the presence of the Northern soldiers in our midst, but our relief from this annoyance will not be long as they have brought boats to the wharf and will of course be enabled to cross at their pleasure, it is painfully humiliating to feel one'self a captive, but all sorrow for self is now lost in the deeper feeling of anxiety for our army, for our cause, we have lost everything, regained nothing, our army has fallen back before the superior forces of the enemy until but a small strip of our dear Old Dominion is left to us, our sons are all in the field and we who are now in the hands of the enemy cannot even hear from them, must their precious young lives be sacrificed, their homes made desolate, our cause be lost and all our rights be trampled under the foot of a vindictive foe, Gracious God avert from us these terrible calamities!...[88]

Betty Maury:
Wednesday, April 30, 1862. Went down yesterday evening to see the bridge of canal boats that the Yankees are building at the lower wharf. The boats are laid close together side by side, the length of the boat being the width of the bridge. Eight boats are in place and it already reached more than half way across the river...The Generals made a requisition upon town yesterday for tools to build the [railroad] car bridge. The Mayor replied that as our authorities had seen fit to destroy the bridges we could not assist in building one.[89]

Gen. Marsena R. Patrick, USA, Provost Marshal of Fredericksburg

(Library of Congress)

For his own headquarters, Gen. McDowell chose *Chatham*, on Stafford Heights, across the river from Fredericksburg and Gen. Rufus King chose the nearby *Phillips House.* McDowell designated Gen. Marsena R. Patrick as military governor, and on the evening of May 2, 1862, Patrick wrote in his diary:

...After the Bridge of Boats was completed, Gen. King & Staff concluded to go through town, with my escort—so we started off & rode through Caroline & Princess Anne Streets, looking at the points to be guarded by sentinels, & property to be secured. The Secesh people

were very indignant at the profanation of the Sacred Soil by Yankees—It was amusing to see the manner in which the Secesh women showed us their Backs---They were all looking until about the time the Cavalcade would get opposite their doors, then, with a grand air they would throw back their Crinoline, as Stage Ladies do...In general every body was disgust[ed].[90]

The Farmer's Bank of Virginia, at 400 George Street, Provost Marshal Gen. Patrick's Headquarters in the summer of 1862. The building is still standing.

(Library of Congress)

On May 7, 1862, Patrick took possession of the *Farmer's Bank* building in town. Ordering his 23rd N.Y. Volunteer Regiment headed by Col. Henry C. Hoffman[91] to occupy Fredericksburg, it took up its line of March from camp near Falmouth, and arrived in town at 9:00 a.m. on May 7th. Sensitive to the inhabitants, Hoffman ordered the regiment to dispense with its usual martial music and the 23rd marched silently to its quarters. Then, by order of Hoffman, the color corporal hung the *Stars and Stripes* over headquarters, opposite the railroad depot.[92]

"Rebuilding the railroad bridge across the Rappahannock to Fredericksburg, Va." Drawing by Edwin Forbes, May 6, 1862

(Library of Congress).

Col. Herman Haupt, Chief of Military Construction and Transportation on the staff of McDowell, was ordered to restore the Fredericksburg railroad line and bridges in the area to facilitate his advance on Richmond. Departing Confederates had destroyed the tracks beginning from Aquia Landing, the northern terminus of the RF&PRR in Stafford County, to the railroad bridge spanning the river into town.

On Colonel Haupt's first visit to Fredericksburg, he observed one method of Patrick's discipline to his troops occupying the town. He saw standing at the street curbs 15 or 20 soldiers with boards on their backs stating their various offenses, i.e., *I stole a ham,* and, *I broke into a private house*, etc. Haupt also reported an incident where a general officer had taken possession of a house occupied by a widow and two daughters, requiring them to seek other shelter. When Gen.

McDowell heard this, he personally reprimanded the officer and ordered him to relinquish the house to its former occupants.[93]

By May 18th, Haupt had made good progress in repairing the railroad from Aquia Creek to Fredericksburg.[94] On that date, Gen. Patrick wrote: *His cars are running today from Acquia to this place – I do not know whether they will cross the Creek (Rappahannock) or not, tonight…*

John Lawrence "Jack" Marye Jr. of *Brompton,* Mayor of Fredericksburg 1853-54 and Lt. Governor of Virginia 1870-73

(Courtesy City of Fredericksburg, Virginia)

Three days later, Patrick was visited by Mayor Slaughter, John L. "Jack" Marye, Jr. of "Brompton," among others and wrote: *It is beginning to be feared, very much, that I am about to leave the Command in Fredericksburg—they are in trouble.*

61

May 25th, 1862 Explosion at Fredericksburg RF&P Railroad Depot Grounds.

(Sketch out of Frank Leslie's *The Soldiers of Our Civil War*, 1893)

      Tipped off by *friendly contrabands* staying in town, Haupt discovered that several artillery shells, *torpedoes,* had been placed under the railroad tracks by departing Confederates to blow up trains entering the depot. He wrote: *The soldiers had removed quite a number and placed them in a small brick building detached from the station that had been used as a powder magazine...A sentinel on duty one day probably handled one of these torpedoes carelessly and caused an explosion of the whole number. The report was startling. The city was shaken and the building blown to atoms—not a brick left. Nothing was ever seen of the sentinel except a piece of his gun at a considerable distance from the spot.*

      As it was not certain that all the torpedoes had been removed, the first train was made up by putting the engine behind and a car very heavily loaded with scrap iron in front, so as to explode any torpedoes before the engine reached them; but none were found.[95]

Lincoln's continued frustration with the Army of the Potomac's stalled campaign led him to schedule a personal visit to the area. On the morning of May 23, 1862, the President and his party arrived by boat at Aquia Landing in Stafford County where they were greeted by Colonel Haupt. From there they transferred to the U.S. military rail line, which had just been rebuilt under Haupt's supervision. At Potomac Creek, the party was met by General McDowell who in turn escorted them to his headquarters at *Chatham*.

Gen. Marsena Patrick, who had learned the day before that he was to be replaced by Brig. Gen. Abner Doubleday of Gen. John F. Reynolds' command, was summoned by McDowell to *Chatham* to meet President Lincoln and discuss the presidential party's visit into Fredericksburg that day. Patrick wrote on Friday night, May 23, 1862:

I went over & found them there & all the Generals...Staid longer than I desired, returned & prepared to receive the President & Cortege at the [canal-boat] *Bridge—Took them through town to my Camp, saw the men under Arms only at the Guard, but the others only turned out—We came back to my Quarters & staid half an hour, when I escorted them to the Bridges & said Adieu—Doubleday has arrived & made a fool of himself before he had been here an hour. There is a feeling of sadness in the whole community & I feel sad myself, at the thought that these helpless families are to be left to the tender mercies of an Abolitionist...*[96]

(1881 Stereoptican image of Fredericksburg Court House courtesy HFFI)

    The previous day, Betty Maury recorded one of Patrick's last acts to preserve law and order prior to the change of command ...*Two soldiers are now tied back to back to a tree in front of the Court house with a board over their heads on which is written: 'For entering private houses without orders.'* On May 25th, she jotted just two lines regarding the Presidential visit: ...*Abraham Lincoln was in town on Friday. Our Mayor did not call on him and I did not hear a cheer as he passed along the streets.* And later that evening: *The Yankees are building their fifth bridge across the Rappahannock. The cars have been running between here and the* [Aquia] *Creek for more than a week.*[97]

Fredericksburg resident Ann Eliza (Pleasants) Gordon, wife of wealthy
Douglas Hamilton Gordon, Esq.

(Photo courtesy The Virginia Historical Society)

Provost Marshal Gen. Marsena R. Patrick, USA, mounted up.

(Library of Congress)

Having received orders to proceed west to the Shenandoah Valley *with all dispatch,* Gen. Patrick was mounted up and moving his troops out on May 29th when he found it necessary to halt in town: *While I was there some time—The Mayor & many others called while I was halting & paid their respects—I sat down on the steps of the Gordon House*[98] *(as I was told) a very Aristocratic Mansion, to watch the movement of my Troops, near the head of the Bridge—While there, Servants came from that house & another, bringing nice pie & cool milk, with the compliments of their Mistresses to Gen. Patrick, & say that 'Although we are Southern Ladies, we wish to show our regard for Gen. Patrick & to express our thanks for the kindness he has shown us, the protection he has given us & the perfect quietness & order he has preserved in the Town.' The refreshments were very acceptable & the spirit of the ladies still more gratifying—*[99]

With repairs to the railroad and bridges completed and rolling stock moving through the Fredericksburg station grounds by the end of May 1862, Colonel Haupt moved his headquarters into town[100] and took possession of one of the residences that had been recently abandoned.

Perceiving a conflict of his authority however, by letter to Gen. McDowell datelined *Fredericksburg, May 26, 1862*, Haupt tendered his resignation. Two days later, Haupt received a response from Secretary of War Stanton, which clarified and expanded his current duties, including an authorization to appoint *civilian* employees.[101]

Chapter V—A Northern Spy Boards at the Wells' House

Joseph Andrew (Orton) Kerbey later in the war as a
2nd Lt., Signal Corps, U.S. Vol.[102]

(Courtesy "The Signal Corps U.S.A. in the War of the Rebellion")

Declaring himself *on duty as a spy from the beginning of the war,* Joseph Andrew (Orton) Kerbey later wrote that he was on a scouting campaign that lasted, in effect, until the war ended. He was born Feb. 4, 1841 at Fort Loudon, Franklin County, in Pennsylvania's Cumberland Valley.

A son of longtime Pennsylvania Railroad ticket and freight agent George W. Kerbey of Wilmore, Pennsylvania, he had been a student of telegraphy in the office of Thomas A. Scott, later United States Assistant Secretary of War and President of the Pennsylvania Railroad. Scott hired young Andrew Carnegie as a personal telegrapher and secretary and, under Carnegie's tutelage while working as an office boy and telegraph messenger, Kerbey became a proficient telegraph operator.

On his self-appointed "scouting campaign," Kerbey showed up at the first Confederate Capital in Montgomery, Alabama, then down to Florida where, by his account, he prevented the capture of Fort Pickens. He managed to alert the fort commander of a planned firing by a masked Confederate battery on shore, thereby thwarting Confederate plans to capture the Federally held fort.[103]

Infiltrating Confederate lines in Richmond in the fall of 1861, Kerbey fell in with some Maryland refugees looking to join the southern cause. Recruited with the Marylanders at Camp Lee on Jan. 14, 1862, "Joseph A. Kerbey" was mustered into the Confederate Army as a Private in the 3rd Battery, Maryland Artillery[104] and detailed as company clerk. When the Battery was ordered to Knoxville the next month, Kerbey deserted and headed north through the lines, returning safely without being captured.

In the latter part of May 1862, Kerbey traveled to then Federally occupied Fredericksburg. He was to report to Col. Haupt, and carried with him a letter from the influential Pennsylvania Congressman John Covode.[105] Col. Haupt had just moved his headquarters into town and Kerbey would work for him as a civilian employee. In later years, Kerbey reflected that the position was created *just to prevent my getting in trouble again.*

Kerbey later wrote about his wartime spy adventures in *The Boy Spy,* published in 1889. Gen. Theophilus F. Rodenbough, USA Ret., and Kerbey's wartime cavalry commander, provided a contemporary review:

> ...*One of the latest and most important of these 'literary bricks' is 'The Boy Spy' -- a title hardly worthy of the mass of valuable information contained in its 500+ pages...a description of the author's personal experience, first as a wild youth rushing into the enemy's country from pure love of adventure, and afterward taking his own life in his hands as an experienced soldier and scout...eventually sent North as a friend of the Union; at once re-entering the enemy's country in Virginia. Imprisoned in the*

Old Capitol – as he says – for no other offense than having fallen in love with a pretty little girl...who lived between the two armies at Fredericksburg; was enlisted in the regular cavalry, detailed on special service before Fredericksburg, at Burnside's headquarters...The author writes as he acted in war time – quickly and intuitively, as well as fearlessly...Through the course web of privation, wounds and war, runs the silken thread of the tender passion, giving the story a touch of romance so often omitted...Besides its historical data, this book contains interesting biographical material...We tip our fatigue cap with grateful thanks.

Brig. Gen. Theophilus F. Rodenbough, USA Ret.[106]

Bvt. Brig.-Gen. T. F. Rodenbough, U. S. A., in 1865; Wounded at Trevilian and Winchester; Later Secretary U. S. Military Service Institution ("Cavalry" Editor).

Brig. Gen. Theophilus F. Rodenbough, USA

(Francis Trevelyan Miller, Ed. *The Photographic History of the Civil War: The Armies and the Leaders*)

Kerbey assumed several different names during his colorful career. When queried about the discrepancies, he sorted out the details:

> *...I was transferred by enlistment to 2nd U.S. Cavalry by Capt. T. F. Rodenbough, as Joseph A. Kerbey, which is the name I was christened and subsequently known.*
>
> *Some years later while working in Washington in the newspaper business I found another person, J. Andrew Kirby, to be an occasional resident of Washington who sometimes received and opened my mail.*
>
> *In order to avoid any misunderstanding, I dropped the "A" in my name, making it instead "O," to conform to my nom de plume "O.K." – by which I have become known in newspaper correspondence. Some checks coming to me as J. O. Kerbey, I was obliged to so endorse them. On my appointment papers as Consul to Para [Brazil], my name is given as Joseph O. Kerbey of Wilmore [Pa.]. Subsequently, to distinguish my <u>literary</u> signature, I signed my press correspondence J. Orton Kerbey.*
>
> *This is to certify that Joseph A. Kerbey, Joseph O. or J.O. or J. Orton Kerbey are one and the same, as per original descriptive list on Army papers, namely, Born Loudon, Franklin Co. Pa. Feb. 4, 1842-3. Dark blue eyes, light brown hair, 5 ft. 6-1/2.*
>
> *I am very Respectfully,*
> *Joseph A. Kerbey*[107]

Kerbey's first book, *The Boy Spy*, included details of his first day as a civilian in Fredericksburg during the Union army's occupation of the town in the summer of 1862:

> *I rolled over the temporary railroad bridge into the old depot at Fredericksburg on a freight train, dressed---well, in the best store clothes that money would buy at that time in Washington...I was directed by Mr. Covode to report in person, with a letter to the Chief Engineer, or Superintendent of the Richmond & Fredericksburg Military Railroad, General Haupt.* [109]

Hon. John Covode of Pennsylvania, friend of Kerbey (Library of Congress)

Col. Herman Haupt, USA, Chief of Military Construction & Transportation

(Library of Congress)

Kerbey's narrative continues in *Further Adventures of the Boy Spy in Dixie:*[110]

In Fredericksburg, the first thing to do was to find a hotel. I was shown to the Exchange...or maybe it was the Planters[111] ...the best hotel, located on the hillside, on one of the principal streets leading out toward Marye's Heights. It was not an agreeable place for me, because I saw that the young boy who ran the office for his mother was only there to collect all the money he could from the 'Yankee Invaders,' while the father and elder brother were probably in the rebel camps outside the town, only waiting a favorable opportunity to return and scalp the boarders.[112]

The town was full, literally, not only of McDowell's soldiers, who were in camp all around, but of all sorts of strange people in civilian's dress; adventurers, sutlers, traders, whisky smugglers, strange women; in fact the main street of the quiet, sleepy old aristocratic town was a perfect bedlam in May, 1862, as compared with my first visit in August, 1861.[113]

That evening, before dark, I saw on the street a greater variety of life than I had met in Washington on any one evening during my stay there. These numerous hangers-on of the armies had been, to a great degree, excluded from the Peninsula, so they had swarmed up to Fredericksburg as the next best place for them, to be nearest their favorite regiments, and 'on the road to Richmond,' where they all expected to rejoin McClellan's army in a very few days.

In addition to the great number of officers and men of the army, there were several batches of naval officers from one or two gunboats of the Potomac flotilla, which had sailed up the Rappahannock and were anchored below town.

Altogether it was what might be termed a lively town. The ordinary, quiet population had been suddenly increased to 40,000 or 50,000 by McDowell's army and followers, which had settled down *around the hills and the streets in one night like a flock of blue-birds or crows at a roosting place.*

During my walk about the town that evening I ran against a crowd of contrabands on the sidewalk, who were watching with the greatest interest the antics of a pair of New York street Arabs, or newsboys, who were dressed up in their rags doing some song-and-dance act to the great delight of the country soldiers and assembled contrabands. There was even an attempt at a theatrical performance after early candle-lighting. Indeed, it was only after taps that the Provost Marshal's[114] guard made any attempt to suppress the fun.

It did not occur to me until after I had undressed myself and had 'doused the glim'—while looking out the window toward the Virginia hill since so well known as Marye's Heights, that there was any possibility of the rebels making a sudden dash on the town and capturing us all. I seemed to realize only when I was alone that there might be some chance for those rebel fellows getting in there in sufficient force to gobble us all up.

As I gazed through the darkness in the direction of Richmond, I appreciated pretty strongly the fact that I was getting close to the front of that rebel gang again, and I had not the least desire to get inside their lines. I didn't sleep well; so early next morning I started out to find a place to stay which did not impress me so strongly as being the house of my enemy.

It was my good luck or my fate to have met with a clever gentleman in Mr. Jimmy Wilson, of Middletown, Pa. He was one of those happy, companionable persons to whom one naturally attaches one's self on first acquaintance. His business in Fredericksburg was that of a trader to the army, and he had secured some special privileges in this direction through his townsman, Gen. Simon Cameron,[115] while he was yet Secretary of War.

It may be that Mr. Wilson was attracted to me by something of a selfish motive, through a knowledge of my connection with the railroad *in an official capacity, by which he might be able to better facilitate his business interests in the transportation of his 'supplies' over the road and evading too close inspections. Anyway, Jimmy Wilson was a clever gentleman, to whom I was indebted for some great favors at that time. In the shrewd manner peculiar to the business of traveling salesman, he had discovered* **the very best place in the town to live,** *to which he kindly consented to introduce me. It was through him that I first met my 'fate,' in the family of Captain Wells.[116] There were in this happy and accomplished household quite a bevy of young ladies. All were young, but one was beautiful.*

It is quite a long, and I think may be interesting, story, which is indeed quite too romantic for this narrative of facts. I will only say that Geno the youngest, was to my eyes all that may be described as a beautiful, budding girl.

The eldest, Miss Sue, had been a belle in Georgetown before the war; another, Miss Mary, was noted for her sweet disposition.

The father, I grieve to add, was suspected by our officers of being a blockade runner for the rebels. He had been engaged on the regular underground line between Richmond and Washington, via the Potomac River, since the commencement of the war. Previous to this he had been the owner and Captain of a steamer plying between Washington and the Lower Potomac. Through this means he had gained valuable information of the rivers and little bays of that part of Virginia, and knew all about the inlets and outlets of the adjacent water, and was in consequence of this fact, probably suspected of being a most valuable ally to the rebel Government. His sympathies were openly with the South, but as this was the general feeling among the citizens, no one gave the Captain's personal sentiments much thought.

Between my infatuation for Geno and the sense of duty to the Government, I had a troublesome old time of it in the weeks and months and years that followed this first evening in the Wells' home.

It's pretty much the same old story of love at first sight and trouble forever after. I was politely invited to join the family circle in the parlor after tea. The mother was as youthful in her happy manner as her daughters. The genial Captain permitted himself to be prevailed upon by the younger children to sing one or two comical songs, which were received with hilarious applause.

The three daughters vied with each other in their polite efforts to entertain such a dull boy, as I must certainly have become after encountering the apparition of Geno that evening. Jimmy Wilson's presence seemed to help me out a little. A group played cards, while someone banged the piano and sang 'Bonnie Blue Flag,' 'Dixie,' and, by way of a tease, 'Yankee Doodle.'

Miss Sue was a decidedly beautiful girl of perhaps 20, quite lively, and perhaps a little bit of a flirt. I state this opinion generally. I did not entertain it so fully at that time as I did subsequently. Miss Mamie was the good girl of the family.

If I were not writing this story myself, I should be tempted to honestly declare that Geno was not only the prettiest but the sweetest girl I ever saw, and I have been with a great many in my life. She was not tall, but a slender, graceful womanly figure, dressed in a dark-blue calico, with no artificial aids to her fresh young beauty. Her face was sweetly intelligent, and while not lacking in resolution, it was marked by that shyness which belongs to young girls who are well-born and bred in comparative seclusion.

It was decreed that Geno should sit near me that evening on a low sofa[117] located in a corner of the parlor. All the chairs were occupied by the rest of the company, either by accident or through Miss Sue's propensity to tease her younger sister and myself...I believe I should at that time have felt more at my ease if I had been 'scouting' or sitting around a campfire with rebels instead of beside the little girl whose dress touched me. It was a clear case of love at first sight.

The Wells family were natives of my own State, having been embargoed during the war because of the father's steamboat interests on the river; and there hangs another tale... I had been introduced to the family as a civilian employee of the military railway, and had been able to present some flattering letters of introduction from Mr. John W. Forney,[118] *Mr. Covode, and other prominent Pennsylvania gentlemen.*

I may as well admit frankly I was about Geno's house more than duty warranted; so much so, indeed, that the amiable mother must have become tired of me. I seldom went to headquarters, and I had lost all interest in the capture of Richmond and in Capitola.[119] *My habit was to make brief daily visits to the Provost Marshal's office, located in the town, and during one of these I was questioned by one of the staff quite closely about the 'politics' or sympathies and the antecedents of the Wells family. Perhaps I was not in proper frame of mind to dispassionately discuss this question of Geno's family affairs with a strange officer, and it is probable that I somewhat rashly resented the supposed impertinence.*

It was through the usual gossipy information volunteered by some unfriendly Unionists of the town, that this officer at headquarters had learned that Capt. Wells had been engaged in blockade running for the rebels.,[120] *I exclaimed that I knew better; that my relations with the family were of an intimate character; that Capt. Wells was a native of my own State; that all his daughters had been born and educated in the Wyoming Valley, and that he was in Virginia solely and only because his business of steam boating had embargoed him there, and he had chosen to remain himself and sacrifice his boats, rather than abandon his family. All this was said in a positive manner, and with probably a little more animation than the subject justified. It had, however, the undesirable effect of bringing out prominently a trifling affair that occurred in connection with the family, which I must relate as part of my experience which soon followed, just to show that 'to the jealous, trifles light as air become confirmation strong as proofs of Holy Writ.'*

It will be remembered by the old soldiers that early in the war it was the custom to display flags promiscuously wherever they could find a place to string one in a Virginia town. Those who were in Fredericksburg with McDowell in 1862 will know that over the main streets of the town hung innumerable flags, so that the natives must either walk under the flag or stay indoors altogether.

Miss Sue Wells, like most bright girls her age, was fond of tormenting our officers, 'just for fun, you know.' She insisted, in the company of Union officers, that she was a rebel, but I was quietly informed by the family that when the Confederates first had possession of the town she was a Union girl to them. On this and several other questions Miss Sue and I differed quite decidedly. The sequence and truthfulness of this story compels me to say here that Miss Sue and I quarreled all the time (after I had become fairly established in the family). One day, while walking with her along the main street of the town, we encountered one of the numerous flags that were suspended over the sidewalk. Miss Sue put her little foot down...refusing in her very decided manner to walk under 'that flag.'

What could I do? The street was full of soldiers and officers, whose attention was being attracted toward us, by my taking her arm and attempting to force her to accompany me under the flag. I explained that there were flags on the other side of the street, and flags every place; that we would not dare to go around it; but the more I talked and urged, the more contrary she grew, and to prevent a further scene on the street[121] we retraced our steps.

That little act on the streets of Fredericksburg in the summer of 1862 is on record today in the war archives as part of the specifications in a charge of disloyalty against myself, on which I was subsequently arrested and confined in Old Capitol Prison.

It is a shameful fact that my early record for the Union at Fort Pickens and the subsequent year of service with a rope about my neck, was for a short time completely shadowed by this silly performance with a young lady in Fredericksburg. Not only this, but it was perhaps the indirect cause of this young lady's father's banishment from his home and the confiscation of his property.[122]

The officer who had reminded me of this incident undertook to give me some advice as to my association or intimacy in a rebel family. He further astonished me by saying they had information of a piratical scheme being hatched which had for its object the seizure of some of the regular line of steamers plying on the Chesapeake Bay. As I was understood to be in the secret service, the officer explained to me further that the plan, as they had learned of it, was for a party of rebels, disguised as passengers and laborers, to board one of these steamers in Baltimore, and after she was out in the bay at midnight, they were to throw off their masks, seize the boat, confine the officers and under the pilotage of Geno's father, run her into rebel waters as a prize.[123]

This was indeed startling intelligence, that for a moment staggered me. I realized that a more suitable person to do this work could not have been selected than Captain Wells. The officer said as they had no proof of this at all, he had mentioned it to me with a view of having me look the matter up; that my relations with the family were of such a character as to enable me to get on to the real facts. I left the headquarters feeling very much depressed.

After an enjoyable evening spent at the Wells house, following this conversation at Provost headquarters, I went to my quarters quite disturbed in heart and mind as to my duty. With the sweet voice of 'Juanita' still ringing in my ears, and the memory of her beautiful eyes seemingly appealing to my tenderest sympathies, I went to bed with my head in a whirl, and dropped into a restless sleep without having settled the question satisfactorily as to her father's guilt. There was no question as to the Captain's being entirely competent to pilot or even command such an expedition...[and] had he not been the father of a very pretty girl I would have jumped at the same conclusion as the officer and had him arrested at once through information given to Washington officials.

I was however unwilling to believe that the father of such an interesting family...would become the leader of a piratical gang. I concluded at last that I would postpone my action for a while at least...But after having slept over the matter, and while enjoying a walk the next morning among the neighboring camps, over which floated the 'emblem,' I suddenly regained my senses, for a little while at least, and made up my mind that it would be worse than traitorous for me by my silence to permit those Maryland sympathizers to go on and mature a plan to hire a gang of Baltimore plug-uglies to play the pirate on unarmed vessels on the bay, within sight of our armies. I could at least put the officials on their guard.

I walked straight back towards my 'office,' where I briefly wrote the rumor as it had, without my volition, been detailed to me, and at once put the letter in form to reach Mr. Covode through the improvised mail service then existing between Washington and the army of McDowell. I felt better for having done this much. I had also advised Mr. Covode that I was in a position to follow up the matter from this clue, and if it could be confirmed I would give the information directly to himself and no one else.

...This letter was intended as a private communication to my friend Covode, and I had particularly cautioned him not to permit certain War Department influences to get hold of the rumors, as I wanted to work it out myself. I learned subsequently, to my sorrow, that this personal letter, containing both the information and the criticism was sent to the War Office at once as an important paper.

Anybody will see that it was not only a mistake of my own to have written in this way, but also of Mr. Covode's to have shown it; but it was one of that statesman's 'privileges' to mix things up...I was not very much bothered about the consequences of such things at that time. I was in love, which will account for a good many of my mistakes...When I went to my newly-found home at Captain Wells' house the evening of the same day on which I had written and mailed this letter, I was received so kindly and courteously into the house by the genial Captain himself, that I began to feel that I had been guilty of an awfully shabby trick in having reported even privately to Mr.

Covode a private conversation with this staff officer in regard to mine host.

Indeed, I was feeling so uncomfortable over what seemed to have been an ungracious return for favors received, that I took the first opportunity to get out of the Captain's presence, and in the seclusion of my room that night I inwardly resolved that I would, if possible, attempt to modify my report by another letter to follow the first.

The evening was spent in the little parlor, as on many previous occasions. I was treated as one of the family, and entertained in the most agreeable manner by the accomplished ladies of this happy household. Each night we had music. Of course, 'Juanita,' with the guitar, accompanied by Geno, became one feature of all others that was always so charmingly attractive to me. The Captain himself sang a number of comic songs with good effect, while the elder daughter, Miss Sue, exerted herself in a pleasant way to create a little fun for the company at my own and Geno's expense. Colonel Hoffman,[124] Mr. Wilson and myself furnished the only audience, while a happy-faced brisk little mother supplied the refreshments and made us all feel at home.

This general attempt at a description of one evening must suffice for the many, many happy days and evenings that I spent in Fredericksburg during the months of McDowell's occupation of that country[125]...This is an absolutely 'true love' story, and I am giving correct names and actual incidents, realizing that I may be talking to some of the survivors of McDowell's army, who may have been 'thar or tharabouts,' who may read this story.

The Colonel Hoffman referred to above was in command of the regiment that had control of the town at this time. The Colonel having known the Wells family in the North, was glad of the opportunity to meet them, and during his stay in town lived with them in the house, with Mr. Wilson and myself. His regiment had been recruited somewhere in the neighborhood of Elmira New York.

A Boarder at Captain Wells House, Col. Henry C. "Barney" Hoffman
Cdr. 23rd N.Y. Vol. Rgt., USA

(National Archives Photo)

    As soon as I could see the Colonel alone I took the opportunity to tell him the story of the Captain's alleged complicity in the Chesapeake Bay piracy. To my surprise and gratification, he blurted out, rather savagely: 'I don't believe a word of it. Why, I've known Frank Wells all my life. No one at home ever accused him of any such traits of character as this. Why,' continued the Colonel, with a show of disgust, 'it's impossible. He couldn't be a disloyal man; he comes of Puritan stock from away back. I've seen, myself, a family tombstone up in Long Island which shows that his ancestors were buried there as early as 1671.[126] Why, boy, they came over in the Mayflower.'

> HEERE LIES Y BODY OF WILLIAM WELLS OF SOUTHHOLD GEN̄ IVSTICE OF Y PEACE & FIRST SHERIFFE OF NEW YORKE SHIRE
>
> Yea Here Hee Lies who speaketh yet though dead
> on winges of faith his soule to Heaven is fled
> His Pious Deedes And charity was such
> That of His praise no pen can write too much
> As Was His Life so was His blest Decease
> Hee liud in Loue And sweetly dyd in peace
> Upon Long Island This lee Nove 13 1671 Age 63

Tombstone of William Wells I of Southold, Long Island, N.Y., d. Nov. 13, 1671. Captain B. F. Wells was of the 6th generation descending from William Wells I.

(Photo courtesy Rev. Charles Wells Hayes, *William Wells of Southold.*

This seemed to settle it with Colonel Hoffman; but he added in an explanatory way: 'I suppose it's one of those 'Unionist's' stories. Every dog who has a grievance against his neighbor in war times runs to the nearest Provost Marshal to get the army on his enemy.[127] *Wells came down here to run his boat on the Rappahannock; that was his business. He tells me that he, with a majority of the citizens here, did not believe there would be a war, or that Virginia would go out of the Union, and therefore he did not attempt to get away until it was too late. The Confederates wouldn't let him take his boat north. When our fellows got here he ran his boat below town to prevent the rebels burning them, as they did all the rest; and when the gunboats came up the river they allowed a lot of rough sailors to seize and confiscate his boat.*[128] *Their object was prize money, and it is probably to their interest to create an impression that he was disloyal, that they may secure this money. I've told Frank he ought to resist this, but he is mad about it; swears they are robbers and thieves, and it is likely he and the girls have given offense in this way to some of our officers.'*

Col. Henry C. Hoffman, USA, Cdr. 23rd N.Y. Vol. Rgt. USA

(National Archives)

  The Colonel's decided talk fully confirmed me in the belief that the story of the Captain's complicity was the outcome of some personal grievance. Feeling that I had been guilty of a mean action in reporting the names to Mr. Covode, I sat down and wrote him the second letter, retracting all that the first contained, and added that the mistake arose from the desire of some enemies of mine or the Captain to get me mixed up with the War Department.

...Unfortunately, I did not mail the letter in time to overtake the first one. I was delayed by engaging myself to accompany the ladies the next day on a visit to the grave and monument of the mother of General Washington. As is generally known, the mother of President Washington lived, died and is buried in this historic old town. The old house,[129] or all that is left of it, still stands on one of the streets. The tomb and monument[130] is situated on rising ground some distance in the outskirts.

Wartime view of Mary Ball Washington tomb and monument off Washington Avenue in Fredericksburg, Virginia

(Library of Congress)

Most of the soldiers of the Army of the Potomac have visited this spot—at least all who were interested in such matters did who were about Fredericksburg. It was arranged that we should make a select picnic party of our visit to the tomb of the Mother of our Country, and as we expected to make a day of it, one day's rations for a dozen, composed of the usual girls' rations of sweet cake and sour pickle, were packed in a big lunch basket.

The picnic was a pleasant affair, of course because Geno was there. For the time being I had entirely forgotten or at least lost interest in the letter of explanation which I had intended to send to Mr. Covode on that day, as well as everything else but Geno.

Ninth New York Infantry, "Hawkins Zouaves," leaving New York City, June 6, 1861.

(Watercolor by Herbert Knoetel, Courtesy West Point Museum)

On our return through town that same evening I saw for the first time a New York regiment in full Zouave[131] uniform marching in their cat-like or tip-toe step, carrying their guns in a graceful, easy manner as they marched along in their picturesque style. The band played and seemingly the whole regiment of a thousand bass voices sang 'John Brown's Body' as I have never heard it since. The effect upon our party and the few loyal citizens was magical, and I leave the reader to imagine the sensations of the rebel occupants of the houses along the line of march. The shades were closed—they always were—

but that did not entirely conceal a number of bright, flashing eyes that one could always find on close inspection peeping through the cracks.

After relieving my mind by sending the letter I turned in to enjoy myself freely in the society of the ladies, and became so immersed in the pursuit of this new-found delight that I lost sight of all other business. Every day was a picnic and every evening a party.

One day while loafing about my office down at the Depot, I observed a strange-looking fellow hanging about. Every time I would look toward him I discovered his eyes had been upon me. He was not a good spy or detective because he at once gave himself away by his too-naked manner of observing things. I got onto him at once, because he did not seem to do anything but shadow me.

There was also a telegraph office at the Depot; the wire extending, I believe, only as far as the railroad was operated—to Aquia creek. I had not met the operator personally, and as had been my invariable practice, I had carefully concealed from all strangers, even friends, the fact that I was also a sound operator. I knew that neither the detective nor the operator suspected me of being an operator. As soon as I discovered that a suspicious watch had been put upon me it stirred me all up, and served most effectively to recall me to some sense of the duties or obligations that were expected of me. For the day or two following I passed more of my time within the hearing of the telegraph instrument and less in the parlor of Captain Wells.

One morning I saw the Pinkerton detective hand a piece of paper to the operator, who quietly put it on his telegraph desk. I had to wait a long, long time, and was forced to manufacture a good many excuses for lying around the office so closely.

Col. Lafayette C. Baker, War Department Secretary Stanton's Chief of Detectives

(National Archives)

...I was satisfied in my own mind, instinctively, as it were, that this fellow was a War Department spy[132] on Captain Wells and perhaps myself...He walked off some distance while I hung to the office, apparently very much interested in reading a copy of the Christian Commission Army Bible which had found its way into the office there. I heard the operator call up his office and after doing some routine railroad business, he sent the message to some one of the chief detectives in Washington, and was in effect, as nearly as I can remember, a sort of report or excuse for the failure to arrest a certain party, because he was absent that day, but was expected to return at night, when the arrest would be made.

Of course, I saw that I was not the party referred to because I was not absent. It did not take long, however to conclude, after some investigation and private talk with the operator, that Mr. Pinkerton had sent a man down there to look after the matter referred to in my letter to Covode. Of course Covode had indiscreetly rushed to the office and presented my letter without once thinking of the severe reflections...He only thought of the proposed scheme to get possession of the steamers.

I suppose that he felt in his honest, patriotic heart that it must be thwarted at once. That's the way Mr. Covode did things...

But I was not willing that the detectives of Pinkerton should have the credit of unearthing this plan, and, aside from little personal feelings and my sympathies and sentiment for the father of Geno, I at once determined to defeat their aspirations; and I succeeded—to my own subsequent discomfiture.

Determined to prevent the arrest of Geno's father, because I believed him innocent, and realizing that I was responsible for the espionage that had been placed upon the family, and without a single thought as to the consequences to myself, I went quietly from the telegraph office to the Wells house, only a few blocks distant.

Geno smilingly welcomed me as she opened the door (she had learned to look for my coming, I have since thought) and to her pleasant greeting I abruptly demanded, in a tone and with an agitation that must have seemed strange, 'I want to see your father right away.' To the polite response, 'Why, there is nobody at home but me. Come in,' I could only say, 'I must see your father or your mother on private business. I cannot talk to you now. I must get this matter settled first.'

Geno turned her big, black eyes on me quickly, quizzically; looked into my heart, seemingly satisfied herself that I was not crazy or intoxicated and she observed, with a smile: 'You can see father tonight, if you wish.' 'I must see him before night. Where is he?'

My animated manner, or perhaps urgent demands in the hallway had attracted Mrs. Well's attention in an upper room. Making an appearance at the head of the stairway, she asked pleasantly: 'What in the world is the matter with you?' 'Oh, nothing much. Come down, please. I have something to say to you and the Captain privately.'

Wells House interior, center stairway.

(2003 Photo by Robert A. Martin)

The happy mother descended only to the landing where she halted long enough to see whether it would be safe for her to come any closer. Geno, on hearing me express a desire to talk privately to her parents, had suddenly disappeared through a side door; while Mrs. Wells, laughingly stepped down, and without waiting to hear from me, said in her gentle motherly way: 'Now, my dear boy, don't you talk to me about that. Why, Geno is only a child.' 'Oh, no; not that—not now.

I came to tell you that the Captain will be arrested tonight. He must leave town at once.'

With a few words more of explanation, the loyal wife and mother was alive to the gravity of the situation. I left the house as suddenly as I had entered it, after cautioning them under no circumstances to admit that I gave this information, as I would be hanged too. I was back at the station before they had discovered that I had been away. They didn't arrest Captain Wells that night, but they did arrest me a few days subsequently.

It was a mistake, as will be seen hereafter, for the Washington Secret Service people to have acted against my advice and attempt to arrest Captain Wells. It would have been better to have quietly waited and watched for some tangible proofs of the rumored piracy, as I had suggested to Covode...I was the least bit afraid that the family might accidentally give away to some one who would report to the detective the fact that I was responsible for the escape of his intended victim.

I learned by my telegraph connection that this Pinkerton spy was continuing to report to his chief daily that 'Wells has not yet returned,' or that 'the party was still absent,' and later that he had 'escaped South.' Luckily for me he did not learn of the short and interesting return visit the Captain made, and in consequence he had no occasion to immediately investigate the Captain's taking off, so that several days elapsed before he found it out. The Captain did not go South to join the rebels, but instead went North, visiting during his exile a married daughter living in Baltimore.

I felt that I had made my way clear in thus 'breaking the ice' when I should want to ask for Geno's hand. I had killed two or three birds at one shot that day. I had beaten or thwarted Assistant Secretary of War Watson and his Pinkerton crowd in their attempt at arresting Captain Wells on mere rumors; I had established myself in the good graces of Geno's entire family; I had prevented her father from being imprisoned. In addition to all this, I succeeded in getting myself into Old Capitol Prison by order of Secretary of War E. M.

Stanton, and became a companion of Belle Boyd[133] and numerous other rebel spies...

I need not say that after this episode I felt that the fate of the entire Wells family was in my hands. From that day on I was what may be slangily termed 'solid' with the Wells family. I believe I have mentioned the fact previously that Geno was a strikingly beautiful girl of 16 and that I was 20.[134] I may be permitted to even say parenthetically that there has been nothing in my adventurous life nearly so fascinating as were the summer days in which I was 'isolated' in company with the little girl who lived, as it were, **between the two armies at Fredericksburg.**

To be sure, the soldiers were there, or there about, in force. The crack of the picket's rifle, almost the distant boom of McClellan's battles around Richmond[135]—indeed the smoke of war was in the air at the time, and no one knew what a day would bring forth. This was not exactly a period well adapted to sincere love making.[136] No one who has known of Geno could be made to believe that she could be insincere, or that anyone could insincerely make love to her. We were together all the time, but I do not think we were sentimental in our talk.

...Geno was a pretty little girl, but at the risk of repetition I will say that her beauty was a kind that may not be easily described or portrayed. It was her eyes—her beautiful dark-brown eyes—that 'were in themselves a soul.'[137]

There was this difference to me between Geno and all my other girls: in her presence it did not seem to be at all necessary to do any sentimental talking. I was always impressed by her soul-piercing eyes, with the feeling that she knew it all anyhow, and it was no use in talking—I had almost written <u>lying</u>. I believe I told Geno more of my life than I ever intended anybody to know. I simply couldn't help it...

In every man's life there is one moment, or one single memory, that is more cherished than all others. I shall have to tell of this one moment of my life, which occurred the day before I left.

One pleasant afternoon in August 1862, I happened around to the Wells house, as usual, knowing very well that Geno, dressed in her most becoming of Summer toilettes, would soon join me on the veranda. Perhaps I was a little earlier than usual at my accustomed seat; anyway, I became a little impatient at Geno not putting in an appearance promptly, and thinking perhaps she might not have become aware of my presence, stepped into the hall to try to make it known to her.

The windows had all been closely shaded to exclude the bright August sunlight, giving the hallway that cool and inviting half-darkened appearance. Stepping into the parlor affecting a little cough as a signal that I was around the house, I had scarcely seated myself when my quick ear caught the sound of her footsteps as she quickly tripped down the stairway.

...a sweet girl, with beautiful eyes, and moreover she was womanly in figure and graceful in action, in that hers was the ethereal style of beauty so aptly described by Longfellow's 'Evangeline.'[138] *...Rising to greet her, I advanced to the door just as her lithe figure darkened it. She looked so nice, and the parlor and hallway were shrouded by that dim, religious light one reads about. I was tempted and, yielding to the youthful impulse, grasped both her hands in mind and attempted to steal a kiss, the first kiss of love.*

I had by her quiet dignity of manner been repelled from attempting anything of a too familiar kind on such a short war acquaintance. She quickly dropped her head, turning her face from me, while I held both hands tightly in my own, and uttered only that one little word of four letters, 'Geno.' Whether it was the tone of voice, the imploring or entreating manner and earnest emphasis, or a mild reproach, I knew not. She answered not a word, but turned her blushing face up to mine, while her beautiful eyes pierced to my soul, and I—I—oh!

Here I drop my pen, put my feet on the desk on which I have been writing this, lay my head back in my lazy chair, and with both hands pressed on my face I bring back this one blissful moment of my life 30 years ago as if it were but yesterday. I cannot write of it. It's a 'true love' story...

Before I could do it again she had deftly slipped away from me, and like a frightened deer glided to a dark corner of the parlor; from behind a chair she blushingly cast reproachful glances toward me, while she rearranged the hair that she had taken so much pains to bewitchingly do up, and that had so long delayed her appearance.

There is a song, and of course plenty of poetry in it, which I have frequently asked my wife and daughter to sing—'Il Bacio'[139]—which more aptly describes this one blissful moment than my pen can write.

After this there was a sort of an understanding between us that all lovers who have been there will understand—and it is not necessary for me to explain. I had Geno's first love, and it is a true saying that in a woman's first love she loves her lover; in all the rest she loves love.

I have been in love—oh, often—so many times...but Geno was my <u>war-girl</u>, and all old soldiers will agree with me that there is a something in the very memories of love and war that touch the heart in a way that is not reached by any other feeling.

Do not for a moment imagine that there was any attempt on the part of this truly happy family to take any advantages of the tender susceptibilities of the 'Boy Spy.' They knew absolutely nothing of my past record.

Through the rifted smoke clouds of the great rebellion of 30 years ago I am relating a little love story from real life that seems almost like a dream now, but which is the best remembered incident of all the war to me. 'The ways of fate are very diverse,' and it has truly happened to me that this sweet face looked into so long since has never been forgotten in all the years that have passed or are yet to come.[140]

...I was under surveillance, or in a manner suspected of disloyalty by some of the officials of the War Office. My brother Spencer, who was regularly on duty in the War Department Telegraph Office, had written me a note of caution...

Miss Mamie Wells, the second daughter, had gone to her sister's home in Baltimore under my charge a few days...Her war history, I venture to say here, would present one of the most attractive yet written. She was during the bombardment and battles [of Fredericksburg] *a Florence Nightingale to both sides, and to her parents and family in the subsequent terrible sufferings consequent upon their exposed position between the two armies, became a heroine in deed and in truth.*

My personal acquaintance with this remarkable young lady was confined to the few days of 1862. The incident which is best remembered occurred while riding up the Potomac from Aquia Creek as her escort, enroute to Baltimore. In reply to something that I had said on the subject that was uppermost in my heart, she took occasion to say to me in a kind, sisterly way about Geno that produced a lasting effect upon me.

'You must not trifle with that child.' That I was sincere and very much in earnest she soon discovered, because from her charming manner I was impelled to tell her right there much more of my love for her sister than I had told Geno herself. Her smiling approval, when I mentioned my ambition to make Geno an officer's wife, was: 'You love like a boy, but I believe you would fight like a man.'

Miss Sue was of an entirely different disposition. She was a born coquette and flirting was natural to her. I never made love to Miss Sue...after having met Geno; but she evidently felt that I was her legitimate game, simply because she was the oldest daughter. In fact, she told me plainly that Geno was entirely too young to be spending so much time with strange young gentlemen.

Naturally enough I resented her advice and talked to Geno about it, but my little girl only laughed sweetly at my earnestness, and not once that I can recall said a single word in reply that reflected on her elder sister's judgment. Geno's voice was mild, her manner of speaking slow, but with a charming hesitating manner that made everything she said, or left unsaid, impressive.

My excellent wife, who looks at matters in a practical way, and has heard me talk about love affairs with Geno, always takes Sue's part in the discussion, declaring that I didn't like Sue because she was too smart for me.

That is only partly correct. My trouble was that Sue would not permit Geno and I to be alone together at all. The father being absent in exile, Miss Sue prevailed upon the mother to allow her to 'manage this affair,' as she haughtily termed it. We were being restricted somewhat arbitrarily by Miss Sue's management, and to get around it I had recourse to smuggling little notes to Geno through her little brother George and sister Jennie.[141]

I recall now, with a laugh, with what slyness and caution Geno managed this little secret service of our own. There was not any ciphers used, but Geno had a way of inserting quotations in French in her notes that embarrassed me, because I couldn't interpret myself, and of course dare not appeal to anyone else.

One day we all came to grief by Miss Sue getting hold of one of my notes to Geno, in which I impulsively intimated that the animus or motive of Sue's opposition was based on the fact that she desired all the attention bestowed on herself. That was a very indiscreet thing to put on a piece of paper; but, as I have said before, I was 20 and Geno was 16.

Entering the parlor one afternoon, I found both the sisters sobbing and crying as if their hearts were breaking over some sudden intelligence of a dreadful character. I hurriedly asked if their father had been caught. But to my eager interest Sue replied through her tears, by taking me to task about this note. I tried to explain, but she did all the talking for an hour, and I had no chance to say a word, until she said something about Geno being too young to take care of herself, when I blurted out: 'Geno is better able to take care of herself than you are, and I know it.' That put my foot into it deeper than ever.

It took me a week to get this affair straightened out, and I verily believe the words uttered so thoughtlessly at this moment were treasured up against me in wrath by Miss Sue for 20 years, though she pretended to 'make up,' and I kissed both the sisters that time before we broke up the conference or love feast.

There remains in existence today a neatly written, faded letter, addressed to 'The friend of an hour,' which my sisters have preserved. The smart, sharp, stinging words of this letter have served as a model for more than one communication under similar circumstances.

There was this peculiarity about the Wells family: they were all loyal and true to each other, and to their parents. More than one outsider has learned to their sorrow, touch one, and all of them were touched.

As serving to indicate this, and to show the innocence and purity of Geno, I will relate at my own expense an incident. Shortly after the Captain and father had 'escaped' through my connivance,[142] Geno, in her sweet, hesitating voice said to me in reply to something I had been saying or doing: 'Father said to me as he bid me good bye: **'Geno, look out for Mr. O.K.***'[143]*

I was stunned. Perhaps I was presuming too far on my being solid with the family, and in my usual impulsive way I earnestly resented the Captain's caution, probably because I realized that he was right, and said something harsh in reply. Geno looked up into my face in a surprised way, while she defended her father. I shall never forget the words and the manner in which they were uttered: 'Why, father knows best; I would not have him angry with me for anything. It was a lesson to me. I was angry at the moment, but I loved her all the more for this evidence of loyalty to her parents....

To pick up the tangled love-knot in the thread of this narrative, I will say during the pleasant evening spent with the Wells family I was so happy and contented that I became wholly oblivious to everything that was going on in the army outside.

It was late the next day when I walked down to the railroad office as usual to see if there was any news for me. It was then that I received the note of warning from my brother Spencer, which had come during my absence...

Col. Daniel C. McCallum, USA, Stanton's Superintendent of U.S. Military Railroads
(Library of Congress)

While in or around this office or station, about which were always congregated a great crowd of officers and soldiers off duty, as well as sutlers, newsboys, etc., I was pleasantly approached by Gen. McCallum,[144] who had charge of all military railroads as the successor of Col. Thos. A. Scott,[145] and who, after talking agreeably about some of the work I had previously undertaken, told me in his gruff way: 'Railroad and telegraph employees have been required by the Secretary of War to take the oath of allegiance. All have signed but you, and I have left a blank in the office for your signature.'

I was an employee, and as such was perfectly willing to sign all the oaths they required, and expressed my willingness to comply at once. I found a written blank form had been prepared for me in the office. I signed it without thinking it necessary to read. When handing the paper back to the clerk, he remarked jocularly: 'They have made you sign a mighty tight paper, haven't they?'

It was only when my curiosity was aroused by this remark that I thought of reading over the form of the oath. I think it was what was known in the year after as the cow-catcher bond or iron-clad oath. It was purposely made strong enough to catch any supposed case of disloyalty. It contained one simple clause that at the time seemed to perplex me a little. It read in substance: "I have never belonged to any organization or borne arms against the Government of the United States, voluntarily or involuntarily.'

I could not conscientiously or truthfully swear to that. I was willing enough to do almost anything to get around the ugly point that seemed like a rock in my path, without being forced to explain that I had voluntarily united with the rebel army and involuntarily borne arms against the Government. I dreaded very much putting my name to a paper which could in any event be brought up against me as proof that I was 'a perjurer.'

I was loyal to the core, as everybody who has read this must know; but I had—I may say voluntarily—united myself with the 3d battalion of rebel Maryland artillery. To be sure, I was forced by the necessities of my peculiar work and the situation during my sickness in Richmond, as well as prompted by a desire to further and better aid the United States Government, to do this; but the stubborn fact was, I had taken their oath and I had in reality borne rebel arms.[146] I had not told anyone in Fredericksburg about this, and none of the railroad employees knew anything of my former experiences. Perhaps Geno had my confidence, but none of the family ever received any intimation from her of my true character. To them all I was, as Sue put it, 'A nice little fellow from Pennsylvania, and that's all we know.'

I saw at the first glance of this new oath that I was in a tight place, and in a moment of hasty impulse, prompted solely by a desire to be truthful and honorable to myself, I scratched my name from the paper. Without a word of explanation to the astonished clerk I took it to Gen. McCallum, and in a few words explained my action, and desired him to try and find some way out of the trouble for me. He had understood in a general way something of my experiences, and when I told him my action he agreed with me, and said it was right and honorable in me to protect my name. Further, on his return to Washington the day following, he said he would report the matter to the Secretary of War and ask that I be permitted to remain in the service without being compelled to sign that iron clad paper.

I thought then that the matter was settled, and in the evening went home from my office to pass another, only one more, of the enjoyable, happy nights in the company of the ladies.

Thomas T. Eckert, Stanton's Chief of the War Dept. Telegraph Office

(Library of Congress)

In the meantime the leaven I had sent to Washington previously, in the shape of a telegram to Covode, had begun to work; so that when Gen. McCallum got back to Washington city the next day and reported my case to the Assistant Secretaries P. H. Watson and Gen. [Thomas T.] Eckert,[147] these two officials put their wise heads together, and with only the evidence in their possession which was additionally overbalanced by Gen Eckert's former prejudice, they came to the hasty conclusion, without giving me a chance to be heard, that 'I was a very dangerous man,' and so reported their conclusion to Mr. [Edwin M.] Stanton, whose attention was at the same time called to my reports to Covode.

The telegrapher at Fredericksburg at that time was a Mr. Gentry of Kentucky, a clever gentleman—as all Kentuckians are that I have ever met.

That afternoon while lounging in the cool parlor with Geno and Miss Sue, I was called to the door by a visit from Mr. Gentry, who politely informed me that he had an intimation from my brother and

friends in Washington that I would get into trouble unless I signed that oath. Mr. Gentry very kindly advised me, to use his own words, which made such a lasting impression on me that I have not forgotten them: 'Now, don't you be carried away by infatuation for this pretty little girl; act sensibly for the present. Why, I'd sign anything, and I'm from Kentucky.'

He was very courteous and I felt he had been sent after me...He knew nothing of my reasons for declining the oath, and when he desired a reply from me to telegraph back to Washington, I merely said: 'Just tell them I won't do it. They will understand that.'...I felt at that time that it was not Mr. Stanton personally who was insisting upon cornering me in this way. He certainly knew of my former services, and that I could not be disloyal if I wanted to. If he had given the subject a moment's consideration he would have surmised the reason for my 'recalcitrancy'...

I believed then, and I have always entertained the opinion, that Mr. Eckert, through Assistant Secretary Watson, was instrumental in creating this misunderstanding. Perhaps I am mistaken, but I shall die without changing my mind on this subject. Mr. Gentry probably went direct to his office after his short interview with me and reported the failure of his effort to 'reconstruct me.'...

Secretary of War, Edwin M. Stanton

(Library of Congress)

In an hour or two Mr. Gentry returned to the house—they all knew very well where to find me—called me to the door again, and in the most feeling manner told me privately that he had received and at the same time held in his possession a telegraph order from the Secretary of War, E. M. Stanton, to Provost-Marshal-General [Marsena R.] Patrick[148] for my arrest.

Mr. Gentry very kindly kept the fact that he had received such a message entirely to himself, considerately bringing to me first the ugly intelligence. He did not say so, but I have always believed his object was to give me an opportunity of escaping. I could easily have done so without having any suspicion attached to him of having advised me of this intention.

I had no thought of attempting anything of this kind. We sat down on the porch together while I read the order, which is today on file in the War Office, in these words:

> 'Arrest and keep in the closest confinement, O. K., and send to Washington in charge of sufficient guard to prevent any communication.'

Mr. Gentry endeavored to ease the 'disagreeable duty' as he termed it, by saying that the receipt of such an order was a great surprise to him, and he felt sure there was some mistake, and that all would be righted when I should reach Washington.

When I realized the full purport of such an order from the Secretary of War, I was almost stunned at the direct prospect. My first thoughts were of the distressing effect of such news upon my father and relatives at home, who were expecting that I should receive very soon a promotion from the Secretary of War to the Regular Army. How then could I explain this arrest to them? I don't know now whether or not I even thanked Mr. Gentry for his kind thoughtfulness at the time, I hope he may be living and see from this after the lapse of 25 years I have not *forgotten his generous and thoughtful consideration for me on that hot Summer day in 1862.*

Asking to be excused for a moment, I briefly told Mrs. Wells of the sudden intelligence, which she received in her motherly, sympathetic manner, with both hands raised in astonishment. Without trusting myself to talk further to her or anyone else in my agitated condition, I rejoined Mr. Gentry, and we walked together up the hill to Gen. Patrick's office,[149] where Gentry handed the order to Gen. Patrick while I stood by. After he read the telegram, Mr. Gentry astonished the old man by introducing his prisoner. The General was kind, indeed he was very sympathetic, and explained that as the order was direct from the Secretary of War, he should have to give it especial attention, and see that it was executed to the letter; but he would make it as pleasant for me as possible.

I was given one of the vacant rooms in the private mansion[150] then occupied as Provost-Marshal's headquarters. A sentry with a loaded musket stood guard in the large hallway at my open door, with positive orders, as I was courteously informed by the officer who placed him there, not to allow anyone to see me, and under no circumstances was I to communicate with any person, except through himself as officer of the guard.

As there were no boats leaving for Washington city from Aquia Creek so late in the day, I was obliged to remain a solitary prisoner, under strict order of the War Department, until the following day.

I shall not waste any paper...in the way of analysis of my feelings during all that long evening and night, in which I was closely guarded by a sentry, who I was informed had orders not to permit any communication with me. He stood within a few feet of me during the evening, and while I slept on a cot, paced about like a guardian angel, conducting himself in a grum sort of a way that was not at all calculated to promote a feeling of sociability. In fact, his bearing rather impressed me with a sort of an overwhelming sensation that the gun he carried was loaded to the muzzle, and the fellow that had *command of it looked for all the world as if he were just aching for a chance to try it on something.*

He wasn't a companionable fellow, so I acted toward him as he did to me, with silent contempt. And that's the way I spent the evening. I knew very well that there were plenty of friends in town who would have called to see me in this my time of need if they had been permitted to do so. As it was, I was all alone in my glory until late in the evening, when an officer, accompanied by a soldier, came to my prison door, the soldier carrying a little basket which I was told contained my supper, which kind and motherly Mrs. Wells had sent to me; but not a word of sympathy or regret accompanied it. I don't know for sure, but I think that the contents had been not only inspected by the officer of the guard on the lookout for contraband communications, but that the different little dainties had been sampled as well...

This generous and thoughtful remembrance from Mrs. Wells was the only indication I received in my solitary confinement during all that beautiful, but lonely long Summer evening in Fredericksburg that there were any persons outside of my four walls except the grim old sentry.

Of course I knew that at our house there would be assembled the usual crowd of happy young folks, and that their conversation and thoughts would naturally be with me in my confinement. This comforting reflection was, however somewhat disturbed by the fear that the entire family might either have been arrested or dispersed; so that the discomforts of my close confinement were greatly increased by this fear until I was, in a manner, assured of their safety by the arrival of the daintily-served lunch.

...We will not dwell on this subject, because the less said about it the better. Indeed, after 25 years have elapsed and though the unpleasant mistake was corrected by President Lincoln and Mr. Stanton—who subsequently ante-dated my commission to cover this time[151]*—I yet think of it with a feeling akin to the sickening heartaches I experienced at the time.*

I slept that night—if I slept at all—on a bed of misery. At every turn I was made to realize that I was a prisoner to our own side. Though the officers of Gen. Patrick's staff[152] who had charge of me were accomplished gentlemen, and seemed apparently to sympathize with me, I could not conceal, and they must have seen, my distress; they were obliged by the strict orders they had received...

The morning following my arrest, after a hasty and solitary breakfast, I was personally visited by Gen. Patrick, who was then Provost-Marshal for that army,[153] who in the most kindly manner possible expressed his regrets for the necessity of putting me to so much inconvenience; further explaining that once in Washington I could no doubt get everything fixed up. He then showed me two letters and a small pocket Bible that had been sent to me, but which he could not deliver to me, under his strict orders to permit no communication. When I recognized the address of one letter to be in the well-known handwriting of my father, the very sight of it seemed to be like a thrust of a knife into my heart, as I at once realized how distressing to him would be the news of my arrest—especially as he, with all other of my friends, had been expecting in its stead a promotion, by way of recompense for my past services. The other note I knew was from Geno, while the Bible was the last, best gift of Mrs. Wells, and remains to this day one of my most valued relics of those unforgotten days. I was assured by Gen. Patrick that they should be sent along with me to Washington in the care of the officer in charge, and he hoped and expressed the belief that I should soon be free and get possession of them.

With a kind good bye, he introduced me to Capt____, whose name I have now forgotten, and a Lieutenant, 'who would kindly accompany me to Washington.[154] The Captain considerately observed that it had been arranged that we should get out of town quietly; that is, without attracting any attention from the crowds about the streets, who had no doubt heard of my arrest.

I thought this very nice of the Captain at the time, but I'm inclined now to think it was done partly at least, to save himself any annoyance and to better prevent or avoid any attempt at communication. To accomplish this and to avoid the depot, we crossed the river together at a ferry, in order to take the train for Aquia Creek from the other side, and in so doing we passed within a half block of Geno's house, but not within sight of it.[155]

...The incidents of which I have been writing are, strictly speaking, all facts which actually occurred during June and July, 1862.[156] *This is now June, 1887; about 25 years have elapsed since, but those are 'unforgotten days' that are treasured in my memory and heart as fresh and as sweet—and at the same time as bitter—as if it were but yesterday.*[157]

Chapter VI – Running the Blockade

During the first Union occupation of Fredericksburg in the summer of 1862, Kerbey escorted Mamie Wells, aboard a steamer from Aquia Creek, to visit her married sister Harriet (Wells) Crawford in Baltimore, Maryland. There, Mamie was reunited with her exiled father who, no thanks to Kerbey and under threat of arrest, had fled to Baltimore. Waiting for the Federal army's departure from the Fredericksburg area in August 1862, Mamie and her father devised a plan to run the blockade and reunite with their family.

One October evening in 1862, shortly before Gen. Burnside's Union troops returned to reoccupy Stafford Heights opposite Fredericksburg, Captain Wells and Mamie left Washington, D.C. to board an awaiting schooner on the Potomac River, and begin their treacherous journey across enemy lines. Debarking the schooner, in a small boat they rowed to the mouth of Potomac Creek, continuing up the creek to Belle Plain. From that point, they set off on foot and lost their way in the darkness. They walked a total of sixteen miles before arriving in Fredericksburg just as the town clock struck 5:00 a.m. Mamie Wells relates their story:[158]

> ...I stepped into the bateau and took a seat in the stern. We pushed out into the stream, and having reached the schooner's side, climbed to its deck. There we remained for some time in silent contemplation of the scene around us—those mighty Monitors, with their heavy guns quietly resting on the bosom of the beautiful Potomac—and many self-congratulations that we had left the Capitol in safety we offered to ourselves as we lingered.
>
> ... I slept well and felt refreshed in the morning...The sun shone brightly, and promised a fair day; and the schooner continued to glide smoothly on with a light breeze. For myself, I was very happy, because I was fairly on my way home, from which I had been separated for four months in consequence of its evacuation, by the Federal forces in the month of August

previous. I shall never forget that bright happy October day—the recollection is like a beautiful dream.

It was between eight and nine o'clock when the captain gave the order to bring the bateau to the schooner's side... "All ready now," whispered the captain." A few moments later when he handed me into the bateau he whispered: "God bless you! I hope you have good luck."

My father took up the oars and we were soon being rapidly carried toward the Virginia shore. A row of two miles brought us to the mouth of a creek[159] into which we turned..."The stars are just bright enough for our purpose." "I am glad there is no moon." "How far have we to go up this creek?" "About three miles." "And then we will have nine to walk."

... Keep a good lookout, for there is a fog rising which may prevent us from finding the point we want. Look for a small wharf on the left bank." 'How wide is the creek!" "About a mile and a half; but we are near the left shore." ... "The fog grows denser." Smoothly the bateau glided on "I can distinguish bushes along the shore. And now I see a wharf. Look!" "It is the place." "Belle Plain?"[160] "Yes."

The boat was directed to the shore. "Remain in the boat until I have secured the baggage. I will hide it among the brush..."Now we will proceed upon our journey... First, let us ascertain the hour if possible. I should say half past ten." "Light a match." "I dare not. Can you see the time?" "Half past ten, I think." "We will allow ourselves four hours to reach home." "That will be half past two."

We pursued our journey for five miles. "How little they think at home that we will be there to-night." "Do not raise your hopes too high; we are not sure of the pickets yet." "Yes; but it would be very hard to be captured now, when we are doing no harm to any one—only trying to go home." ..."But still, father, the hope of reaching home to-night seems too bright to be realized. I am afraid the worst of our journey is not over. And yet everything around is so peaceful, as though the enemy had fled to give place to rest and quietude once more." "To-morrow may make this spot a battlefield"

At the end of a half mile, or there-abouts, the road we had followed terminated in a cross road. "Which way shall we turn?" "I do not know. By the stars neither appear right." "I think the left." "So say I."

Twenty minutes passed. "We have walked about a mile on this road." "Yes; but I begin to fear we are wrong. It turns too much to the north. See the stars!" "Yes; I have been watching the dipper, and thinking so, too. "I don't like to turn back until I know we are wrong. Suppose we walk on a little farther."

...We trudged on. "Another house. I will endeavor to learn something from these good people.

"...Who dar?" The voice came from a cabin a short distance from the house. We drew near it, and discovered the head of an aged negro woman protruding from the window. "Who dar?" "We are strangers, Auntie. Can you tell the way to Fredericksburg." "Yes, sir. Right back dat road what you come. "How far are we from the Belle Plain road?" "Two miles, Massa." "And how far from Fredericksburg?" "Five miles 'zactly." "Thank you." "You're welcome, Massa. You see as how I was feared the Yankees done come 'gin. Dey served us powerful bad, dey did." "Good night, Auntie." "Good night, Miss Sarvint, Massa."

"And we have walked two miles out of the way, father?" "Yes, making in all, four extra miles." ...Back in the direction we had come we journeyed until we reached the Belle Plain. "The army has cut up the whole country into roads. We will follow the one with the most wagon tracks," said my father.

Accordingly, we bent our heads to the ground, to ascertain the direct route, when we journeyed on.

The night was still as death. Not a sound broke upon our ear save the tramp of our own weary feet, and the soft rustle of the autumn leaves when bestirred by the breeze. ... "Surely we have walked five miles since we left that house." "Making in all twelve and a half miles... "I must confess I am somewhat discouraged myself; but there is only one course left us—push on." "Yes, while there continues the faintest hope of being on the right road."

A moment more and I had paused in my walk. Clasping my hands in that moment of joy, I cried: "Oh, father!" The sentence was incomplete, but revealed, more than words, what I felt. And I now recall that moment as one of the happiest of my life. The old town clock[161] struck three. Who can describe its effect upon us in that uncertain moment! Its tones pealed forth like sweet music in the dead silence of the night.

We soon reached the Phillips house[162] (since burned by the Federals) and shortly afterward the Lacy mansion.[163] Then we quickened our steps to the bank of the river.[164] "The bridges are destroyed as I feared. Nothing remains but the broken piers." "How will we cross the river?" "At the ferry. We must walk around the hills." "How far?" "By the path, one mile and a half." "And we are directly opposite home now." "Try to bear up a little longer."

As we walked to the ferry, the town clock struck four. "Now our walk is most ended." "Ho! ferryman!" "Who's there?" "Mr. [Wells]. Where is the boat?" "There is no boat here." "No boat!" repeated my father. "No boat!" I faintly murmured. "No boat, sir. The ferry has been removed up the river." "How far!" "Above the Lacy house, where the Yankees had their pontoon bridge." "Is it possible?" "Where have you come from, Mr. [Wells]?" "Washington, and we have been walking since half past ten." "The lady with you?" "Yes; my daughter. We have come here from the Lacy house." "Well, the ferry is not far above that."

1881 Stereopticon image of Fredericksburg looking northeast across the Chatham Bridge

(Courtesy HFFI)

Our disappointment at hearing this news was so great that, for a few moments, we hardly had courage to move. But it soon came back to us, and we retraced our steps around the Stafford hills.

"This must be the spot, but the fog is so heavy, I can distinguish nothing across the river. There is no boat here, and it is growing very cold." "I think there is a faint light opposite. Do you see—there?" "I will call. Perhaps some one may hear me. At all events we cannot remain here until daylight; for we are too cold and damp. Hollos, ferryman!" The echo of his voice died away, but no answer was returned. "Hollos, the guard!" Still no answer. "Bring over your boat!" "No reply, father." "Yet I think the light grows brighter. Ho o-o-o; Ho: ferryman." " I am afraid they will not come until daylight; they have no pickets on this side." "Ho! the guar-r-r-d! Bring over your boat." Twenty minutes, and no response. "Hollos, picket!

There is a lady to go over." "Ho! ho!" came from the opposite shore. "Bring over the boat." All right."

In a short time a light was seen approaching thro' the fog, and a flat boat struck the shore. We stepped aboard, and were carried to the opposite shore as that dear, old town clock struck five. I will not attempt a discussion of what followed. Our arrival home is sacred to us. Neither is it necessary to state that we survived our walk of sixteen miles, which was only the beginning of the hardships and trials we endured during the remaining two and a half years of the war.

Chapter VII – The Northern Invaders Arrive

Barely a fortnight had passed from when Mamie Wells and her father ran the blockade to reunite with their family. On November 17, 1862, they would witness the arrival of Gen. Edwin V. Sumner's Right Grand Division, the first of Gen. Burnside's army to arrive on the opposite side of the Rappahannock River.

Fredericksburg was held by a small force led by Col. William B. Ball of the 15th Virginia Cavalry who Gen. Robert E. Lee had placed in charge of guarding the town. In a November 14th telegram, Lee directed him to destroy the railroad track and bridges between Aquia Creek and Fredericksburg.[165] Ball's troops had just barely finished the task when, on November 16, his scouts signaled the approach of Sumner's army through Stafford County. Under threat of the enemy crossing the Rappahannock River into Fredericksburg, Ball's small army set up riverfront defenses at the upper end of town, opposite Falmouth.

Of the November 17th events, diarist Jane Beale wrote:

Our little army here was augmented by the arrival of a small force from Richmond. A considerable number of the enemy appeared above the town of Falmouth and towards evening commenced firing upon our battery stationed in the field beyond White Plains. Col. Ball who was in command here returned the fire and there was an artillery duel kept up for about an hour. We watched the firing with intense interest until warned by the near approach of a shot we left our station at the window and came downstairs when we came into our front porch we found the whole neighborhood in a great state of excitement. The poor people from the upper part of the town had fled from their homes and were running wildly along with children in their arms, a shot had gone thro the paper factory and frightened the poor girls who where at work there terribly and they had joined the stampede, we yielded to the advice of the gentlemen of the neighborhood and went to another part of the town until night came on when we returned home to await the events of another day, we learned then that the Yankees had got the range of our batteries and had disabled our guns killing one man and wounding several, one boy who had gone from curiosity to witness the fight had his foot shot and terribly shattered.[166] Several horses were killed and the battery was withdrawn from the open field and hid behind the house at White Plains.[167]

Arriving the following day, Gen. Marsena R. Patrick wrote: *...Found that Hancock's Division was here in Falmouth, having taken possession Yesterday, after an Artillery duel with the Batteries on the other side of the River, which they knocked to pieces & forced to retire, while, it is said, the enemy retreated from the heights to the cellars of the town –It is not known how many Troops are there, but not any large force, & I do not know what our plans will be about taking possession of the town...*[168]

The day following the artillery duel, Jane Beale had company: *Rose early and the first object that met my eyes upon looking out was a line of cavalry drawn up behind my schoolroom and stable, I soon learned they had been there for hours and by a little concert of action among the neighbours we determined to give them their breakfasts and my boys and servants fed and watered fifteen by 9 o'clock. They were so grateful did my very heart good to give it to them...*[169]

The next day, Mrs. Beale wrote: *Watched with trembling hearts the long line of Yankees pouring over the Chatham hills to take the same station they occupied last summer, they come in countless numbers and our hearts sank within us as we thought of our little Spartan band who holds the fords, why do they remain to be sacrificed? And to bring destruction upon our town were queries that forced themselves upon us, nor did our wonder cease much when we heard Gen. Lee had telegraphed to Col. Ball "to hold the passage of the River at Fred'g at all hazards."*[170]

On the morning of November 20th, Generals Lee, Longstreet, and staff arrived outside of Fredericksburg and proceeded to "Snowden," the hilltop mansion of John L. Stansbury. Held in "Snowden's" parlor, Gen. Lee called a meeting with Mayor Slaughter and other town officials. Described as grave and serious, Lee spoke plainly regarding the real dangers threatening the town now that the two great armies were positioned face to face. Responding to Mayor Slaughter's question as to whether the townspeople must fear the worst, Lee replied *Yes, they must fear the worst.* General Longstreet then added, *But let them hope for the best.*[171]

The next day, under a flag of truce, Gen. Sumner sent Gen. Patrick across the river with a letter to the mayor. Col. William B. Ball received Patrick at a wharf at the foot of Hawke Street where Patrick delivered Gen. Sumner's letter:

Headquarters Army of the Potomac, November 21, 1862.

Mayor and Common Council of Fredericksburg:
GENTLEMEN: Under cover of the houses of your city, shots have been fired upon the troops of my command. Your mills and manufactories are furnishing provisions and the material for clothing for armed bodies in rebellion against the Government of the United States. Your railroads and other means of transportation are removing supplies to the depots of such troops. This condition of things must terminate, and, by direction of General Burnside, I accordingly demand the surrender of the city into my hands, as the representative of the Government of the United States, at or before 5 o'clock this afternoon.

Failing an affirmative reply to this demand by the hour indicated, sixteen hours will be permitted to elapse for the removal from the city of women and children, the sick and wounded and aged, &c., which period having expired, I shall proceed to shell the town. Upon obtaining possession of the city, every necessary means will be taken to preserve order and secure the protective operation of the laws and policy of the United States Government.

I am, very respectfully, your obedient servant,
E. V. SUMNER,
Bvt. Maj. Gen., U.S. Army, Commanding Right Grand Division.[172]

Col. Ball informed Patrick that, before he delivered Sumner's letter to Mayor Slaughter, he had to refer it to his commanding officer. Subsequently, Major G. Moxley Sorrel of Gen. Longstreet's staff, visited Patrick and informed him the letter was now in the mayor's hands.[173] Unknown to Patrick, the letter had been taken to Gen. Lee, who with a large part of his army, was waiting hidden on the heights at the rear of the town. Patrick waited at *French John's* log house at the foot of Hawke Street until 7 p.m when the mayor handed his reply to Patrick: [174]

MAYOR'S OFFICE,
Fredericksburg, November 21, 1862.

Bvt. Maj. Gen. E. V. SUMNER,
Commanding U.S. Army:
SIR: I have received, at 4:40 o'clock this afternoon, your communication of this date. In it you state that, under cover of the houses of the town, shots have been fired upon the troops of your command; that our mills and manufactories are furnishing provisions and the material for clothing for armed bodies in rebellion against the Government of the United States; that our railroads and other means of transportation are removing supplies to the depots of such troops; that this condition of things must terminate; that, by command of Major-General Burnside, you demand the surrender of this town into your hands, as the representative of the Government of the United States, at or before 5 o'clock this afternoon; that, failing an affirmative reply to this demand by the time indicated, sixteen hours will be permitted to elapse for the removal from the town of the women and children, the sick, wounded, and aged, which period having elapsed, you will proceed to shell the town.

In reply, I have to say that this communication did not reach me in time to convene the council for its consideration, and to furnish a reply by the hour indicated (5 p.m.). It was sent to me through the hands of the commanding officer of the army of the Confederate States near this town, to whom it was first delivered, by consent of General Patrick, who bore it from you, as I am informed, and I am authorized by the commander of the Confederate Army to say that there was no delay in passing it through his hands to me.

In regard to the matters complained of by you, the firing of shots upon your troops occurred upon the northern suburbs of the town, and was the act of the military officer commanding the Confederate forces near here, for which matter [neither] the citizens nor civil authorities of this town are responsible. In regard to the other matters of complaint, I am authorized by the latter officer to say that the condition of things therein complained of shall no longer exist; that your troops shall not be fired on from this town; that the mills and manufactories here will not furnish any further supplies of provisions or material for clothing for the Confederate troops, nor will the railroads or other means of transportation here convey supplies from the town to the depots of said troops.

Outside of the town the civil authorities of Fredericksburg have no control, but I am assured by the military authorities of the Confederate Army near here that nothing will be done by them to infringe the conditions herein named as to matters within the town. But the latter authorities inform us that, while their troops will not occupy the town, they will not permit yours to do so.

You must be aware that there will not be more than three or four hours of daylight within the sixteen hours given by you for the removal of the sick and wounded, the women and children, the aged and infirm from this place; and I have to inform you that, while there is no railroad transportation accessible to the town, because of the interruption thereof by your batteries, all other means of transportation within the town are so limited as to render the removal of the classes of persons spoken of, within the time indicated, an utter impossibility.

I have convened the council, which will remain in session awaiting any further communications you may have to make.
Very respectfully, your obedient servant.
M. SLAUGHTER,
Mayor.[175]

Gen. Sumner's response to Mayor Slaughter's letter:

HEADQUARTERS RIGHT GRAND DIVISION
Camp near Falmouth, November 21, 1862
Mayor and Common Council of Fredericksburg, Va.:
Your letter of this afternoon is at hand, and, in consideration of your pledges that the acts complained of shall cease, and that your town shall not be occupied by any of the enemy's forces, and your assertion that a lack of transportation renders it impossible to remove the women, children, sick, wounded, and aged, I am authorized to say to you that our batteries will not open upon your town at the hour designated.

General Patrick will meet a committee or representative from your town to-morrow morning at 9 o'clock, at the Lacy house.

Very respectfully, your obedient servant,
E. V. SUMNER
Brevet Major-General, U.S. Army, Commanding Division[176]

As a consequence of the bombardment threats, General Lee recommended that the women and children be at once removed from the town. Lee furnished them army wagons and ambulances throughout the night of November 21st and the next day to carry them out of harms way.[177] In a 22 Nov. 1862 letter to his wife, Lee wrote: *I was moving out the women & children all last night & today. It was a piteous sight. But they have brave hearts. What is to become of them God only knows.*
[178]

Chapter VIII – McLaws' Mississippians Defend the Town

Pickets of Gen. Barksdale's Mississippi Brigade pose on burned railroad bridge in Fredericksburg.

Photo taken by Andrew J. Russell during informal truce in April 1863.

(Library of Congress)

Mamie Wells continued: ...*We had decided to weather the storm, one of our household being sick with typhoid fever...Nineteen days passed during which time we busied ourselves feeding and caring for the soldiers who came to picket the town. These pickets were relieved every second night by another brigade from McLaws' Division.*
Mamie L. Wells

On the morning of the 22nd of November, Gen. Patrick received the Mayor and his deputies at "Chatham," the Lacy mansion, whereupon it was agreed that the Mayor was given until 11 o'clock the following day, the 23rd, to remove the rest of his people---*and that the town would not be shelled until she fires.*[179] Fleeing the town by any means available, the townspeople piled into the train cars, which were loaded to capacity, family wagons and vehicles, and many others were forced to leave by foot, following the roads leading into the countryside.

As one of the last train cars full of refugees was slowly steaming out of town on the 22nd, a Union artillery gun, against orders, opened fire upon the cars, fortunately causing no injury.[180] A soldier with the 19th Mississippi Infantry, which was that day marching into town wrote: *Just as we came in view, the Yankees shelled back a train approaching from Richmond. The enemy's camps and wagons in plain view across the river. Many families from town passed us going to the rear.* [181]

After the mass exodus of November 21-23, 1862, Captain Wells and his family were among the very few townspeople left in town. With the majority of the residents fleeing from harms way, General Lee's plan was to hold off the Union Army's crossing of the Rappahannock River into Fredericksburg until the rest of his forces arrived upon the scene.

Upon their arrival, soldiers of Richard H. Anderson's division of Longstreet's First Corps were the first ordered to set up defenses. Gen. Lafayette McLaws sent Gen. William Barksdale to occupy the town with a brigade, posting pickets along the river above Falmouth and running down to Deep Creek south of town. Barksdale chose the 17th

Mississippi Infantry Regiment,[182] three companies of the 18th Mississippi Infantry,[183] and the ten best sharpshooters of the 13th Mississippi Infantry,[184] to deploy in the houses and outbuildings nearest the Rappahannock.

Maj. Gen. Lafayette McLaws, CSA

(Library of Congress)

McLaws wrote:

Detachments were immediately set at work digging rifle-pits close to the edge of the bank, so close that our men, when in them, could command the river and the shores on each side. The cellars of the houses near the river were made available for the use of riflemen, and zigzags were constructed to enable the men to get in and out of the rifle-pits under cover. All this was done at night, and so secretly and quietly that I do not believe the enemy had any conception of the minute and careful preparations that had been made to defeat any attempt to cross the river in my front.[185]

The rest of Barksdale's brigade took position in rifle pits and houses farther in from the river with orders to contest each street. From these points, the Mississippians awaited the move of the Union Army across the river.

"Union and Rebel Soldiers on Opposite Sides of the Burned Railway Bridge"

Alfred R. Waud sketch published in Harper's Weekly of Dec. 13, 1862 (Library of Congress)

During this period, an artist for a Northern newspaper described the ongoing verbal sparring, and sometimes abusive language known as "blackguarding" heard from opposite sides of the burned railroad bridge: *This is a favorite spot for the soldiers of either army to meet within speaking distance and exchange remarks, frequently of uncomplimentary character. Proposals for all sorts of exchange (impossible of accomplishment) are made--such as offers to barter coffee or tea for whiskey or tobacco, gray coats for blue ones—the rebels walking about in the clothes they have taken from Uncle Sam's men prompting the proposal. The seceshers show a laudable anxiety to get New York papers for Richmond publications...they generally express a belief that they 'will whack the Union army now that M'Clellan is gone.'...Some witty remarks are made on both sides, but it usually ends in a general black-guarding. One of them told a Zouave that they should shortly come over to look after us. 'Yes,' he answered; 'so you will, under a guard.'*[186]

Although the girls were Northern by birth, Confederate soldiers thrived on the *feeding and caring* administered by Sue, Mamie and Geno Wells. With regard to the *Southern beaus* courting his daughters, Capt. Wells wrote[187]

...There were several came to my house. Major Hard of S.C.[188] *was a beau of Sue; Capt. Govan of Miss.*[189] *was Mamie's beau; and Lieutenant Crump of Miss.*[190] *for Geno. They were all killed at Chickamauga in Battle. There was a Capt. Martin*[191] *of Gen. Barksdale's staff. Geno didn't like him but I think he was fond of her.*

The Peel Brothers of Mississippi

(c.1860 photo by permission of Peel descendant Kevin Hudson, courtesy Jack Durham.)

Seated, left to right: Lt. Albert L. Peel, Adjutant, 19th Miss Inf., Co. I, killed May 12, 1864 in Battle of Spotsylvania Court House, buried in Spotsylvania Confederate Cemetery (no stone); Thomas Jefferson Peel (1837-1862) 19th Miss Inf., Co. J, wounded in action around Richmond, left on battlefield in rain and died of pneumonia July 6, 1862; Dr. Robert Hunter Peel, Surgeon (1832-1903) 19th Miss Inf. Rgt. (beau of Sue ("Susie") Wells);
Standing, left to right: Lt. William Hunter Peel (___-1865) 11th Miss Inf. Co. C, died in prison at Johnson's Island, Ohio, Feb. 17, 1865; Volney Peel (1846-after 1885) 3d Miss. Cavalry, Co. I, POW May 4, 1865 at Citronella, Ala.; Addison Peel (1843-after 1870) 19th Miss Inf., Co. I.

Dr. Robert Hunter Peel,[192] a Regimental Surgeon with the 19th Mississippi Infantry,[193] also became attached to the eldest Wells daughter, whom he called *Susie,* the *black-eyed beauty* and *a sweet little flower.*

Dr. Peel told of his lady friends in town the previous winter in a June 10, 1863 letter[194] written at a "Field Hospital, Posey's Brigade, near Fredericksburg," He wrote that he had become quite attached to one in particular by the name of "Susie" from the Wyoming Valley area of Pennsylvania, and that while he was near town he visited her at her home:

See below: A page of letter written by Dr. Robert Hunter Peel, 19th Miss. Infantry, while at a *Field Hospital, Posey's Brigade, near Fredericksburg, June 10, 1863.*
(Peel Family Papers, Kevin Hudson, courtesy Jack Durham.)

corn and rye for biscuit and ginger bread of which it is very fond, thus resembling my dear little Sister in another point. I had some lady friends in town last winter, who used to ride the pony sometimes and frequently called on me at my little tent in the green wood near by, to drink egg-nog and eat peanuts with me. One black eyed beauty (Susie) was so much pleased with the pony, that she even agreed to take the owner to get possession of it, and had she not been a Pennsylvania girl by birth I fear I should have given up pony rides and all, for Susie was a sweet little flower from the valey of Wyoming, and used to sing songs to me, and call me her dear Brother. She found me sensei, and for that reason I called her Sister, and became quite attached to her while I was near town and could visit her at home. I have one other lady friend in this state, in whom I feel deep interest because of her peculiar circumstances, and because she has ever shown such a disposition to confide in me though I

128

Peel brothers with 19th Mississippi Rgt. Dr. Robert Hunter Peel, regimental surgeon (left); Adjutant Albert L. Peel (in Confederate uniform), killed in Battle of Spotsylvania Court House

Dr. Peel wrote:...*I had some lady friends in town* [Fredericksburg] *last winter, who used to ride the pony sometimes and frequently called on me at my little tent in the green wood near by, to drink egg-nog and eat peanuts with me. One black eyed beauty (Susie) was so much pleased with the pony that she even agreed to take the owner to get possession of it and had she not been a Pennsylvania girl by birth, I fear I should have given up pony rides and all, for Susie was a sweet little flower from the Valley of Wyoming and used to sing songs to me, and call me her dear Brother. She favored you some and for that reason I called her Sister, and became quite attached to her while I was near town and could visit her at home...should I get sick again in Virginia these new sisters of mine have promised to nurse me until I am 'all right' and ready for duty.*[195]

There was a great religious revival among the troops of Gen. Barksdale's Mississippi Brigade after the December 1862 battle. The revival had its strongest surge in Fredericksburg among soldiers of the Mississippi regiments that were now on picket in and around the war-torn town. The Mississippi men first congregated in the Presbyterian Church in meetings organized by the Rev. W. B. Owen, a Methodist chaplain of the Peel brothers' 17th Infantry Regiment. On occasion Rev. Owen was assisted by other ministers, including the Rev. Joseph C. Stiles, a Presbyterian minister, and the Rev. J. William Jones. Rev. Jones, who served as a chaplain in the Army of Northern Virginia, visited Fredericksburg in late March 1863 to *participate in exercises of the glorious revival…there…I have never preached under more impressive circumstances. The Episcopal Church—capable of seating about twelve hundred—was well filled with attentive listeners.*[196]

When Rev. Stiles came to Fredericksburg at the end of February 1863, he wrote: *After my arrival we held three meetings a day—a morning and afternoon prayer-meeting and a preaching service at night. We could scarcely ask of delightful religious interest more than we received. Our sanctuary has been crowded—lower floor and gallery. Loud, animating singing always hailed our approach to the house of God; and a closely packed audience of men, amongst whom you might have searched in vain for one white hair, were leaning upon the voice of the preacher, as if God Himself had called them together to hear of life and death eternal.*[197]

Photo in later life of Capt. Silvanus J. Quinn, with Barksdale's Brigade, 13th Regiment, Co. A at Fredericksburg.

(Frontispiece photo c. 1908, *The History of the City of Fredericksburg*)

Another Mississippi officer, Capt. Silvanus J. Quinn with Co. A of the 13th Mississippi Infantry, Barksdale's Brigade, became enamored with young Josephine Duvall, the daughter of William Street grocer James Duvall. Capt. Quinn survived the war and returned to Fredericksburg to marry Josephine Duvall in May 1866. He became a town leader and in later years was commissioned by the town council to write a history of Fredericksburg.[198]

A Richmond paper reported the Mississippians' role in Fredericksburg's municipal election held in March 1863: *...Protected by Barksdale's Brigade, under the very guns of the Yankees, this election was conducted with unusual quiet and order. M. Slaughter, Esq., who for several terms and especially during the war has discharged the onerous and important outlets of the office with honor and credit to the community and himself, was re-elected Mayor...*[199]

Captain Quinn's regimental band joined in the election celebration...*The Mayor was serenaded at night by the admirable Band of the 13th Mississippi regiment, whose leader is Prof. T. D. Nutting, who performed several beautiful airs and were thanked by the Mayor both as soldiers and musicians.*[200]

Above: Rufus Bainbridge Merchant, Cobbs Ga. Legion, Cavalry, Cobbs Brigade, for 14 months served as a scout under Gen. Wade Hampton.

(Photo of Merchant in later life, courtesy Fredericksburg Area Museum)

Yet another romance blossomed involving a soldier from McLaws' division. Across the street from the Wells House resided Fannie and Henrietta (Rhetta) Mills, daughters of clothing merchant and master tailor Walter M. Mills and his wife Pamelia, a seamstress. Calling to court Rhetta was Rufus B. Merchant, a cavalry soldier with Cobb's Brigade, and a native of Dumfries in Prince William County, Virginia.

Merchant enlisted in Cobb's Georgia Legion Cavalry before Virginia seceded from the Union. Thoroughly familiar with the Virginia countryside, Merchant was detailed as a scout under Gen. Wade Hampton of S.C., and served as a spy inside the Union lines for fourteen months of the war.[201]

While in Fredericksburg, Merchant fell in love with young Rhetta Mills, then just fourteen years old. He vowed that he would return after the war to marry her. He kept his promise and they were married in 1866 and settled in Fredericksburg. Their first child, a son born the next year, was named Wade Hampton Merchant. In 1869 Merchant established the Fredericksburg Star newspaper and was for more than twenty-six years its proprietor and editor. He had the distinction of founding the first successful daily newspaper in Fredericksburg.

ESTABLISHED 1869—LARGEST CIRCULATION.

Leading Local Paper—Semi-Weekly—$1.50 a Year.

FREDERICKSBURG STAR,

(Published Every Wednesday and Saturday Mornings—Thirty-two Columns.)

RUFUS B. MERCHANT, EDITOR AND OWNER.

ALL KINDS OF PLAIN AND FANCY JOB PRINTING DONE.

Star Iron Front Building, Commerce Street.

Fredericksburg, Va., 1890.

133

Chapter IX – Between Two Armies: The Bombardment

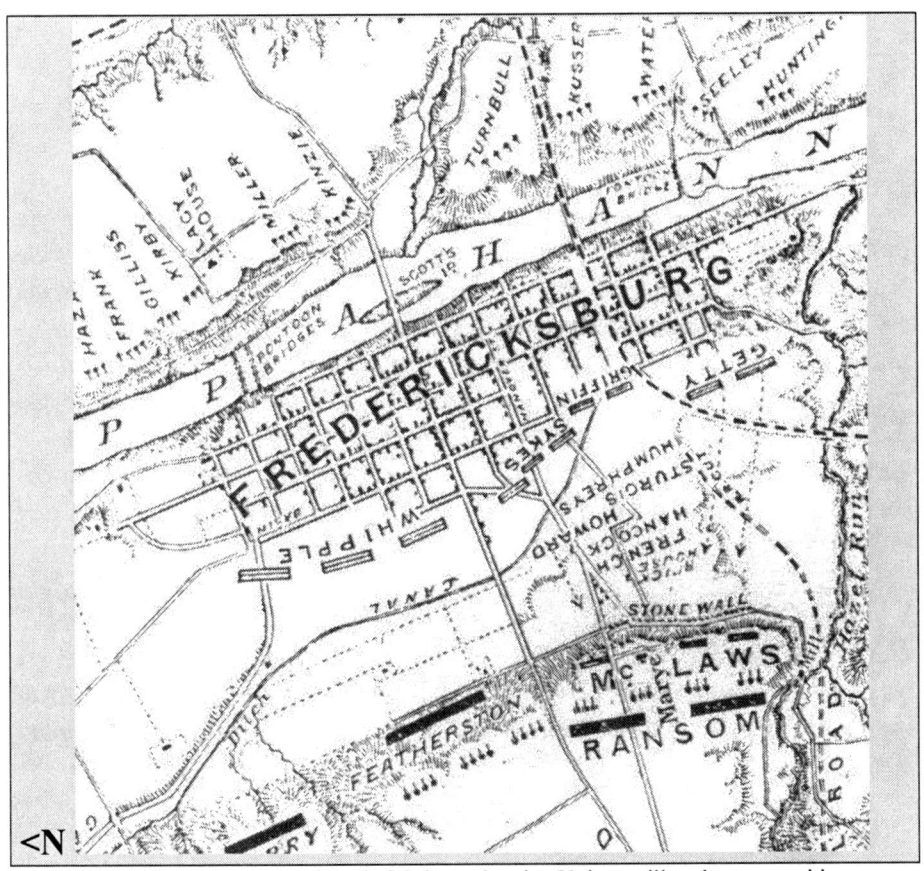

Map of the 1862 Battle of Fredericksburg showing Union artillery battery positions

Along the banks of the Rappahannock River facing the town.

(The Wells House faces the southern tip of Scott's Island.)

The following is a chapter of Mamie Wells *Reminiscences of the Late War,*[202] entitled *The Bombardment:*

> Mankind have felt their strength and made it felt.
> They might have used it better, but allured
> By their new vigor, sternly have they dealt
> On one another; pity ceased to melt
> With her once natural charities.
> —Byron

I cannot positively assert whether the order to surrender the city of Fredericksburg on the twenty-first day of November, 1862, came from Gen. Burnside; but I know that the Army of the Potomac under his command, was stationed on and back of Stafford Heights on that day, and that the demand to surrender the city at nine o'clock that night, or be shelled by five o'clock the following morning, was made by a Federal officer who crossed the river that afternoon under a flag of truce. I know that there were a few Confederate soldiers in the town; and that the reply of the Mayor was: 'The town is in the hands of the military."

At nine o'clock that night the Mayor proclaimed to the people in the streets that the bombardment would not take place the next day, as threatened—not until further notice, unless some hostile demonstration was made by the Confederates. But this could not stay those terror-stricken people.

Fredericksburg civilians *fled... to the woods where hunger and cold overtook them in helplessness.* (Mamie Wells)

(Painting by D. E. Henderson, courtesy Gettysburg National Military Park.)

They fled—some to the Capitol,[203] some to the South—and some to the woods where hunger and cold overtook them in helplessness. Crowded in wayside cabins and churches the children of these poor fugitives cried for bread, while the cellars of their own comfortable homes were supplied with all the necessities of life for months to come.

A few of the citizens were forced to remain—those who had no means of escape, and those who from sickness, and other causes, could not go.

Before the Mayor had communicated to the people the latest intention of the Federal commander, we had decided to weather the storm, one of our household being sick with typhoid fever. Accordingly, we packed our clothing and other necessaries in trunks, buried some valuables, and made up our minds to gather together in the cellar whenever the storm burst upon us. We knew that there was an All-Seeing One above, whose merciful love would shield us from harm; and, with this blessed conviction, we felt resigned to whatever fate awaited us.

Nineteen days passed away, during which time we busied ourselves in feeding and caring for the soldiers who came to picket the town. These pickets were relieved every second night by another brigade from McLaws' Division.[204] Some of the citizens had returned in the meantime, believing as we likewise did, that after such a delay it was far from the intention of the enemy to molest us. Satisfied upon this point, we gradually unpacked our clothing and restored it to it place; and when we were asked the question: 'Do you think the town will be shelled?' we invariably answered: 'No.' Besides, had we not the assurance of the Federals that it would not be, until further notice?

We retired, as usual, on the night of the tenth of December, and slept well, with the exception of my mother, who was kept awake most of the night by a continuous rumbling of wagons across the river.[205] Feeling anxious lest the noise portended something approaching trouble, she did not close her eyes but kept on the alert until a little before five, when two heavy guns firing in rapid succession, awoke us all and she advised us to rise and dress.

Henri Lovie sketch: "Bombardment of Fredericksburg by the
Army of the Potomac, Dec. 11, 1862"

(Library of Congress)

It was not long before the whole line of batteries upon Stafford Hills was opened upon us.[206] *The river having a bend at the upper end of town, the enemy had a crossfire upon it.*

My mother gathered the younger members of our household into the cellar, where she made a fire in the old fireplace and spread carpets to keep them warm. My father assisted my elder sister and myself in gathering together and packing several trunks and in removing them to the lower floor. This we deemed necessary in case the house should take fire; for clothing, as well as everything else, was not very easy to obtain at that period, and most uncomfortable to do without in the month of December. In the midst of all these preparations, while the shot and shell were whizzing with fearful

138

rapidity by and over the house, we could not but pause to contemplate the scene. The flash of one cannon after another as they were arranged along the hills beyond, lighting up the scenery around, and the deafening shouts that followed were sights and sounds which the novel spectator must have viewed and listened to with eager eyes and ears. It was a beautiful but awful sight.

In the streets the confusion was dreadful. Here, a child was left, its frantic mother having fled; and there a husband, who in the excitement of the moment, had become separated from his wife, ran madly about in search of her while she was being safely conveyed from the scene of terror on a wood cart. Here families were crouching in their dark cellars for protection from the ruthless shells; while there, the more reckless ascended to the house-top to view the impossible grandeur of the scene before the daybreak.

Cellar fireplace in the Wells House, Fredericksburg, Virginia.

(*Free Lance Star* photograph, *March* 5, 1966)

The Wells House cellar fireplace, Fredericksburg, Virginia

(2003 photograph by Robert A. Martin)

Reader, imagine an old cellar covered with planks, where the water had entered and remained two feet deep at each river flood; which had a window on either side one pane deep, upon which the mud has spattered from recent hard rains; which has a large old fashioned fireplace, with its giant crane; a low ceiling, with smoky rafters; numerous holes for the December winds to enter, and huge piles of wood occupying half the space. Imagine a bright fire upon that old-fashioned hearth, a dim candle burning in the darker corner of this underground habitation, and you are acquainted with our rendezvous during that terrible bombardment, lasting thirteen hours. Beside our own family of ten, several poor out-casts had sought shelter with us.

In the further corner, where the candle flickered and burned, a poor half-witted woman crouched, hugging her knees as she rocked to and fro, exclaiming: 'Oh, my son John! Oh, John! If I only knew where he was! And he's got my best blanket, too! Poor John! Ohhh..!'

Near her two bright-eyed African boys sat, at one moment grinning at the poor creature, and the next opening their eyes and mouths in fear and astonishment at the bursting of a shell in the yard surrounding the house.

On one side of the fireplace a young man was seated upon a rude bench. His right elbow rested upon his knee, and his cheek in the palm of his hand. His eyes were bent with a mournful gaze into the fire, and his hair 'stood on end.' Whether the latter fact resulted from excessive fear, or from a continuous running of his fingers through his prominent locks, I am not prepared to say; certain I am that this eccentric individual's hair stood aloft. Whenever a shot or shell passed through the house, and we, curious and reckless as most young people are, wanted to go up and see what damage had been done, the individual alluded to would raise his head, spread his right arm to its full length, (which was not to be sneered at) expand his fingers and expostulate with us upon our 'madness.' His manner, tone and look, in these moments, would have provoked a smile from the soberest of people. The effect upon us may be imagined. I am not quite sure that we did not feign a goodly part of our bravery for the sake of a remonstrance from our dejected guest. Poor fellow! He has since married a widow with two children, and I sincerely hope he watches over them as tenderly as he guarded us on that truly fearful day.

We managed to cook in the fireplace what we wanted to eat—a few boiled potatoes, some coffee and bread. I believe we had some pickles and preserves in the adjoining cellar which we did not spare.

In the meantime how fared the soldiers who inhabited the town? Barksdale's brigade of Mississippians were on picket the night of the tenth, as brave and noble a set of men as ever graced an army. Firm in the belief that they were executing their duty, they guarded our town.

Henri Lovie sketch: "Volunteer Storming Parties… Crossing the Rappahannock in Advance of the Grand Army to drive off the Confederate Sharpshooters Annoying the Pontooniers"

(Library of Congress)

During the night it was discovered, through the fog, that the enemy was constructing a pontoon bridge across the river at the lower end of the town; and this fact was communicated to Captain G[ovan][207] whose men were on picket at that point. A bridge was likewise being built at the upper end of the town, and Colonel F[iser][208] summoned to the spot. Accordingly, toward five o'clock, regarding the building of bridges as a hostile demonstration, the companies at each point, two in number, were ordered to fire upon the bridge-builders, which they did—the effect being the opening of the batteries on the opposite hills.

When hundreds of shot and shell had been expended upon these points sufficient to have buried to eternity a thousand times as many men as lay upon the shore, without a rifle pit or embankment of any

142

kind to protect them, the bridges were again manned and work begun. As if from their graves, those brave Southrons arose once more and fired. They were not so numerous as at first but their courage was the same. So it continued throughout the day. Two hundred men under command of the heroic officers mentioned, prevented the 'Army of the Potomac' from crossing the Rappahannock on that ever to be remembered 11th day of December. Many of them passed away from earth in that severe struggle; but in the belief, I am sure, that they were faithfully performing their duty; that they were manfully driving the enemy from their home. Thanks be to our Heavenly Father that with him alone rests their forgiveness.

Henri Lovie sketch: "Burnside's Army Crossing the Rappahannock"

(Library of Congress)

At night, when the cannonading ceased, it was discovered that the town was on fire in several places and rumored that the enemy had effected a crossing still further up the river. At about seven o'clock, hearing the sound of musketry close at hand, I stepped into an adjoining cellar under a corner of the house in order to hear more distinctly. At that moment a squad of men came rushing down the street,[209] uttering fearful oaths about the rebels. The order was given to fire. A volley of musketry and a heart-rending death cry from a Southern officer[210] followed. Though the shelling had been fearful, and had lasted so many hours, it had not unnerved me; but that poor human cry pierced my very heart.

Wells House, front entrance

(Photo courtesy University of Mary Washington, Fredericksburg, Virginia)

A moment after, my father came through the back door of the hall, having been across the street to look after a lady[211] and her children—her husband having gone to Richmond a few days before. As he walked toward the front door to see if it was securely fastened, another volley of musketry was poured into the house; one of the slugs falling upon the oilcloth at his feet.

Below: Alfred R. Waud sketch, *Harper's Weekly* of Jan. 3, 1863:

Our Soldiers in the Streets of Fredericksburg[212]

Arthur Lumley sketch showing Union troops pillaging the Wallace house and store, southeast corner of Main (Caroline) and Commerce (William) Streets, December 12, 1862.

(Library of Congress)

The night that followed was one that I shudder to recall. I pause when I reach this period; for I feel how utterly unfit I am to attempt a description of those five days and nights in which the 'Army of the Potomac' occupied our town.

Henri Lovie sketch: "Destruction of Fredericksburg by Union bombardment and looting."

(Library of Congress)

    Where shall I find language to picture the scenes of desolation and woe that met the eye wherever it rested after that night's plunder! But that night! The pounding at our doors; the peering in the cellar windows by eyes red with intoxication; the oaths and curses; the ringing of axes and hammers; breaking in the tenantless houses; the firing of the buildings opposite; the insults heaped upon the occupants; the streets literally packed with soldiers in a complete state of moral demoralization (I make a few exceptions, for I saw one of the soldiers assist a poor widow and her daughter in saving some of their furniture from the flames, only to be destroyed by the men without; and our own merciful escape is due to a Federal colonel from Philadelphia—I think his name is Ormes;)[213] the attempt to plunder our house; and, finally, the carrying off of my father at the point of a bayonet, at the moment when we were told our house was on fire.[214]

147

Now, when I recall all these harrowing scenes, I ask myself: How did we live through them? And I sometimes wonder if it is not all a dream—so incomprehensible does such human depravity appear.

But our Creator is provident. One prayer to Him will furnish strength and comfort for the weakest of His creatures. In this faith lies our strength; and, through it, the final accomplishment of the heart's pure desire.

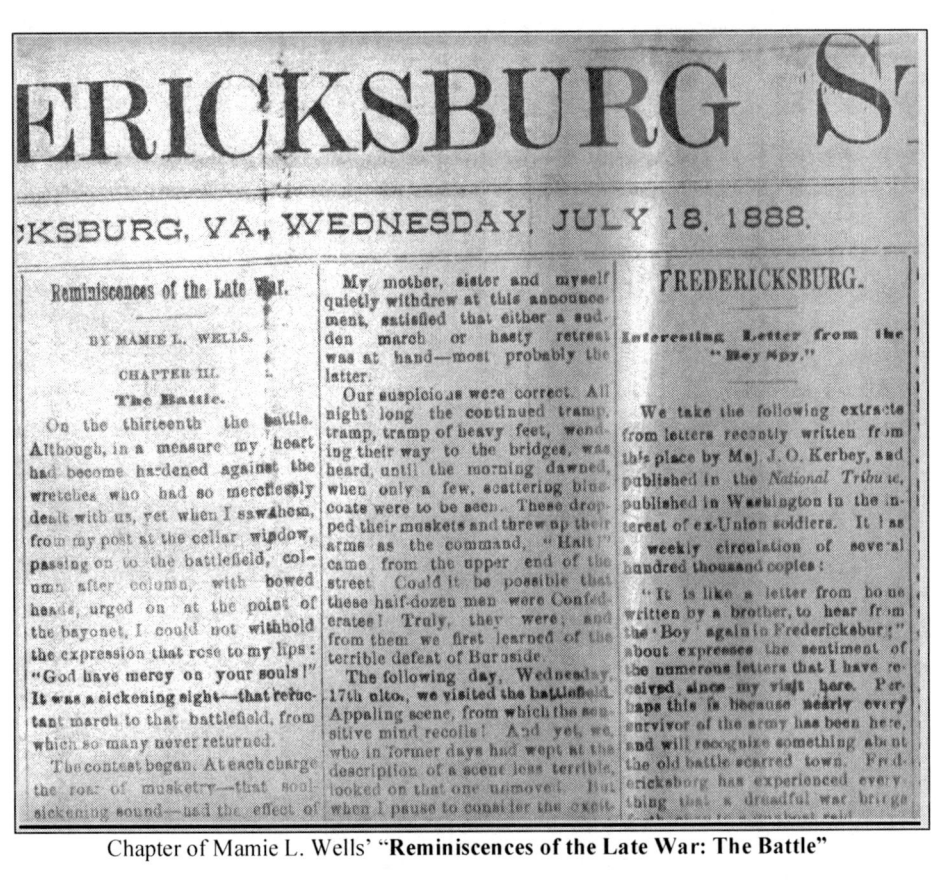

Chapter of Mamie L. Wells' **"Reminiscences of the Late War: The Battle"**

Shown on the front page of the July 18, 1888 issue of the *Fredericksburg Star*, alongside *Interesting Letter from the "Boy Spy"* (Maj. J. O. Kerbey)

Chapter X—Between Two Armies: The Battle

Federal Officers including a Union Army General and his staff, take the Wells House as their Headquarters

Mamie Wells continues her story:

On the thirteenth the battle. Although in a measure my heart had become hardened against the wretches who had so mercilessly dealt with us, yet when I saw them from my post at the cellar window, passing on to the battlefield, column after column, with bowed heads, urged on at the point of the bayonet, I could not withhold the expression that rose to my lips: 'God have mercy on your souls!' It was a sickening sight—that reluctant march to that battlefield, from which so many never returned.

The contest began. At each charge the roar of musketry—that soul-sickening sound—had the effect of almost stopping my breath. In those moments I pictured to myself the dead and the dying, and wondered why such a cruel thing as war should ever be allowed in a civilized country. That childish wonder still clings to me. We spent that Saturday afternoon huddled together beneath the windows, silently gazing at each other's mournful countenance as we strained our ears to catch every sound, even though they chilled us to the heart.

Brig. Gen. James Nagle, USA, Cdr. 9th Army Corps, 2nd Div., 1st Brigade

Col. Joshua K. Sigfried, USA, Commander 48th Pennsylvania Infantry

MAJOR JAMES WREN.

Capt. James Wren, USA, Co. B, 48th Pa. Infantry, wrote in his diary that he camped in Capt. Wells house on the nights of December 12 and 13, 1862.

. (Photo courtesy Oliver Christian Bosbyshell, *The 48th in the War* (Phila. 1895)

At nightfall, when the officers who occupied our dining-room as headquarters[215] *(it being the only habitable room in the house in consequence of the passage of shells) returned, we were told they had gained the first hill. We could not ascertain what hill; but lay down that night as upon the previous ones, on our bedding spread upon the pile of wood in the cellar, in dread anticipation of the battle being renewed upon the morrow.*

Upon the following morning[216] *I had occasion to go to a pantry leading from the dining-room, and hearing no sound, ventured within. I had gone about half-way across the room when my step was arrested by a low moan. I turned quickly and discovered an officer laying upon the lounge in the rear of the door by which I had entered. Perceiving that his wrist and thumb were bandaged, I approached him and inquired whether he was wounded very badly. I shall never forget the look of astonishment pictured by his face, as he replied: 'I am not wounded externally. I was knocked down by the passage of a shell near me, and lay for several hours upon the field insensible. I have had hemorrhages to-day and fear I am injured inwardly.' 'What is the matter with your hand?' 'Only a couple of boils. I have not been able to attend to them for two or three days and the cloths are very much soiled.'*

He replied to my questions hurriedly; at the same time looking at me with the most intense surprise. Before I had time to question him further, he asked: 'Do you live in this house?' 'Yes, sir' 'But you were not here during the bombardment?' 'Yes, sir.' 'Were you not afraid to remain? I did not suppose there was a lady in the city.' 'We remained because we had no chance to escape, even if we had desired to go.' 'But you had warning to leave the city.' 'No, sir.[217] *I will get some water and clean cloths and dress your sores for you if you desire it.' 'I am not so sure that I deserve such attention from a citizen of this unfortunate town.'*

I left the room rather abruptly, perhaps, and soon returned with water and soap. While I was washing and dressing his hand and wrist the officer continued to question and sympathize with me in reference to the treatment we had received at the hands of the Federals. In conclusion, he said: 'If I were a Southerner I would fight to the end.'

When I had finished dressing the boils with some salve he took from his pocket, I asked him if he had eaten anything, and, his reply being in the negative, I left the room to provide something a little more delicate than 'hard tack' and such coarse food as had been offered him. My mother prepared a delicate breakfast from what we had, and took it to him. He seemed very grateful, and we continued to attend him whenever the other officers were absent from the house.

On Sunday the battle was not renewed. Neither was it on Monday. On that evening the General[218] *and his Staff having left the house, we went up to see the sick lieutenant. We found him, according to his own information, quite feeble. He had tried to walk about the room, but his strength was not equal to the performance. A few minutes later a messenger came hurriedly in and addressed him thus: 'Lieutenant, are you not going on picket to-night?' It was a strange question to put to a sick man, and the answer was equally strange. 'Why, no; I am—yes, I will go if you will assist me a little.' He looked earnestly in the messenger's face as he finished the sentence, and raised himself to a sitting posture. My mother, sister and myself quietly withdrew at this announcement, satisfied that either a sudden march or hasty retreat was at hand—most probably the latter.*

Henri Lovie sketch: "The Grand Army Recrossing the Rappahannock from Fredericksburg,, Monday Night, Dec. 15, 1862"

(Library of Congress)

Our suspicions were correct. All night long the continued tramp, tramp, tramp of heavy feet, wending their way to the bridges, was heard, until the morning dawned, when only a few, scattering blue-

coats were to be seen.[219] *These dropped their muskets and threw up their arms as the command, 'Halt!' came up from the upper end of the street. Could it be possible that these half-dozen men were Confederates! Truly, they were; and from them we first learned of the terrible defeat of Burnside.*

The following day, Wednesday, 17th ulto., we visited the battlefield. Appalling scene, from which the sensitive mind recoils! And yet, we, who in former days had wept at the description of a scene less terrible, looked on that one unmoved. But when I pause to consider the exciting days and nights through which we had passed, I no longer wonder that we did not shrink from the sight of that field of dead. First, the terrific bombardment, followed by the night of plunder, insult, incendiarism, and arrest. Second, the day of destruction and carnage, accompanied with shell from the Confederate side, and the night of raillery and carousing. Third, the day of the battle, and the night in which the cries of the wounded rent the air in piteous groans. Fourth, the day in which the wounded were borne through the streets on litters and in ambulances, with the blood dripping from their mingled bodies, and another night in which the mind gathered no rest.

We had visited different portions of the town before going to Marye's Heights, and had looked with pain and surprise at the dire destruction of almost every house we saw. In giving a description of the condition of one of the dwellings we entered, I am only giving the idea of all. To sum up the devastation perpetrated by the Federal troops upon the town of Fredericksburg during their sojourn there of five nights, I can only say that unless they had burned every building to the ground, I do not know what more they could have done.

Let us enter this house. It belongs to an intelligent, enterprising citizen, who fled with his wife the morning of the eleventh. See the empty portrait frames upon the wall! Upon the floor lies a portion of the canvas, an aged face, may-hap one long since buried beneath the sod. We cannot enter this room, for a barrel of molasses has been poured upon the velvet carpet. The piano is covered with salt pork, the keys are broken and the wires cut. The mirrors are shattered; gas fixtures trampled upon; the bottoms of the sofas are cut out; chairs split with axes, and the plastering, even the laths, torn from the wall. We will go up stairs. Here are the relics of handsome dresses torn to ribbons. There is no bedding—that lies in the street in the mud. This carpet has been spread with butter. The doors of the wardrobes and washstands are broken off, and ruin stamped upon everything around. There is no silver to be found anywhere—a portion of that we have already seen in possession of a Federal officer.[220] The owner of this once pleasant home will return in a few days to find but the shadow of a house; not a change of garments for himself, wife or child; not an article of value left him either at his house or store.

As about every fifth house had been occupied as a hospital, there were many dead bodies to be found in these dwellings. In one small enclosure, by the side of a building, a dozen or more dead soldiers were piled together. Amputated limbs lay all through the streets, which were in a most lamentable condition. One house we saw had been used as a stable. The old negro woman[221] who had been killed by a shell on the Thursday previous, six days before, still lay unburied. Poor old creature! She had crept beneath her bed for safety. But as though that fatal ball had sought her life only, it came in the room near the ceiling and shot downwards, thereby severing her body in twain. To relate all that we saw as we wandered through that unfortunate town would only be relating the most unheard of indecencies. Moscow never fared worse.

As I am only giving a few simple facts, as they fell under my own observation, I do not pretend to say whether the officers in command of the forces under Burnside could have prevented the plundering of Fredericksburg. I know that in some cases the officers joined in the plunder; for we were advised by a Federal colonel[222] to keep our doors securely locked and to appeal to him if disturbed, for there would be plundering that night—the first night of their occupation. The men were heard to say at different times that they were promised eight hours of plunder if they would cross the river under the Confederate fire. And a citizen who appealed to a Federal general (I will not give his name or rank) for protection from the vandals, received the reply: "They are not half as bad as I want them to be.'

Extract of Mamie Wells' letter to a neighbor refugeeing in Lynchburg, Virginia, published on page 1 of the *Richmond Daily Dispatch* on Jan. 1, 1863. (Typescript on following page):

"Horrors of a Bombardment"[223]

"The following are extracts from a private letter of a young lady who remained in Fredericksburg during the late bombardment, to a neighbor, at present sojourning as a refugee in Lynchburg. They possess deep interest for our readers:

"On Thursday, December 11th, we were awakened by two cannon. At 5 o'clock we arose and dressed. About six the firing began in earnest—We packed our trunks amid it all, made a fire in the cellar, and thither repaired. We had not been there an hour, when a shell went through our attic room, breaking bedsteads, etc. One shot went through the parlor; five in all through the house. As they passed, the crash they made seemed to threaten instant death to all; it sounded as though the house were tumbling in, and would bury us in its ruins. We knew the danger, but our trust was in God, and we were calm. Aunt Clara (the colored woman who lives opposite)[224] was with us. Darkness came on, and the cannonading ceased.

"Barksdale's Mississippians opposing the laying of the pontoon bridges"

(Sketch by Allen Christian Redwood, *Battles and Leaders of the Civil War*)

B[enjamin][225] *went to the gate and returned with the news that there was a fire in different parts of the town, and that* **a company of our men were at the corner firing on the pontoon bridge.** *Though the bombardment had ceased, the musketry* *sounded to my ears yet more awful, for I knew they were fighting in the streets. My ears are suddenly shocked by a shout of demoniacal glee—'Here are the rebels! Here are the d—d rebels! Fire, boys! Fire!' Two dreadful cries rend the air—our gallant Capt. Cook[226] is killed at our corner.—To hear the fiendish cry of the enemy unnerved me more than the explosion of the thousands of shell that burst around us.*

"*All being now quiet for a time, we lie down, but not to sleep; for hark! They are breaking into houses like so many demons. With terrible force they throw themselves against our doors, back and front, but an officer[227] (Yankee, though he was,) saved us. We hear them break into your house, but dare not utter a word, lest they slay us. Oh! Who can tell the horrors of that night?...They order my father out, declare that he has wine in his cellar, &c. He assures them he has only his unoffending wife and eight children there.*

"*Thus passes the night, the fire still raging.—About 8 o'clock the flames burst forth in our vicinity, and we expect every moment to find our own roof on fire. In the midst of the excitement a soldier rushed in with his bayonet, which he pointed at my father's breast, and ordered him to follow him. My father asked why? But the manner in which he repeated the order convinced him that he must follow or die. This occurred in the back porch; I was at that time in the front porch watching the sparks and expecting our house every moment to take fire. They carried father to headquarters, and, after accusing him of firing on them from his house, he was released, the officer before whom he was arraigned reading a lie in the face of the accuser, and innocence in that of the accused. While he was gone, soldiers came to me at the front door, and to mother behind, and assured us that the house was on fire; but such was not the case. The trick did not succeed, nor did the story afford them the opportunity they sought to rob the house...*

"The next day every unoccupied house was plundered and every piece of furniture destroyed. In order to save your furniture we told Aunt Clara to move into your house, which she did. You would have had nothing left but for this. The first night they took a crock of lard, and ate up your preserves and pickles. Your candles, also, they made way with but we do not know of anything else. They pulled everything out of your drawers and trunks, burst open closets, etc. No shell went through your house, and if you saw the sufferings of most of the people you would think you had indeed fared well. Mr. A.___ lost everything—his store, furniture, etc.; his house is riddled with shell and his wife and child with nothing to wear but what they have on. Hundreds are in the same situation. As shell were being thrown by our men on Friday, Saturday, Sunday, and Monday, we spent each of those days chiefly in the cellar, as well as Thursday; thus, _five_ days in all.

Mary Price, a black woman, was killed by a shell—cut quite in two. She had gotten, for protection, under a bed in a room through which a shell passed. I saw her on Wednesday. She had been killed the previous Thursday, but there was no one to bury her...Every house not inhabited has been sacked and ruined inside. They committed every species of outrage."

(End of letter extract published in the
Richmond Daily Dispatch, January 2, 1863)

Fredericksburg Houses destroyed in the Dec. 1862 Battle of Fredericksburg

(National Archives)

Chapter XI—1863: Living in a Ruined Town

> *...It was rumored that a certain old Negro was making a snug little income by the...selling of rats to the soldiers for fifty cents apiece.* (Mamie Wells)

"The winter succeeding the battle of the thirteenth of December was one of comparative suffering to the remaining citizens of Fredericksburg. Surrounded as we were by the armies of Lee and Hooker, it was almost impossible to procure food. The Federals on the opposite side of the river prevented communication with the lower counties; and almost every article of food transported from Richmond was required for the Confederates.

I remember well how eagerly some of the citizens gathered the few greens[228] that grew in the open lots as the spring advanced; and it was rumored that a certain old Negro was making a snug little income by the entrapping and selling of rats to the soldiers for fifty cents apiece.[229] I cannot vouch for the truth of this, although I never could understand why rats should not be tolerated as an article of food. At the same time, I do not propose such a reform of taste.

Hooker's well known defeat in May[230] brought about a happy change for us. There is a little circumstance connected with that battle which returns forcibly to me. Noticing that a soldier was deliberately tearing some planks from our garden fence, my father requested him to cease his wanton destruction. 'Sir,' said he, 'I would not disturb your fence, but I want to make a coffin to bury my brother.'

Photo by Timothy H. O'Sullivan: "View of Town from East bank of the Rappahannock, February 1863."

(Library of Congress)

In June the Federal army retreated into Maryland, and as Lee had already begun his march to Gettysburg, we were once more open to the surrounding country. Naturally enough, when the way was open to procure something more, and perhaps something better, to eat, we felt a keen desire to do so. We had neither tasted butter nor milk the most of the winter nor spring. Fresh meat had come to us like 'angels visits;' and aside from these luxuries, for they were luxuries then, we needed flour and corn. Accordingly, a canoe was procured and my father, accompanied by my brothers, made a trip down the Rappahannock in search of provisions. They returned in a few days with a fair supply; and in a short time, these being exhausted, prepared for a similar excursion. On one of these trips he was captured by a Federal gunboat,[231] and afterwards carried to Washington. My

163

brothers,[232] after some delay, were allowed to return home with the news. This occurred in August.

Harry B. Derr photo of boat on Potomac River Bank

(Courtesy Fairfax County Virginia Public Library)

Timothy H. O'Sullivan photo of pontoon boat

(Library of Congress)

In October, seeing that the coming winter in town would be one of great privations, we resolved to carry out my father's plans by removing to Lancaster County[233] about one hundred and twenty-five miles down the river.

Having procured a pontoon boat in which we placed such necessaries as we would need until some favorable opportunity occurred for removing the remainder of our worldly goods, and hoisted sail on the little canoe, we secured the pontoon to the stern and started on our way.

For six days and five nights we traveled in that little open boat, only resting at each flood tide when the wind was unfair. During one of the days the rain poured in torrents. At night, the tide having changed to flood, we anchored near the shore, and perceiving a light, apparently not very far off, resolved to go in search of it, hoping to find some human habitation wherein we could dry our wet garments, for we were drenched with rain. After having extended our walk some distance, and becoming almost buried in the mud, the light suddenly disappeared, and we were left to grope our way back to the boat in a worse situation than we had left it. And as nine people in a canoe could not at any time, be disposed of very comfortably for a night's sleep, it may be well understood how we passed that night. My brothers were all lads, the youngest being but six years old[234]; but they labored faithfully for our comfort, and deserved our praises.

Weary and hungry we reached our destination on the sixth day, just as the sun was setting. Having refreshed ourselves with some delicious oysters, fresh from the river, and corn bread furnished us by the old Negroes on the place, we prepared for rest by spreading our beds upon the floor.

165

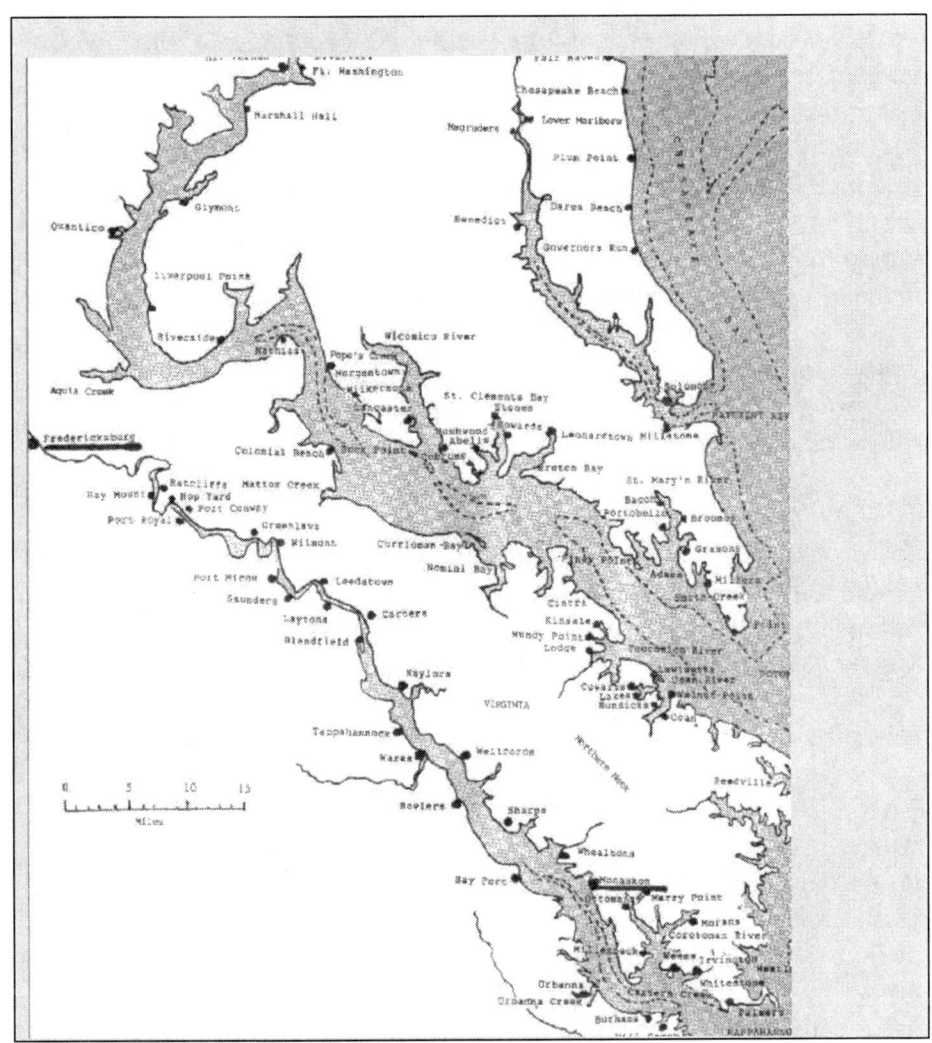

Above: Rappahannock River route of Capt. Wells wife Jane Wells and eight children by canoe, towing a pontoon boat from Fredericksburg to Lancaster County, Va. in October 1863.

(Holly, David C., *Tidewater by Steamboat: A Saga of the Chesapeake*, p.263, c1991 David C. Holly. Reprinted with permission of the John Hopkins Univ. Press)

For many weeks after our arrival at M [onaskon][235] we did not see a white face; and having received no news from my father since his unwarranted arrest, the time passed away drearily. Yet in recalling those hours spent on that old plantation, I am reminded of the pleasant moments passed with good old Uncle Jesse. Many an evening he has sat at our fireside and filled our eager ears with tales of his boyhood, his courtship and marriage, and his general great consequence. And many an evening we have sat at his fireplace and enjoyed the good oyster roasts he had prepared for us. How proud he was to have 'de young ladies take supper wid de ole man!' And old Aunt Bettie who brought us the fresh eggs, and taught us to card and spin cotton! God bless her! How well I remember the night when we were gathered around the bright wood fire, seeding cotton, and Aunt Bettie, close by, with her cards making snowy heaps upon the floor, giving us the following account of herself and affairs generally:

'Yes, honey, you see as how we dem didn't card an' spin 'fore de war; for den Massa he buyed all de close for de people; but now, you see, honey, dat's what we women does. We cards and spins, an' Massa he hires a weaver for to spin de clos for we dems close. You see, he has so many pounds for to spin and card in a fortnight, and den, if we's smart, we can do dat in a week, so de oder week we can do what we dem please.'

'Did you always belong to Mr. C[arter] Aunt Bettie?' 'La! No, honey! My ole Misses was a ole England lady! She was a great lady my missis; and she was very rich—we had so many people, you see, chile. An' Missis had great dresses, she did, great dresses, wid long trailers behind her, an' den dere was a boy for to hold dem off de groun' ever she went out de door. She was a great lady, my missis, an' I was brought up in de house under her 'spection. I is 'spectable, I is, cause I was brought up wid white folks. Bress God! I don't 'long wid someo' dese yere common people o' Massa John's [Chewning]. Why, honey, I 'member when all dese yere plantations 'way up to Glenwood, and 'way down to de Curtoman[236] all 'longed to us. An' dis here was Ole Misses' Mansion House. Dere was all marble steps up to de doors den, and de floors was waxed ebery day; and' dey was so bright you *could a'most see your faces in dem. An' den, you know, Ole Missis she died an' Ole Massa Jonas he got de place, an' he was a powerful wicked man, he was. You see, Ole Massa Jonas he got three daughters. Dere was Miss Rosie, an' dere was Miss Arabellar, an' dere was Miss Lucy. An' so Miss Lucy was her father's favorite chile. Den Miss Arabellar, she died; but, you know, de ole gentelleman he didn't say much. Den Miss Lucy she took sick, and she died. Den Old' Massa Jonas he did walk up an' down de floor in dis yere room, an' he did walk out to de hall, an' so his hands dey would go dis a way—all a rubbin' 'gainst one anudder. An' den when Miss Lucy she was in de coffin, Ole Massa Jonas he writ a letter to God.'*

'Wrote a letter to God, Aunt Bettie?' 'Yes, honey, he writ a letter to God, an' axed God why fore he did take away his favorite child.' 'Oh, wasn't he wicked?' 'Yes, chile, an he was a great swearer, too. But den, you see, Miss Lucy she was dead just about one week, when, sure as you live, Ole Massa Jonas he died.'

'Who got the property then, Aunt Bettie?' 'Why, you see, Ole Missis, when she died, she aired de property to Miss Fanny, her only dear chile, and Massa Jonas he got de 'state 'till she growed up. 'Fore she growed up, she died, and de 'state fell to Doctor Green—he was kin to Missis. Den he died an' his wife she got married again, and had heaps of children, an' so de 'state was divided, and I fell to Miss Ella, an' dat's how it was.

'Who is Miss Ella?' 'Dat's my Missis—Massa John's. She's done gone down to de government now 'cause de war's done frightened her away. But my Ole Missis was a ole England lady, an' when de Britishers comed up dis yere river in de oder war, she said dey wouldn't gib it up, dat de war would come agin, an' so it did cum.'

'Do you remember the War of 1812, Aunt Bettie?' 'La, yes! Missis was sittin in dis yere room, an' de Britishers come up de river in dere boats. So de redcoats dey come to de house, an' all de people had to wait on de gemmen an' fotch de wine out de cellar. But some o'de

people dey was powerful scared an' run to de pines, jus' like they do now ever the Yankees come up de river in dem bum-shellboats."[237]

Chapter XII—Running the Blockade - Again

*'Man, proud man,
Dressed in a little brief authority
Plays such a fantastic trick before high heaven,
As make the angels weep.'*

Mamie Wells:

It was approaching sunset, one of those gorgeous August sunsets on the Rappahannock, when, having bidden adieu to the dear ones at home.[238] I stepped into the 'dug out' that was waiting to carry me to a neighboring plantation, from which I intended an early start in the morning. I did so with a hopeful heart, although the enterprise I had undertaken was one fraught with danger and probable disappointment. The matter had been well considered. My father had been absent a year; and more than nine months had passed since we had received any tidings of him. He was then in the Old Capitol Prison[239] at Washington. For days, weeks and months we had waited for his return; but in vain.

Old Capitol War Prison, Washington, D.C., where Capt. Wells was held prisoner.

(National Archives)

At last, in our despair, I gained my mother's consent to cross the line, hoping to return in a few weeks and allay the fear that filled her mind—that my father was dead. The raids that had been perpetrated upon the 'Northern Neck' by the Northern troops—mostly Negro regiments commanded by white officers—by whom the most horrible outrages had been committed, had prevented her from making the trip I was destined to make.

And, with no other motive than to reach Washington and ascertain my father's fate, then to relieve the minds of our anxious family, I left Lancaster County early in the morning of the fourth of August, 1864, in company with a lady and her little son, from Richmond, and a gentleman who had promised my mother to accompany me to the Maryland shore.

The ride across the country to the Potomac, which we reached at nightfall, was a delightful one; and the hospitable reception at the house of Mr. H__ by himself and daughters, somewhat dispelled the gloom that naturally followed my departure from home.

On the succeeding day my escort accompanied me to a cabin a few miles distant, in search of a man who we had reason to think would assist us in crossing the river. Although reluctant at first to carry out our plans, the 'blockade runner,' upon hearing my name and my purpose in crossing the lines, decided to aid us. He informed me that he had been confined in the Old Capitol Prison and there had seen my father; but he could give me no later intelligence of him than we had already received. Although he promised to cross the river with us, he was uncertain as to the time. 'It was very risky business,' he said, 'and the price would be twenty dollars apiece, in greenbacks.'

Not until the night of the eighth inst. did we receive the anxiously expected message: 'to leave the house at nine o'clock and drive to Beach Point.' After having lost our way several times, we, at last, secured a Negro guide who, the night being very dark, led our horses over the secluded road to the point mentioned. Arriving there, my lady companion and myself were left alone in the carriage while our guide and protector went in search of the boatmen. It was a dreary place in which to be left alone, and when a gang of men approached the side of the carriage and one of them demanded who was within, I must say my heart beat somewhat faster than it was wont to upon ordinary occasions. However, the intruder proved to be only our uncouth friend, 'the blockader,' who informed us that he had 'about given us up.'

Between 11 and 12 o'clock, the Captain having carried me to the barge and anchored some seven or eight rods from the shore, and placed me in the bow, beside Mrs. C__, the four oarsmen took their places—the captain at the helm—and we struck out boldly. The Potomac was filled with lights. There was indeed great fear of our being run down by one of the many gun-boats plodding their way up and down the stream. Finally, the heavy fog that arose so obscured the lights and horizon that the captain and men seemed quite bewildered as to their course. At one time we were not sure that we were not returning to the Virginia shore. The river being ten miles wide at that point it was not very pleasant to be rowing in an uncertain direction; neither was it safe for blockade runners to be drifting around until daylight.

At last the lights from Point Lookout being detected, the captain, in an undertone, gave the order to 'row on.' It was within an hour of daylight when we struck the Maryland shore, tired and sleepy. Our escort went in search of a house wherein we could procure some breakfast, and we remained seated upon the bank until he returned and conducted us through a field to a house where the boatmen were already assembled.

After a substantial meal of fried chicken and good bread, we parted with our escort, who returned with the boatmen that night to Virginia, and, having settled ourselves in a large box wagon, on the top of Mrs. C.'s trunk (I was wise enough to have but a satchel myself), we were jolted to Leonardtown, behind a negro driver, for the sum of fifteen dollars—a distance of five miles. It was a generous price, *especially as the equipage was a stylish one (for Long Island fish hauling) in which to draw up before a Hotel filled with boarders. Mrs. C__ and myself drew our veils closely down over our faces as the clerk ran down the steps, with a chair, to assist us from our establishment. We entered the parlor looking tired and forlorn. I say forlorn, for I suppose we must have appeared so to the gaily dressed ladies assembled there. In truth, our dress was not exactly in accordance with the prevailing style—a most lamentable circumstance it would have been to many of our fashionable girls; not so to us. I cannot call to mind how Mrs. C__ was attired; but I remember that my hat was particularly low crowned when the fashion appeared to be in a directly opposite direction. I wore upon my feet a pair of shoes for which I had paid, before leaving home, one hundred and five dollars; but they were rough calfskin, and had been manufactured by a country shoemaker. But, if any of my readers were within the Southern lines during the war, they will readily understand how glad I was to get them. I was indeed accounted very lucky in getting them at all, there being several applicants for the same. With this knowledge I blame myself very much for allowing myself, when I arrived at Leonardtown, to wish I had changed them for a finer pair in my satchel. The finer pair alluded to had been hoarded up since the earlier part of the war for extra occasions. Oh, what a treasure a good pair of shoes was! But I am digressing.*

We had hardly reached our room at the Hotel when we were summoned to the parlor to meet a Federal officer, who ordered us to report immediately to the Provost Marshal. We obeyed by accompanying him to the quarters mentioned, which proved to be but a short distance from the hotel. There we were questioned and scrutinized closely—the color of our hair and eyes and general appearance being noted with our ages and general account of ourselves. When all this disagreeable performance was ended, we were commanded not to leave Leonardtown until we had orders. Under the pleasant reflection that we might be held to await orders a much longer time than our patience demanded, we returned to our room at our hotel.

Fortunately, we were only detained at Leonardtown two days. I have wondered since if we had been kept there for any length of time, if there would have been any provision made for our board.

On the morning of the eleventh we were conveyed by an officer to the steamboat landing, and placed on board of a tug en route for Point Lookout. Descending to the cabin, we found ourselves in the midst of a crowd of females—the very scum of Richmond women, whose husbands had already fled from the Southern Conscription Law. I looked around me for one intelligent countenance, one face to assure me that I had not been brought to the level of the creatures before me; but I saw not one. I turned to my companion and asked her to return with me to the deck. There I sought the captain of the tug, and asked him if there was any place we could go away from the motley group that crowded in the cabin. The countenance of the rough man lighted up kindly as he replied: 'Certainly, certainly, Miss! You shall have my office.'

So, saying, he conducted us to the cozy little apartment in the centre of the deck, and giving us the key, told us to lock the door if we chose. We were between four and five hours going down the Potomac, and reached Point Lookout at twelve o'clock. Scarcely had we struck the wharf, when an officer rushed aboard, and, after a hurried conversation with another officer on board, hurriedly approached the office wherein we sat. In a tyrannical voice he ordered us not to leave the boat until further orders. No sooner had he left us than the captain of the boat, coming close to my side, whispered: 'Look out for that man; he is a villian.' 'Can you tell me his name?' I asked. 'Lieutenant Phelps.' (The Captain may have said Phillips.)

At two o'clock a body of men came marching down the street (if it may be called so) and drew up in line on the wharf. 'I have orders to conduct the prisoners to the Provost Marshal.' At this announcement, Mrs. C__ and myself, with the former's little son, stepped ashore and started in the direction the men had come. But we had not taken many steps when we were ordered to 'Halt!'

I think I never suffered such mortification as when I found myself at the head of that ignorant group of females, guarded on either side by soldiers, marching to the Provost Marshal's office at Point Lookout. In one moment the tears rushing to my eyes would almost render me powerless to move; but in the next my indignation would rise to such a pitch that I would force them back and resolve to bear the indignities heaped upon me as submissive as possible.

The walk to the Provost Marshal's office was about three-quarters of a mile. The house in front of which we were drawn up was a long, one-story frame building, with a porch in front running the whole length of the building, off of which there were doors leading to some three or four different offices. I stepped upon the porch, although I was expected, no doubt, to stand among the crowd in the rays of the hot August sun. Mrs. C__ followed me. The door of the central office was open, and in the rear, directly opposite the door, lounging back in his chair, with his left elbow resting on a small table at this side, sat the Assistant Provost Marshal. He was a man quite young in years, with a heavy, black mustache, and he wore a linen duster extending well down to his heels. It needed but one glance at his countenance to assure you that his bump of self-esteem must have attained an enormous size, especially since his appointment to that office. Some fifteen or twenty minutes must have elapsed before the gentleman alluded to thought fit to undertake the examination. Then, with a lazy nod of the head, he said, in an affected voice: 'You can come in.'

I raised myself to a proud height, for I felt the most utter contempt for the man before me, and asked him if he addressed me. His reply, or nod, being in the affirmative, I advanced into the room. There were some three or four clerks at their desks, who looked at me somewhat compassionately, I fancied, as I entered.

Withdrawing to one side of the office, the Assistant put the question: 'What is your name?' This was executed in a tone that would have done credit to many of his superiors. I suppose my lips curled slightly as I replied to the question, although I endeavored to be respectful. I confess I did so through policy—I certainly could not feel any respect for the man before me.

'Where did you come from?' 'Lancaster County, Virginia.' Then followed those endless interrogatories, such as: 'What is your business here?' 'When did you leave Virginia?' 'How did you cross the lines?' 'Who brought you across the river?' The latter question I could not answer, not knowing the blockade runner's real name, which I had taken pains not to ascertain, having no disposition to betray a man who had befriended me. 'What is your destination?' 'How old are you?' etc., etc.

Then, in a decidedly pleasant, almost persuasive tone, the officer put the following question: 'Do you desire to take the oath of allegiance?' 'I do not.' 'What did you come here for?' he almost screamed. 'You cross the lines; claim protection from our government, and then refuse to take the oath. We will see you again.' I asked to be allowed to see one of the forms of oath, and upon being handed one, retired to the porch to await my fate.

A chair was handed me through the window by one of the clerks. Mrs. C__ was then called in for examination. I took up the printed oath to read, and as I did so one of the most intelligent looking of the crowd of females leaned over the railing of the porch and whispered: 'Shure, ye don't have to take the oath, do ye?' I replied that I supposed it was necessary, when she added: 'Oh, if I had knowed that, I'd never left Richmond in the world.'

The document I held in my hand contained the usual formula of an oath, with the addition of two clauses, which read thus: 'That I will abide by any proclamation the President may issue in reference to slaves.' How was I to know how materially the future proclamations of the President might affect me or mine? With this question revolving in my mind, I remarked to Mrs. C__, who had returned to the porch, that such an oath could only emanate from a despot. In reply she said: 'that the clause respecting slaves was the only objectionable one to her.' For myself, I regarded the latter clause in by far the worst light, and so remarked.

Lieutenant Phelps, who stood near, his evil eye keeping watch over us, probably heard a portion of our conversation; for he advanced to my side, and asked in the most uncouth manner: 'What is the matter with that oath?' 'I regard it as despotic, sir,' I answered candidly, in defiance of his authority. 'You'd better stayed where you came from,' he answered threateningly. I made no reply to him. I felt satisfied that if my examination was left to him, I stood a poor chance of escape; but of this I had no fear.

I had learned before leaving Leonardtown, that if sent to Point Lookout I had no alternative but to take the oath or be imprisoned for an indefinite length of time; and although it had cost me many tears, I had resolved to take the 'oath of allegiance' rather than expose myself to the insults and diseases of imprisonment, thereby abandoning my project of finding my father and returning home to relieve our unhappy family. I say I had resolved to take the oath of allegiance to the United States if necessary; but with a mental reservation. I considered that upon my return to Virginia I was liable to be similarly forced to swear allegiance to the Confederacy, and as I had no disposition to refuse 'aid and comfort' to an afflicted creature North or South, I reserved to myself the right to bestow my sympathy upon such of God's creatures as I saw fit. But when the Assistant Provost Marshal put the question: 'Do you desire to take the oath of allegiance?' I answered candidly that I did not.

I had not sat long upon the porch when an officer, who proved to be Major__, the Provost Marshal, emerged from the office at the right of us, and rushing up in front of me, demanded: 'You refuse to take the oath, I understand?' 'No, sir, I have not refused'—I was about to add that I would take a reasonable oath if necessary, when the evil minded lieutenant interfered. 'She lies; she refused to take the oath in my presence.' 'How much money have you?' demanded the Major. 'I cannot tell exactly, but within a few dollars.' 'Well, if you don't know we'll very soon find out. Walk in that office! I'll see you again.'

I did as ordered. The doors, both front and rear, were closed upon me, and a guard placed at the outside of each. I must acknowledge I felt many misgivings regarding my fate at this juncture; but, offering up a prayer to the God who directed my destiny, I awaited as calmly as possible the entrance of the Major. Remembering the threat that had been made relative to my funds, I counted the pieces over and when the Provost entered I named the exact sum in my possession.

Although Major__ had accosted me in such an eat-you-up way upon the porch, when he was alone he was both kind and gentlemanly, that is: he conducted the examination officially but respectfully. In conclusion, he said: 'Miss __, you were reported to me before you reached the Point. You are suspected of being a spy, and I have orders to investigate your case thoroughly. These people outside we care nothing about—they are crossing the lines all the time—but ladies of your appearance, and I may add, intelligence, are not often detected running the blockade, and, when detected, we always suspect them. I should consider that I had neglected a most important duty if I allowed you to leave the office without a thorough examination of your person. Of course, there is nothing to be found among your baggage. Have you any objection to being searched? I will procure a lady to do so.'

I replied that, if by submitting to such an examination I would be furnishing any proof of my innocence, I was ready to do so. A call-bell summoned the guard at the entrance, and after some conversation with a soldier, who afterwards entered, I concluded that a messenger had been dispatched for a lady. The Major then said: 'Understand, this will be a thorough search of your person. You will be compelled to take down your hair, remove your shoes, &c.'

I remained in the office until six o'clock—Mrs. C__, at my request, had been allowed to join me in the meantime—and still the Provost's attempts to procure a female to search me had proved ineffectual. At that time Lieut. Phelps entered, and bending down to the major's desk, whispered something in his ear. I could not hear what he said; but I distinctly heard the Provost's reply: 'No; I will not insult her.'

'What can the man have proposed?' I tremblingly asked myself. 'Can it be to search me himself?' Tears filled my eyes as the question arose in my mind; and my hands clasped so tightly together that the nails penetrated the flesh. The lieutenant being dismissed, the Major turned to me and said; 'Have no fears. I would not allow you to be searched by a black woman.' I felt relieved at this, although the Lieutenant's proposition proved to be insulting. 'No, Major,' I returned, 'I cannot submit to such an outrage. Humiliating as it is, a lady of my own color can execute your demands—no other.' 'I am very sorry, for your sake, that I have not been successful in my attempts to procure a lady to search you,' said the Provost. 'Am I to be detained here until such time as you can do so?' 'I see no alternative. I should be neglecting a most important duty if I allowed you to go without.'

'Sir, it is unnecessary for me to assure you again that I am upon no illegal errand. You will not credit it. I have referred you to responsible parties from whom, by telegraph, you can soon learn the truth of my statements: and am ready and willing to have my person searched. What more can I do? I am not pleading my innocence in the matter charged against me; that would be useless. But if there is anything more I can do to be allowed to resume my journey, I would like to know what it is. I have been eight days endeavoring to go from Lancaster County to Washington, to my father; and I am tired and exhausted from fatigue and excitement.'

The Major regarded my face earnestly as I spoke, and when I had concluded drawled out slowly: 'Your story is very plausible; but I don't like to trust you. 'Is it possible?' I ejaculated, somewhat despairingly. 'Why did you not take the oath?' 'I would prefer not to take an oath to any government; but if it is necessary, I will do so.' 'What do you consider necessary?' 'If by such means only I can reach my destination.' 'You speak candidly.' After a moment he continued: 'There is but one oath I would allow you to take, only one that I consider binding enough.'

Having asked the nature of the oath referred to, I received the reply: 'It requires you to take it without mental reservation.' I gave the Major some penetration after he had announced this. And as the oath was a simple one which I had no disposition to break, I took it, without mental reservation. The Provost, having signed the papers and handed them over for my signature, left the offices and did not return for at least a half hour.

As Mrs. C__'s fate seemed to depend upon mine, we felt considerable anxiety lest we should be detained as prisoners. But when the Provost returned and addressed us in the following way, we were relieved of our unpleasant fears: 'Ladies, I will give you a pass on the tug that leaves the wharf tonight, at eleven o'clock, to meet the 'Louisiana' coming up the Chesapeake from Fortress Monroe. As you have money you will be required to pay fifty cents a piece for your fare on board the tug. If you had not, you could go free.' Turning to me, he continued. 'I shall give you a pass; but I am not satisfied.' 'I am sorry to learn that I am suspected,' I returned. 'Although I have my suspicions regarding your interest in the rebellion, yet I respect you; and it affords me pleasure to allow you to return to your friends.'

Notwithstanding I puzzled considerably over the Provost Marshal's last words to me, and marveled that I should be allowed to leave Point Lookout under such suspicion, I did not imagine the investigation would pursue me on my journey. Therefore, when we had been transferred about midnight from the tug to the 'Louisiana,' and had settled ourselves upon a 'tete-tete' in the center of the handsome saloon to lament over our misfortune in not being able to secure a state-room, a young man, in naval uniform, approached and endeavored to open conversation with Mrs. C_'s little son, I was happily unconscious that he was a spy upon my movements. This young man reported himself as from Fortress Monroe, on a furlough, and offered to give little Willie a berth in the bow of the boat. To this Mrs. C__ gladly consented, the child being weary and almost overpowered by sleep. The officer having disposed of the boy comfortably, as he informed my companion, returned to the saloon and expressed many regrets that herself and friend had not been able to secure a state-room.

Mrs. C__, feeling under obligations to him for his kindness to her son, chatted pleasantly with him until a state-room door about midway of the saloon opened, and a man in his shirt sleeves with his coat hanging over his arm, approached us. 'Ladies, if you will accept of my state-room, I will go in with a friend,' he said. We thanked him politely, declining to disturb him. But, finally, yielding to his persuasion, took the offered key and retired, only too glad to have an opportunity to get a few hours sleep before reaching Baltimore. As I turned to go in the room I saw the gentleman in the shirt-sleeves in earnest conversation with the naval officer already mentioned. I was a little surprised on entering the state-room to find it had not been disturbed; but being too tired to take into notice anything that did not concern me, I undressed and climbed into the upper berth.

Before doing so, Mrs. C__ and myself had examined the outside of the window to ascertain if we could with safety leave it open, the night being very warm. Our examination satisfied us that there was no possibility of intrusion there. Consequently, we left the window open. I do not know how long I had been in my berth endeavoring to go to sleep, keeping my eyes closed for that purpose, when Mrs. C__, who occupied the lower berth, of course, in a frightened tone of voice called my name, adding: 'There is some one at the window.'

I raised my head and saw by the light, reflected through the glass over our door from the saloon, a man, whose figure was partially hid in the shade of the window. I was very much alarmed, so much so that I could form no sane conclusion as to the course we should pursue. As I am endeavoring to give a faithful account of events in connection with this trip, I will not shrink from an explanation of my conduct on this occasion, however ridiculous it may appear.

Mrs. C__, it is a man! I am going to scream.' 'What shall we do?' returned Mrs. C__. 'I tell you I am going to scream.' But, although I persisted in my intention to give an alarm, I did no such *thing, feeling somewhat reluctant to have anybody and everybody demanding admittance to our state-room in our present situation. Neither had I the courage or boldness to leave my berth in the face of the intruder, to shove the window and bolt it. So I persisted in a most determined voice, raising myself still further on my elbow: 'I tell you, Mrs. C__, I am going to scream murder.' Whether it was the determined tone I assumed that frightened the intruder from his position or not I cannot say; but he moved away after my most alarming threat; and Mrs. C__ hastily rose and secured the sash.*

In the morning when we awoke the 'Louisiana' lay at the wharf at Baltimore. The first thought we had was to examine the boat outside of the window. We discovered that, being in the centre of the boat, we were separated from all the other state-rooms except one, which was unintentionally connected with ours by a short platform running beneath the window of each, separating us from the works of the boat. We had not time to examine the situation perfectly, for we were anxious to leave the boat; but we satisfied ourselves that the man who had for some purpose been watching us the night before, occupied the adjoining state-room.

It would be too tedious to relate the manner in which the carriage I occupied was followed after leaving the steamboat until I was safe among my friends. The subsequent interception of my letters, together with other transactions, proved to me that the Provost Marshal at Point Lookout had not allowed me to escape without being 'satisfied' that I was innocent of the cause ascribed to me.

Mamie Wells was spied upon through her stateroom window while aboard the *USS Louisiana*.

(Sketch of *USS Louisiana* from Frank Leslie's Illus., 1861)

ERICKSBURG S

⊃SKBURG, VA., WEDNESDAY, AUGUST 1, 1888.

Reminiscences of the Late War.

BY MAMIE L. WELLS.

CHAPTER VI.

Trials and Disappointments.

"Since then it is entailed upon humanity to submit, and some are born to command, and others to obey, the question is : as there must be tyrants, whether it is better to have them in the same house with us, or in the same vicinage, or still further off in the metropolis." — *Oliver Goldsmith*.

The "City Jail" of Baltimore is a large stone structure, with two huge wings spreading out on either side of the main entrance. In the apartments of the South wing, in the year 1864, were gathered the criminals of the city and county of Baltimore; but in the North wing were quartered men of a different stamp called by the officials of that day "Political prisoners." The walk in front of the building, leading

some strategy for the relief of those tedious hours of prison life. Thus : (I am not ashamed to confess it, for I am sure I did my duty) upon every Thursday I contrived to have some choice fruit concealed in my parasol or pocket, which I likewise contrived to drop between the bars into my father's outside coat pocket. Papers and books were similarly administered. Mayhap some of the visitors may have observed these transactions; but, if they did, they only pressed more closely to my side to hide the gaze of the armed guards at our backs. Yet we were not contented with this small bestowal of comforts. An acquaintance, in confinement near my father, having the heart disease, was allowed more liberties in consequence; among others, once a week, he was the recipient of a basket of provisions from his friends. We were not long in making arrangements with the mother of this gentleman to double the amount of provender. The surplus was conveyed, little by little, in the gentle-

appearance, first approached the President, whose business it was to release her son from the army, he having entered the service at the age of fifteen without her knowledge or consent.

"What do you come to me for ?" rudely questioned Mr. Lincoln. "How do I know anything about it ? Where are the papers ?"

"At the War Department, sir."

"Well, why don't you go there ?"

"I have been to the War Department, sir, and was then directed to you."

"Get the papers. Until then I can do nothing for you."

The lady departed; but soon returned with the information that the papers could not be delivered into her hands without the President's order.

The second advance was made by a woman of rather handsome appearance who wanted a pass to visit her brother in prison.

"I can't give you a pass" said Mr. Lincoln.

"But, Mr. Lincoln, how would

Chapter of Mamie L. Wells' **Reminiscences of the Late War: Trials and Disappointments,**
on front page of the August 1, 1888 issue of the *Fredericksburg Star*.

Chapter XIII—Trials and Disappointments

> 'Since then it is entailed upon humanity to submit, and some are born to command and others to obey, the question is, as there must be tyrants, whether it is better to have them in the same house with us, or in the same village, or still further off, in the metropolis.'--Oliver Goldsmith

Mamie Wells:

"The 'City Jail' of Baltimore is a large stone structure, with two huge wings spreading out on either side of the main entrance. In the apartments of the South wing, in the year 1864, were gathered the criminals of the city and county of Baltimore; but in the North wing were quartered men of a different stamp called by the officials of that day 'Political prisoners.' The walk in front of the building leading from the gate to the entrance I observed, as I tread it for the first time, was well tended, and sweet flowers grew beneath the gloomy windows. These sweet, pretty flowers! They seemed to offer comfort to my suffering heart.

I reached the top of the long flight of stone steps, and there I paused. How I moved on I cannot tell unless supported by the friend who accompanied me. I entered the immense quadrangular apartment and tremblingly looked around me. A row of iron bars running up and down from the floor to the partition above, some few inches apart, separated me from either wing; behind which I could see the upper and lower corridors stretching in front of the different cells. It was Thursday—visiting day to those who could, by proving themselves loyal, procure a pass to visit their friends confined within these walls.

Upon that day, the eighteenth of August, one year before, I had parted from my father at Fredericksburg—now I sought him in the cells of that gloomy prison. I had promised my companion to be calm and collected to bear the meeting with as little emotion as possible; but, Oh! what a struggle! I stood beneath one of the tall windows, with my back to the bars, pressing my hand hard upon my heart to still its wild beatings, while my friend remained at the bars to announce my arrival before I presented myself. Once I turned; and in that short, eager glance I saw my father descending the steps. Oh, God! What a trial! I turned away to renew the struggle over my heart; but only for a moment. Then I pressed through the crowd of visitors and took my father's hand, extended toward me between these unrelenting bars of iron.

Only those who have been called upon to undergo a similar trial can understand the joy and the misery occasioned by such a meeting. It was joy to me to be able to look upon my father's face once more; joy to him to see one member of his family so recently from the home circle, to learn that those most dear to us on earth were still alive. But when we reflected that we were both so widely separated from them with such a faint hope of being reunited, our sadness overcame our short period of happiness.

It may not be amiss here to state the circumstances connected with my father's imprisonment in the City Jail of Baltimore. After a month's confinement in the Old Capitol Prison at Washington, whither he had been taken shortly after his capture by the gun-boat 'Currituck,' in August 1863, he was taken before the Judge Advocate (Capt. Parker)[240] for trial. But, although the Judge, according to his own words, believed him innocent of the charge laid upon him (that of carrying supplies to the Confederate government) he was thrust back into prison because he would not take an oath that would separate him from his family during the remainder of the war—a most uncertain period it was then. At the expiration of a little less than four months, at the entreaty of his eldest daughter, Mrs. C[rawford][241] of Baltimore, he was released on condition that he was not to go South during the war, without permission from the authorities. He returned with her to Baltimore, at which place he remained over five months, endeavoring to gain permission to go to his family from whom he had been separated nine months. Failing in this and suffering untold anxiety regarding them, for they were not in the land of plenty he well knew, he left Baltimore in a little sailboat, intending to go down the Patapsco and Chesapeake and enter the Rappahannock under cover of the night. You who have wives and families, tell me, was there any crime in this?

Unfortunately, upon the eve of the success of his plan, he was picked up by a sailing vessel with a crew of armed men and, after three weeks of hard labor, was lodged in the City Jail, where he was awaiting his trial when I arrived in Baltimore. Here he was kept in solitary confinement excepting an hour and a half each day when he was allowed to walk in the gallery. My sister had not been permitted to send him anything to eat, although his food was scanty and poor; neither was he allowed any book or periodicals. But, as 'all is fair in love and war,' I confess we resorted to some strategy for the relief of those tedious hours of prison life. Thus: (I am not ashamed to confess it, for I am sure I did my duty) upon every Thursday I contrived to have some choice fruit concealed in my parasol or pocket, which I likewise contrived to drop between the bars into my father's outside coat pocket. Papers and books were similarly administered. Mayhap some of the visitors may have observed these transactions; but, if they did, they only pressed more closely to my side to hide the gaze of the armed guards at our backs. Yet we were not contented with this small bestowal of comforts. An acquaintance, in confinement near my father, having the heart disease, was allowed more liberties in consequence; among others, once a week he was the recipient of a basket of provisions from his friends. We were not long in making arrangements with the mother of this gentleman to double the amount of provender. The surplus was conveyed, little by little, in the gentleman's pockets to his fellow prisoner during his walk in the corridor. Aside from the pleasure of knowing when I saw my father each week that he had not been half starved. I must acknowledge it afforded me the most intense satisfaction to know that we had outwitted those prison tyrants.

But, it will be remembered, I left Virginia with the expectation of returning as early as possible to dispel the dread fears of those I left behind. Uncertain that the result of my father's trial which was daily expected might be, but in the belief that he would be released I resolved to await the issue before attempting to return home. The trial took place in the latter part of September, before a Military Commission. It is hardly necessary for me to give an account of that disgraceful affair, as it is well known that such a trial amounts to certain conviction, if the parties in power feel unfavorably disposed toward the accused.

Suspicion, followed by perjury on the part of the sailors who appeared as witnesses, was sufficient to condemn an innocent man.

On the morning of the sixth of October I arose earlier than usual and descended to the sitting room to read the local news. Through that column of the [Baltimore] <u>Sun</u>[242] I learned that my father had been sentenced to three year's hard labor at Fort McHenry, and fined one thousand dollars. I read it over and over again to assure myself that my eyes did not deceive me, then ascended the stairs to my sister's[243] room where I spent with her the hour before breakfast in bitter tears. It being Thursday, I left the house directly after lunch to visit my father. I was attended by my usual companion in these visits; my sister being in poor health did not accompany me. Arriving at the prison we were informed that the prisoner had been conveyed to Fort McHenry that morning, so I returned home sad and disappointed.

Fort McHenry
Portion of a lithograph of Fort McHenry, by E. Sachse, 1862. Peale Museum, Baltimore.
Courtesy of The Library of Congress

187

I had previously determined that if my father's sentence proved unjust, I would take immediate measure towards its repeal. Being satisfied it was perfectly useless to appeal to Gen. Wallace,[244] I went the next morning to Washington to consult with some friends upon the proper course to pursue. But those friends, though popular among their constituents, were not favorites of the President. They were Democrats, and as Mr. D[enison],[245] M__, C__, remarked to me, their influence would only be a drawback. The advice I received from one and all was: 'see the President and enlist his sympathy.'

Therefore my first aim in the effort to release my father from his most unjust confinement was 'to see the President.' Major__ held a position in the War Department, and through an intimacy long existing between his sister and our family I was introduced to him. He expressed a desire to aid me to the extent of his power, and accordingly paved the way for an interview with the President by giving me a note of introduction to Major [John] Hay,[246] his private secretary.

Exterior of White House, c.1860

(Library of Congress)

On Monday, the tenth of October, I went to the White House, and after much difficulty, succeeded in sending my card to the secretary, who soon waited upon me in the Ladies' Reception Room. Major Hay received and treated me with all due politeness, and assured me he would use his utmost endeavors to secure me a private interview with the President, although he had little hope of being successful. I remained in that room four hours. At the expiration of that time a messenger at the door announced: 'that the President would devote the next hour to the reception of all those who desired an interview.' There were at least forty ladies besides myself ready to answer this announcement; and as many gentlemen waited in the lobby extending in front of the President's room to join us as we passed into the presence of the Executive.

Mr. Lincoln[247] sat in front of one of the windows which overlooked the grounds at the rear of the House, and the glittering Potomac beyond. I immediately observed that an unpleasant frown had taken the place of the smile worn upon his face at his first Levee[248] which I had attended in the spring of '61, but for that I could readily account. He leaned his right elbow upon the table beside him, and bent slightly forward as the crowd advanced into the room. A good looking lady, of genteel appearance, first approached the President, whose business it was to release her son from the army, he having entered the service at the age of fifteen without her knowledge or consent. 'What do you come to me for?' rudely questioned Mr. Lincoln. 'How do I know anything about it? Where are the papers?' 'At the War Department, sir.' 'Well, why don't you go there?' 'I have been to the War Department, sir, and was then directed to you. 'Get the papers. Until then I can do nothing for you.' The lady departed; but soon returned with the information that the papers could not be delivered into her hands without the President's order.

The second advance was made by a woman of rather handsome appearance who wanted a pass to visit her brother in prison. 'I can't give you a pass.' Said Mr. Lincoln. 'But, Mr. Lincoln, how would you like to be in prison and not have your sister come to see you?' 'I wouldn't be in prison; I wouldn't be there.' 'But you might. Now I know you are going to give me a pass,' pettishly urged the lady. 'But I know I won't,' replied the President. 'Anyhow, I am not going away until you do.' 'Very well; then I'll get my boys to put you out.' 'Oh, I know you wouldn't do that Mr. Lincoln.' 'Oh, but I know I would.' 'Well, you are going to give me a pass, I know—please, Mr. Lincoln.' 'Will you never bother me again?' 'Not until I want another favor.' 'Well, I'll give you a pass now; but it will be the last one.'

The third applicant was evidently a poor woman of about sixty years of age. 'Well, what do you want?' asked the President, as she modestly advanced to his side. 'Mr. Lincoln, my son has been drafted, and he is the only support I have.' 'Well, what did you come to me for?' 'Because nobody else will do anything for me.' 'There is a law exempting men under such circumstances.' 'But they will not do anything for me without your say so.' 'What can I do? What do you expect me to do?' As the Executive spoke he laughed in the woman's face. She tremblingly faltered in reply: 'Give me a paper, sir.' 'What kind of a paper.' 'Anything, sir, with your name on' 'What good will that do?' 'A great deal, sir.' 'But if your son is your only support he is exempt.' 'I know, sir.' 'Perhaps you are able to support yourself?' 'No, sir; I am not.' 'I don't know but what you are.' 'No, Mr. Lincoln, she is not,' spoke up the companion of the poor supplicant. Then, I tell you, your son is exempt.' 'Will you give me a paper saying so?' 'I can write: if the woman's son is exempt by law from duty as a soldier, let him off. Will that do?' 'Yes, sir, if it will do me any good.' 'But I tell you it won't.' The President then wrote a few words on a slip of paper and handed it to the woman, who, after asking if it would relieve her son and receiving the reply, 'No,' departed.

A soldier next advanced to the President, who greeted him in his accustomed way: 'Well, what do you want?' 'Mr. President, I simply called to pay my respects before leaving the service.' As the soldier spoke he tapped the empty coat sleeve hanging by his side and extended his hand cordially. Mr. Lincoln half noticed, half grunted, barely touched the soldier's hand; then turned to the next in advance.

'Well, what's your business?' To this question the gentleman addressed returned a beaming smile and announced the fact that he was the son of __ from one of the Western States. I gathered enough from the lengthy conversation which followed to satisfy me that the gentleman's father and Mr. Lincoln had indulged in some very extraordinary excursions some time previous, fishing in some hollow, &c., which circumstance was sufficient to allow the gentleman alluded to take up the few moments allotted to those whose business with the President was, in many cases, of vital importance.

Although I have a vivid remembrance of all that transpired up to the moment of approaching the Executive myself, I cannot recall my own conversation with him. I remember that upon seeing the hands of the clock approaching the hour of three, I gathered courage to take the few steps that brought me directly in front of him.

Mr. Lincoln looked up through his glasses, and...demanded: *'Well, what do you want?*

(Anthony Berger photograph Feb. 9, 1864, Library of Congress)

Mr. Lincoln looked up through his glasses, and, in the same uncouth way that had deterred me from presenting myself sooner, demanded: *'Well, what do you want?'* Alas! I wanted more than I had the courage to ask for. I wanted that which I felt should be mine without supplication. I wanted, in default of this, a kind word or look, some encouragement to ask for it. I could not be as one of my own sex had done before me; but I stated my business in a brief manner, adding that, unless something was done to mitigate the sentence inflicted upon my father, he could not possibly survive it. I don't know what Mr. Lincoln's first intentions toward me were; but upon questioning me as to the residence of my mother and receiving the reply, *'Virginia,'* he dismissed me with these words: *'I can't do anything for you.'*

I stood for a moment revolving in my mind whether or not to speak again, then the words of those better informed than myself returned to me—*'Only the President can aid you,'* and I spoke again, trembling, but imploring, in the conviction that it was the last chance offered me for the release of my kind parent. To this reply the President of the United States gave no reply; but, leaning rudely to one side, accosted the person nearest to me with his usual interrogatory: *'Well, what do you want?'*

Shocked, stunned, chilled to the heart, I left his presence. How I reached my friend's house I do not remember. But toward nightfall a delicate arm wound around me and a soft, girlish voice whispered: *'I am so sorry for you! Don't cry!'* There was sympathy in the touch of the hand, and in the tone of the voice, and I yielded to its appeal. Than having bathed my tear-stained face, I sat down to deliberate upon the course I had pursued. The conclusion I came to was, that I had committed a most excusably foolish act. What right had I, a resident of Virginia, to expect any sympathy from one of its bitterest enemies? Yet I could not dismiss the thought that Mr. Lincoln could at least have treated me civilly, or banish the idea that he could have aided me without any encroachment upon his own time.

Upon the following morning I returned to Baltimore, and upon the succeeding day procured a carriage to take me to Fort McHenry, a distance of five miles, in the full expectation of seeing my father. It proved to be entrance day, consequently I had no difficulty in gaining admittance to the fort. Gen. Morris, then in command, was walking with his adjutant when I found him, and upon being informed of my business, told me, in his slow way, that he had no power to admit me to any of the prisons; that I would not see my father without a permit from the Secretary of War. I must have expressed my great disappointment in my face, for the Adjutant, in the kindest voice imaginable, said: 'You just run down to Washington and get a pass from Mr. [Edwin M.] Stanton,[249] then you can see your father.' I thanked the gentleman and turned away to hide my tears of disappointment.

The day after I again went to Washington and applied through my good friend, Major__ for a pass to visit my father. I was unsuccessful; but I returned to Baltimore with Major's assurance that he would continue to strive for a permit. Arriving at Baltimore, I found a note had been received from my father asking for a mattress and blanket. He had laid upon the floor of the prison without covering since his arrival at Fort McHenry; the nights had been unusually cool, and he had contracted a cold, from which he was suffering. Mr. [James B. Crawford],[250] my brother-in-law, prompt and faithful, had attended to his wants.

While I was still puzzling over the next step to pursue in the cause I had undertaken, I received a letter from a near and dear relative, residing in New York asking for a correct statement of events connected with my father's arrest and imprisonment, and stating that a plan had been devised through which, it was hoped, his release would be effected. Mr. Henry J. Raymond,[251] Editor of the <u>New York Times</u> was then a candidate for Congress, and as his influence with the President and Secretary of War was supposed to be very great, it was proposed to enlist his services. Before the election (I do not say the election had anything to do with it) Mr. Raymond appeared much interested in the matter and promised, when he went to Washington in a couple of weeks, to see the President and use his influence in my father's behalf. This promise was made to the relative alluded to. Accordingly, I wrote a letter of thanks to Mr. Raymond, in which I proposed to meet him in Washington upon his arrival there, in order to furnish further details concerning the case.

I waited until after the election, some two weeks, when receiving no reply, I wrote again. To this letter an answer came to the effect that he could not undertake to act in a case of which he was entirely ignorant. He did not know when he would go to Washington—perhaps not in several weeks. I, of course, regarded his letter as a blank refusal to aid me, and abandoned all though of assistance from him.

But at this period of dejection I received good news from Washington. The Major had at last succeeded in procuring a pass for me to visit Fort McHenry by offering to escort me there and be present at the interview. Consequently I was permitted to see my father on the 19th of November in the parlor of Gen. Morris' house, whither he had been conducted, through the kindness of the General, to meet me. He was suffering from a severe cold consequent upon the exposure inflicted upon him immediately after his arrival at the fort, and looked badly. Then I learned that his prison was in the loft of what had once been a stable, that he was there confined with about one hundred fellow-prisoners. His food consisted of six hard crackers, with a very small piece of poor meat for his dinner—not a morsel more. Yet we are ever reminded by those who have had no experience in Federal prisons how excellently well the prisoners were fed. He was not put to hard labor as I had feared, and was allowed to walk in the muddy yard surrounding the buildings, during the day. In the same prison were men who had been in confinement for a year and a half without a trial, without knowing in fact, for what offence they had thus ruthlessly been torn from their home and friends. One of these was so old and feeble that he tottered in his walk and shook with palsy.

In the belief that the removal of our family to Baltimore would aid me very materially in the release of my father, I determined to make an effort toward its accomplishment. Capt. [Foxhall A.] Parker,[252] being in command of the Potomac Flotilla and the blockading fleet on the Rappahannock, I went to Washington in order to see him but failed, he having left the city. Having obtained his address, I wrote him concerning the removal of my mother by one of the federal gunboats.

Failing to elicit a reply, I made a trip to the Relay House, nine miles from Baltimore, and walked from there to Capt. Parker's residence, about a mile distant—a beautiful place overlooking the entire surrounding country, with a broad avenue winding gracefully from the road to the house. I was received by Captain Parker and his wife in the most cordial manner, and gained the former's consent to carry out my plans during the next trip up the Rappahannock.

However, although I left Capt. Parker in the full expectation of soon being united to our broken household, my bright anticipations were of short duration. Not many days after my visit to the Relay House I received the intelligence that Capt. Parker refused to carry out his promise in consequence of having ascertained the fact that my father was a Political Prisoner. He had supposed my mother to be a widow. True, I had not told Capt. Parker that my father was a prisoner for the reason that he had not asked me concerning him. It would certainly have been very impolitic in me to relate, without provocation, facts that would have marred my plans. At the same time, if Capt. Parker was deceived regarding my mother, it was his fault, not mine. However, I give to that gentleman the credit of executing his duty; and his subsequent sympathy and kindness deserve my esteem.

Chapter XIV—More Disappointments

> 'He hated man too much to feel remorse,
> And thought the vice of wrath a sacred call,
> To pay the injuries of some on all.
> He knew himself a villain—but he deem'd
> The rest no better than the thing he seem'd,
> And scorned the best as hypocrites who hid
> Those deeds the bolder spirits plainly did.'
> --Byron

Mamie Wells:

"Although I was not permitted to see my father after the nineteenth of November,[253] I frequently went to Fort McHenry to take him little articles of which he stood in need—paper, envelopes, etc., consequently I was very often compelled to submit to the indignities heaped upon me by the Provost Marshal at that place. Had not Gen. Morris befriended me, I fear I should have been turned away from the fort gates at every application for admission. The Provost, Capt M___, bore among the soldiers the appellation of "Black Jack," which name he richly deserved. I shall never forget his disgusting appearance. Many a time have I turned away to hide the look of scorn which I could not control; and how often I have comforted myself with the reflection that the time would come when he, with many others, would receive his reward.

Having learned, through one of my father's weekly notes, that his cold continued to trouble him, I prepared some medicine and started with it to the fort. I had also purchased a small vial of brandy at a drug store thinking it might be of service in case of exposure. When I reached Fell's Point, I found the river frozen over so that no boats could cross, consequently I walked over on the ice, and by the time I reached the fort gates I was suffering from the cold. But I could not gain admittance until I had dispatched one of the guards with my card to Gen. Morris.

When I entered the Provost's office the salutation I received from him was: 'How did you get into the fort?' 'General Morris admitted me, sir.' 'You have no right to enter the fort on any day but Wednesday.' 'I have brought some medicine for my father, and I would like to send him a note also.' Having delivered the syrup and the note I had written into the Provost's hands for examination, I said: 'Captain, I have a small flask of brandy for my father. He is not addicted to the use of it; but I have brought it in case of exposure.' 'He cannot have it,' replied Capt___; it is against the rules.' 'Very well, sir; I do not wish to interfere with your orders.'

When I rose to leave the office after waiting for a reply to my note he said, in the kindest voice he had ever assumed in my presence: 'Miss, if you like, you can leave that flask. I respect your father very much.' For a moment I paid Capt. M__ the compliment of thinking well of him, and, thanking him, asked: 'You will give it to him?' 'I did not say I would give it to him; but I say you can leave it.'

The significant nod that accompanied his answer spoke as plainly as words, according to my interpretation: 'I will deliver it in person even against the rules.' A few months later I ascertained to my entire satisfaction that Capt. M__ did deliver the brandy in person against the rules—to the first person, himself, against the rules of temperance.

The poor fare furnished to the prisoners at Fort McHenry had, since I saw my father, been a source of great discomfort to my sister and myself and created a keen desire to send a box of provisions to the one we were most interested in. Having consulted our kind friend, Major__, we prepared a list of articles which was submitted to the Secretary of War for approval. Through his kind intercession, permission was granted us to carry a substantial box shortly before Christmas. Upon that visit to the fort I saw my father on the porch at the door of the loft in which he was confined. He was not more than thirty yards from me; but I dared not bow or make any sign of recognition. Too well I knew the nature of the man into whose presence I was then going; too painful was the recollection of a scene I had witnessed in that same office because a wife had presumed to bow her head to her husband as she saw him in the distance. Did such orders proceed from headquarters, or were they only other instances of Capt. M_'s petty tyranny? I ask the question that I may not unjustly accuse him. But, although I dared not bow my head or wave my hand, I looked long and earnestly in the direction my father stood, and when I entered the Provost's office it required all my mental persuasion to be civil to him.

Up to this time I had been working to obtain some foothold in the matter of my father's release. But, although at time my hopes had risen to the very summit of success they had quite as suddenly been dashed to the base of their erection. At last, weary of waiting for the assistance of 'influential friends' whose promises were fair enough, I determined to subdue my pride and court the assistance of some 'Republican.' With this intention I again visited Washington, and being introduced, made known my business to a Member from New York, also one from Massachusetts. This was in the latter part of January, '65. I must give to the gentlemen alluded to the credit of using me with all due politeness and attention. Upon learning that I had held some correspondence with Mr. Raymond, Mr.__ of New York, either to rid himself of the trouble of aiding me or to do me a service (I am not sure which), said: 'Mr. Raymond! Why Mr. Raymond is the very man you want! Mr. Raymond can do anything with the administration! By all means, see Mr. Raymond!'

From the enthusiastic manner in which the above was delivered, I came to the conclusion that it was my business to immediately seek that influential editor of the *New York Times*. The time for resentment had passed. I felt and determined that my father should be released, and was ready to humble myself to gain the assistance of those in power. It was a struggle; but oh! What an object to be attained thereby.

With this conclusion I returned to the hotel, determining to go to New York on the following day in quest of Mr. Raymond; but before I retired I learned through a paragraph in the *Times* that its worthy *editor was at that moment in the Capitol. Failing to ascertain his quarters through the newspapers I had a diligent search for him the next day, but did not succeed in finding him until five o'clock when he returned to Willard's* [Hotel] *to dine.*

Henry J. Raymond, founder and editor of the New York Times

(Photo by Mathew Brady, Library of Congress)

I never was more disappointed in the appearance of any one than I was in Mr. Raymond. I had imagined him of good size, blustering, and noisy. Instead of this I find him of small stature, quiet, and agreeable. In truth, when I left Mr. Raymond after our interview had ended, it was with mingled feelings of gratitude and respect; and in the full belief that I had a powerful agent in him. He had in his quiet, collected way directed me to write a petition to the President; to collect such papers and letters as I knew would be serviceable and send them to him. He would return to Washington in the course of two weeks, and would then place the papers in the hands of the President.

  Acting upon this advice, I immediately returned to Baltimore, and began in good earnest to furnish such proof of my father's innocence as I could obtain. I had no difficulty in securing certificates of his character as a gentleman of honored integrity; but how should I prove that he had at no time taken part in the rebellion? To my knowledge, there was but one man north of the Potomac who could testify to my father's position during the war—a man who had sometimes been in my father's employ at Fredericksburg; a poor but honest man. But where was he? There was no time to lose; and without pausing to repeat the enquiry, I started in search of him. At last I found his family in an obscure part of Baltimore, and learned through his bright little daughter that he was engaged as a nurse in one of the city hospitals, where I would be obliged to go in order to see him. Of course I went to the hospital and saw Mr. M[ontgomery][254] who assured me in his humble way he was ready and anxious to serve me in any way possible. I then asked him to make a statement in writing with regard to my father's position during the war. He expressed himself willing to do so, but finally confessed that he did not consider himself capable of writing the same. I then proposed to draw up the paper myself; and it being executed to his entire satisfaction he added his signature.

  I then held in my hand the most valuable document I could obtain. But whose was the signature? A poor nurse in one of the government hospitals. Feeling that it was absolutely necessary to have the same indorsed, I asked Mr. M[ontgomery] if his acquaintance with Marshal McPhail,[255] who had obtained for him his situation in the hospital, would warrant him in applying for his endorsement. But the hesitating reply I received convinced me I was asking too much; and receiving his full permission to see Mr. McPhail myself, left him feeling that I had accomplished one great purpose in finding that good man. It being late I returned home, determining to call upon the Marshal upon the following day.

Marshal [J.L.] McPhail, Provost General of the State of Maryland, had been represented to me as one of the most depraved, hardened wretches in the whole catalogue of government employees, and I had been advised to avoid him of all others. But, oh! he was influential, and if he could only be induced to sign that one paper in my possession, what a powerful instrument it would be in the hands of Mr. Raymond! Such was my reflection.

Despite my fears regarding the character of the Provost Marshal General, I could not persuade myself but that the paper I held would be perfectly useless without his name, and my reasoning overcoming my fears, I called on him unbeknown to every friend I had. From him I learned of the interception of my letters, and of them being sent to him for examination. But, whatever Marshal McPhail had been guilty of before or after, he befriended me. He not only signed the paper I offered him, but gave me a letter to the Secretary of War, as well as one to Captain Parker in behalf of the removal of my mother. I would give 'Honor to whom honor is due,' and, to do so I must add that Mr. McPhail not only used me kindly and respectfully, but aided me very materially in my efforts to release my father from prison.

When I had collected all the papers and had written my petition to the President, as directed by Mr. Raymond, I dispatched a letter to that gentleman asking when he would go to Washington in order that I might meet him there and deliver them into his hands. But I received no reply. I waited two weeks, then went to Washington myself.

On the eighth day of February,[256] in a most disagreeable storm, I once more entered the White House. In consequence of the storm but three females beside myself waited in the reception room to see the President. I was indeed waiting to see Mr. Lincoln, but with a bolder, stouter heart than before, and with a full determination to accomplish my purpose. I waited three hours, until it wanted but twenty minutes to 2 o'clock, when we were summoned to see the President with the understanding that he would see no one after two.

Northwest façade of the White House with portico at main entrance.

Bell & Brother photograph c. 1862-1868 (Library of Congress)

We were kept waiting outside of the door just eighteen minutes, when I turned to go away rather than seek such an unsatisfactory interview; but I was prevented from doing so by one of the ladies in waiting who said: 'I think you had better stay as there are but four of us; and this lady only accompanies me upon the same errand.' A moment after, we were admitted into the presence of the Executive.

February 8, 1865 Petition of Mary "Mamie" Wells to Abraham Lincoln [257]

To the President of the United States

Honored Sir:

Will you listen to the appeal of an unhappy daughter who sues for her father's liberty? Will you give attention to my petition? I know sir, that as our country's "Executive," you have much to engross your attention, and much to perplex and annoy you, but I trust you will allow a few moments of your time to be given to me, since you alone, can give me what I seek.

At my request, my father sent me a statement of facts which have occurred to him since he has been a prisoner. I submit a copy of the letter to your perusal which I trust you will read with care:

"Cell 266, City Jail
Baltimore, Oct. 1st 1864

My dear daughter Mame:

According to your request, I will endeavor to give you a brief history of what has occurred to me since I left your Mother and the children.

I left Fredericksburg on the 18th day of Aug. 1863, to go down the Rappahannock river in search of provisions, for which the family stood much in need, as you are aware.

The first stop I made was in Totusky Creek Aug. 21st and, while there, the U.S. barges came in and took me prisoner. I was kept onboard the Steamer "Currituck" two days, on the "King Philip" one, and on the "Teaser" one, when I was lodged on the 25th inst. in the "Old Capitol Prison" at Washington, where I remained until the 25th of

Sept. when I was taken before the Judge Advocate, Capt. Parker for trial. I told him my story, and he said he believed I told him the truth, as there was no evidence to the contrary. He asked me if I was willing to take the oath of allegiance. I replied by asking him what would be done with me if I did. He could not tell. I told him that my first duty was to my family – that they were within the rebel lines, and that I was not willing to take an oath which would keep me from <u>them</u> during the war. I remained in the prison until the latter part of Nov. when my daughter Mrs. [James B.] Crawford of Baltimore, came to see me, and stated that she had seen Gen'l. [John Henry] Martindale, who told her that if I would consent to go to Baltimore, and not go south during the war, without permission from the Gen'l. of this Dept., he would release me from prison by taking the oath of allegiance. I told him I could not do so, but on the same day, after she had left me, I received a letter from you stating that the family had removed from Fredericksburg to Monaskon, Lancaster County, when I determined to take the oath, as I believed the Commanding Gen'l. would see no impropriety in allowing me to go to my family in Lancaster Co., it being partially under the protection of the U.S. Gunboats.

On the 3rd day of December I took the oath-of-allegiance in good faith, and had the right to expect good treatment in return. I came to Baltimore, and called to see Gen'l. [Henry Hays] Lockwood, who was, at that time, in command of this Dept. He refused to see me, and of course, I was compelled to remain. A friend told me he thought he could get me a pass to go home, but it never came. I remained here until the 11th day of May 1864 (over five months from the time of my release when, seeing no way to relieve my family, I took a small boat, and started for "Tangier Island" to see Capt. John Evans, who, I had learned, had brought his family from Va. and from whom I hoped to gain information of mine. My object was to see him to learn of my family, and to be governed accordingly.

On the 17th day of May, near Smith's Island – about ten miles from Tangier, I was overhauled by a sailboat, and soldiers on board, who demanded to know where I was going. I told them the truth, not thinking they would take me Prisoner, which they did, keeping me on board their boat that night, and landing me the next day on "Deal's Island" where I was detained seven days, when I was taken to Salisbury [Md.] for three days – placed on board a Steamer for three days more, and landed in Baltimore on the 31st of May. I was taken to the "Military Prison," where I remained until the 7th of June, when I was brought to this Jail where I have been confined since that time.

My trial came off on the 21st of Sept. There was nothing proved against me, yet there was so much prejudice against me that suspicion was enough to condemn me. It is true that I was taken near "Smith's Island," steering in a southerly direction, that I had about $3 worth of spices, $1 worth of notions for family use, $1 worth of medicine, with a pair of scissors and two knives. One of the knives was a very fine one, and may have been worth $3 – it was presented to me by Mr. Joseph Passano [Balt. Md. dry goods dealer] – the other I bought with the scissors for $1, so the whole amount of my loss was about $12 – not including the boat, which was quite small, but new.

Had I done less that I have for family, I should feel that I had neglected my duty, and, as God is my judge, I can see nothing wrong that I have done, except agreeing to remain from my Wife and Children when they, so much, need my services. For that, I hope they will pardon me, as I thought, at the time, it was for the best.

I have never deserved such treatment from my countrymen, yet I have borne it over thirteen months—eight of which I have passed in prison.

I enjoyed liberty forty-nine years of my life, and, should the remnant be spent in prison, my Wife, Children, and Grand-children will be satisfied, from this hasty statement, that I did not deserve such a fate.

I forgot to state that, when I was arrested, I gave my name Franklin Wells, leaving off the B., my first initial and stated that I had been living in Baltimore with my daughter during the Winter and Spring; but that I was a native of New York, when I then claimed my residence I did not tell an untruth, for I have been called by my second name from childhood, and I could not claim my home in Lancaster Co., Va., for my family had been obliged to move there since I had left them, and I felt that I had no home except New York, where my relatives, as well as those of your Mother all reside – the place of our nativity.

My health is not very good, yet I bear up very well, and am usually in excellent spirits.

With love to our friends,
I am,
Truly yours,
B. F. Wells"

Here is the letter – my father's letter – that father from whose lips I received my lessons of truth, honor, and virtue – that father who would rather sink into oblivion than utter falsehood to his child.

On the 6th day of October, his sentence was published – three years imprisonment at Ft. McHenry, to take effect from the time of his arrest, May 17th, 1864 with a fine of one thousand dollars, which, if not paid at the expiration of the three years, would subject him to further imprisonment.

Consider, sir, that he was first taken from his wife and eight children without having given any offence – that, after he was released,

Gen'l. Lockwood would not see him – that he was suffering the most intense anxiety about his family who were in a famishing country, and whom he had sworn before his Maker to protect. Remember that over four months had elapsed from the time of his capture to that of his trial, and that in the interim many things may have occurred to dim the recollection of the soldiers who had bore false witness against him, and then ask yourself if his daughter pleads in vain. Oh no – I do <u>not</u> believe that you will refuse to pardon a father whose wife is nearly broken-hearted, and whose children are suffering because their parents are unhappy – their father in bondage who is a stranger to crime or dishonor. I have applied to Com. Parker, Comm'd'g Potomac Flotilla, for the removal of my mother, sisters and brother by the U.S. gun-boats from their present abode to this city, and I beseech you, the President of the United States, to bid the prisoner come forth to greet his family from whom he has been separated for seventeen months. He only desires to be with his family, and, for his loyal conduct hereafter, I offer myself as security. When you have read the letters which accompany this petition, I feel that you will rely upon my father's word as well as mine, and that you will stretch forth your hand to save ere it is too late.

And when you have done this, I shall not forget to call upon our Maker to bless you for the justice shown to him, whose locks are growing white from sorrow and care, and He will not withhold his mercy from you, who have done unto others as you would have them do unto you.

Once more I entreat you to forgive even as you hope to be forgiven.
    With great respect, I am,

    Your obedient servant,

    Mary Wells

To His Excellency,
Abraham Lincoln

Chapter XV—Capt. Wells Release from Prison: A Family Reunited

> 'Surprise, relief, a joy scarce understood,
> Something, perhaps, of very gratitude,
> And fifty feelings, undefined and new.

Mamie Wells:

"Mr. Lincoln stood in the center of the room as we entered, and appeared to be in an extremely nervous and excitable humor, declaring that he would not see anyone after two o'clock.

The business of two of the ladies, who had entered with me, being to obtain a pardon for a friend, they were dismissed thus: 'I have granted him a reprieve, and will do no more: you need not come to me again.'

The only remaining person besides myself was a young lady from Massachusetts, who made application for a pension for some old man in her native state. I was astonished at the change in Mr. Lincoln's countenance while conversing with her. He was ready to accede to whatever proposition she made, and finally, directed her, with an order, to the Treasury Department.

Mamie Wells' final interview with President Lincoln was on Wed. Feb. 8, 1865.

Alexander Gardner photo, Feb. 5, 1865, Library of Congress

Then, I was left alone with him. Having advanced to the table beside which he sat, I took a seat beside him and handed him the papers with the request that he would examine them. 'What is it all about? I haven't got the time; I have not got the time.' But it will not detain you long, Mr. Lincoln.' 'I tell you, I will not be bored to death.' 'Then, Mr. Lincoln, will you direct me to some one who has the time to examine them—General Wallace who ordered the sentence or any one you choose to name?' 'I've got Judge [Joseph] Holt[258] expressly for that purpose,' said Mr. Lincoln in a most irritable tone of voice. 'Then, sir let me take the papers to Judge Holt?' 'No; I'll send them myself.'

At that moment the admission of some gentleman, who had a long article to read to the President, seemed to change his intention.[259] Cramming the papers in an envelope, he handed it to me saying: 'Here, you can take them yourself.'

I was so overjoyed at this announcement that when I entered the Judge Advocate's office, I was barely able to make known my errand. It was, in truth, such a privilege to be allowed to ask any one else besides the President to examine the papers I had collected. Judge Holt must have observed my emotion, for he questioned me in such a fatherly way that his very kindness brought the tears to my eyes. "The heart must leap kindly back to kindness," and my feelings toward him are those of esteem and gratitude. He, having promised to examine the papers and draw up his report in the course of three days, I returned to the hotel to await the issue. At the expiration of that time I again called at the Advocate's office and found, to my great satisfaction that the report was read as promised.

As it was necessary for the same to pass through the War Department before being sent to the President; and as the delay there was likely to be of great duration, I accompanied the messenger, according to Judge Holt's instruction, into the presence of Colonel C__, in whose hands the report was delivered; and having made the request that it should be copied in as short a time as possible, received that gentleman's promise that it should be forwarded to the President that day. I then determined to wait some three or four days before calling upon the President to urge his examination of Judge Holt's report. In the meantime my anxiety was so great that, even in my dreams, I saw the President read the report, and underwent all the misery of unsuccess.

On Thursday, the sixteenth of February 1865, I again visited the President's House. I communicated my errand to Major Hay, who immediately asked: "Are you sure the report has passed the War Department?' 'I have Colonel C_'s word for it,' I replied. 'However, I do not think it has; but I will see.' In a short time he returned with a bundle of papers in his hand. His countenance wore its usual earnest look, and mistaking it's expression, I arose as he drew nearer, prepared to hear the worst; and as I stood before him, trembling in every limb, he said: 'Miss [Wells], the report has been received and acted upon by the President.'

Then he paused; but I could not bid him proceed. I had no courage to speak, I felt that whatever he had to say would only confirm the fears that filled my mind. But what were my feelings a moment later?

'The President has acted upon it favorably. The prisoner is released unconditionally.'

These were the words that fell from the secretary's lips, and which I seem to hear now. I do not remember what I said to him in reply; I only know that he gave me the papers to carry to the War Department myself, and that when I reached the office of my good friend, Major__, I placed them in his hands without saying a word, and sank into a chair entirely overcome by the joy so unexpectedly mine.

'What! Crying with such good news!' exclaimed the Major after he had read upon the back of the package the following:

"The prisoner is discharged from the unexecuted portion of his sentence.
A. Lincoln"

Of course I insisted that I was not crying, although the tears were rolling down my cheeks; and of course I asked all manner of impatient questions such as: 'When will he be released? Do you think they would allow me to carry the release?' &c. 'Now, now, have a little patience,' said the Major. 'We will go down to Colonel C_'s office first.

When we entered the Colonel's office, the major continued: 'Well, Colonel, Miss [Wells] *has had the good fortune to obtain her father's release.' 'Ah! Allow me to congratulate you,' said Col. C__, offering his hand. 'I am right glad to hear it.' 'But what do you think she wants now?' continued the Major. 'I am sure I can't imagine what more she could desire.' 'To carry the release herself to Fort McHenry.' 'Is it possible!' returned the Colonel, smiling.*

By two o'clock the release was placed in my hands by Col. C__, who said: 'We have granted your request; you may carry this yourself to Fort McHenry.'

The first thought that I then had was: If I can catch the three o'clock train for Baltimore, I can see my father to-night. I was not long in returning to the hotel and settling affairs there, and reached the depot in time. Oh, what a happy passenger there was on that Baltimore and Ohio railroad that afternoon! Truly I was reaping the harvest of my labors, and my joy was unbounded. It was half past four when I reached Baltimore, and securing a carriage I drove to headquarters in order to see General Morris, who officiated in the absence of Gen. Wallace. Not finding him there, I drove to Fort McHenry. It was nearly dark when we entered the gate and drove to the General's house. I must have given the bell a terrible pull for it was speedily answered and I was conducted to the pleasant old-fashioned parlor where a bright wood fire burned cheerfully upon the hearth. The General, being a little indisposed, sat by one of the windows in his gown and slippers and the whole formed a pleasant picture. I was certainly not very long in communicating my business. The General gave a sort of satisfactory grunt, and requested me to be seated.

'Humph! Your father's release,' he continued in his slow way. 'I am very glad to hear it.' 'And I would like to take him with me to-night.' 'To-night, eh? Well, take a seat; we'll have a light presently.' 'A light presently!' I inwardly ejaculated, 'What does he think I am made of?' 'Did you just come from Washington?' 'Yes, sir.' 'Did you see Major___?' 'Yes, sir.' 'The Major belonged to my old regiment.' 'Ah?' I replied, although I had been informed of the fact before.

I suppose it was not a very long time before the General's wife entered, but it seemed so to me. Then the light was brought and placed upon the centre table, after which the General arose slowly and took a seat thereby. 'I haven't my spectacles.' 'They are up stairs,' said Mrs. Morris, 'I will send for them.'

It took a few moments to get the general's spectacles and considerably many more for him to read the order. Then he wanted a pencil, and when that had been given him, oh horrors! He wanted it sharpened. In the meantime Mrs. Morris, being introduced, took a seat beside me and endeavored to entertain me in a most lady-like manner. But I was not in a mood to talk of the state of the country then, and that estimable lady no doubt regarded me as an exceedingly nervous or eccentric individual and was glad when I had taken my departure.

At last, the General summoned his son, Lieutenant Morris, to accompany me to the Provost's office. It was a triumphant moment to me when I entered that office, and stood face to face with the man who ruled there, with the order for my father's release from his power. And in a short time after, when my father and myself left his presence, I instinctively murmured, 'Thank God!'

After seven long months of weary waiting, I had realized my brightest earthly hope. Nothing but my firm trust in the Giver of all good could have sustained me through the trials and disappointments of that period. Into His care I had placed myself, and, through Him, was permitted to reap the harvest I had labored for.

GENERAL COURT MARTIAL, } WAR DEPARTMENT,
ORDERS No. 90.   } ADJUTANT GENERAL'S OFFICE,
                              Washington, February 18, 1865.

I...*Franklin Wells*, citizen, sentenced by a Military Commission "*To be imprisoned at hard labor for and during the period of three (3) years from the day of arrest,* (*May* 17, 1864.) *at such place as the Commanding General may designate, and then to be released upon the payment of one thousand ($1,000) dollars to the Government of the United States, or in default of paying the same to be further imprisoned until the same shall have been paid,*" as promulgated in General Orders, No. 88, Headquarters, Middle Department, 8th Army Corps, Baltimore, Maryland. September 28, 1864, and now in confinement at Fort McHenry, Maryland, is pardoned for the unexecuted portion of his sentence. He has been discharged from custody.

II...*John F. McCarthy*, citizen, sentenced "*To be imprisoned at hard labor for and during the period of three* (3) *years, to date from the day of sentence,* (*December* 12, 1864,) *at such place as the Commanding General may designate,*" as promulgated in General Order, No. 121, Headquarters, Middle Department, 8th Army Corps, Baltimore, Maryland, December 14, 1864, is pardoned, on the ground that the conviction is not sustained by the proof. He will be released from custody and set at liberty.

III...The record of the General Court Martial in the case of 1st Lieutenant *William Henry Boyce*, 15th Maine Volunteers, failing to show that the Court was properly organized, the proceedings are therefore irregular and void, and the sentence "*To be dismissed the service,*" as promulgated in General Orders, No. 29, Headquarters, Department of the Gulf, New Orleans, February 24, 1864, is inoperative.

BY ORDER OF THE PRESIDENT OF THE UNITED STATES:

E. D. TOWNSEND,
Assistant Adjutant General.

OFFICIAL:

Assistant Adjutant General.

Copy of War Department Pardon of "Franklin Wells" dated Feb. 18, 1865, included in Petition of Mary Wells to Abraham Lincoln file (National Archives)

Chapter XVI—Picking Up and Moving On

After the war, Captain Benjamin Franklin Wells took over management of the Mattituck House Hotel, Mattituck, Long Island, N.Y.

(Photo courtesy of Rev. Charles E. Craven, *A History of Mattituck*)

...I was looking in March 1865 for a place to get a living for myself and family. I was in Baltimore and Philadelphia and New York and in the beginning of April while in New York my Brother told me of the Hotel in Mattituck. I came here about the 12th of April 1865 and made arrangements and Leased the Mattituck House for three years and returned to the City for my family on the 15th – so you see I was here on Long Island when the President was Assassinated and in a very few days I was here with all my family.[260] Capt. B. F. Wells

Thus, Captain Wells returned with his family to Mattituck, the place of his birth. Located on Long Island, N.Y. in Suffolk County, Mattituck lies between Long Island Sound and Peconic Bay near the eastern end of the island. The older part of the hotel kept by Captain Wells had been a tavern before the Revolutionary War. As Mattituck House hostesses, daughters Geno, Jennie and Nellie entertained guests by singing old songs with Geno on her guitar.

The first post-war marriage in the Wells family was on November 16, 1865, when eldest daughter, Susan "Sue" Wells, married her first cousin Isaac N. Teed, born in 1841 on Long Island, N.Y. During the Civil War, Teed served as a sergeant with Co. A, (U.S. Lancers), 4th N.Y. Heavy Artillery Rgt. USA. The mother of four surviving children, Sarah F. "Sue" (Wells) Teed died on November 13, 1881.

Next in line was Mary "Mamie" Wells, who on December 4, 1865, married George T. Lorigan, f the Eighth Infantry, N.Y. Volunteers, UA. In 1871, Mamie gave birth to Nellie Eugenia Lorigan, who was deaf. A strong woman ahead of her time like her mother, Nellie was contributing editor of *The Silent Worker*, a popular newspaper for the deaf, which also published her poetry. Mamie Wells Lorigan died in childbirth in 1875. Her infant daughter named Mamie lived only three months and is buried at her side in the Mattituck cemetery.

Never marrying, Sarah Eugenia "Geno" Wells remained at home with her parents in Mattituck, and died in her 30th year on December 11, 1877. She is buried alongside her parents in the Mattituck Parish Presbyterian Church Cemetery in Mattituck, Long Island, N.Y.

On November 6, 1873, Emma Jane "Jennie" Wells, who had celebrated her 10th birthday in Fredericksburg the month the war broke out, married Robert S. Russell. George T. Wells died in June 1875 at age 26, and the youngest sibling, Nelson Thomas Wells, died in March 1877 at age 20. Ella Augusta "Nellie" Wells, was alive at age 25 in 1880 but had died by 1889.

In less than two decades after the war ended, Captain and Mrs. Wells had lost seven of their nine adult children with only the eldest married daughter, Harriet L. (Wells) Crawford, and eldest son, Benjamin Jr., surviving.

Capt. Wells wrote:
It has been my misfortune to have been ruthlessly deprived by Death in a few years of seven of my grown up children – the probable result of the breaking down of their health in consequence of the exposure and suffering during the war. [261]

Captain Wells was back on the water with a new packet steamer according to an 1882 advertisement running in the Southold Long Island, N.Y. newspaper, Wells named the steamer in honor of his wife, Jane Teed Wells:

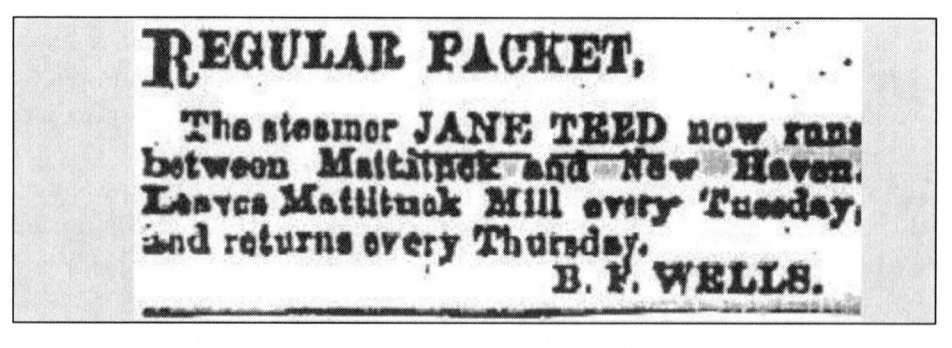

REGULAR PACKET,

The steamer JANE TEED now runs between Mattituck and New Haven. Leaves Mattituck Mill every Tuesday, and returns every Thursday.

B. F. WELLS.

Advertisement in *The Long Island Traveler (Southold) Long Island, N.Y.*, Aug. 11, 1882

In the fall of 1887, ten years after the death of Geno, Captain Wells and Joseph O. Kerbey began an exchange of letters centering on Wells' claim for compensation due to the loss of the *Eureka,* as a war prize.

In reply to Kerbey's queries, Wells wrote:
...I consulted different Lawyers at different times and could not get any encouragement as the Boat was claimed as a prize and taken in Rebel waters. As money was scarce with me I came to the conclusion that without money it was no use. So I let the matter drop and now as much as I need what is my honest due I feel that without money to

spend it won't amount to anything. But yet when I see that the Treasury is overflowing I feel sad to think that a poor man can't get his dues because he is poor.

You ask about Geno. We don't think she or any of the family heard from you since we saw you. With regard to those Southern Beaus I can only say that there was several came to my house. Major Hard[262] of S.C. was a beau of Sue. Capt. Govan[263] of Miss. was Mamie's beau and Lieutenant Crump[264] of Miss. for Geno. They were all killed at Chickamauga in Battle. There was a Capt. Martin of Gen. Barksdale Staff. Geno didn't like him but he was fond of her.

We received the Picture.
                              Yours, B. F. Wells[265]

Now living back in Washington, D.C., Kerbey had evidently offered to facilitate Well's petition to the Congress about to assemble that coming December, and was laying the groundwork for its introduction.

The Petition dated December 9, 1887 *for the relief of Benjamin F. Wells, senior* was introduced by New York Congressman Perry Belmont as H.R. 6436, dated January 31, 1888. With no action taken, on January 17, 1890, the Petition was reintroduced by New York Congressman James Way Covert as H.R. 5258, and referred by the Committee on Claims to the Committee on War Claims where it died.

50TH CONGRESS, } **H. R. 6436.**
1ST SESSION.

IN THE HOUSE OF REPRESENTATIVES.

JANUARY 31, 1888.

Referred to the Committee on Claims and ordered to be printed.

Mr. BELMONT introduced the following bill:

A BILL

For the relief of Benjamin F. Wells, senior.

1 *Be it enacted by the Senate and House of Representa-*
2 *tives of the United States of America in Congress assembled,*
3 That the Secretary of the Treasury be, and he is hereby, au-
4 thorized and directed to pay, out of any money in the Treas-
5 ury not otherwise appropriated, to Benjamin F. Wells, senior,
6 of Mattituck, Long Island, in the State of New York, the
7 sum of five thousand dollars, in compensation for the steam-
8 boat Eureka, taken from him by the officers of the Potomac
9 flotilla of the United States Navy in the Rappahannock River,
10 April twentieth, eighteen hundred and sixty-two, as shown
11 by the records of the Navy Department, and afterward used
12 by the United States Navy, and sold after being damaged
13 and condemned, as further set forth by the affidavit of the
14 captain and owner, and the survivors of the crew of said
15 steamer, and the testimony of Federal officers, who were
16 cognizant of the affair at the time.

Kerbey meanwhile was also promoting his book:

> Mr. Joe Kirby, a well known telegrapher and scout in the late civil war, has published a book entitled "A Boy Spy in Dixie." It is a very readable book and will interest many of our Long Island folks as its heroine is Miss Zeno Wells, who now slumbers in the old "God's Acre" with her beloved and accomplished sisters and brothers. Though dead they are not forgotten, but linger pleasantly in our memories, for their very names conjure up many halcyon days when Capt. Frank Wells conducted the Mattituck House and his daughters, Misses Zeno, Jennie and Nellie, entertained so delightfully his guests.

In December 1887 Kerbey's book received a favorable review in the Southold newspaper, *The Long Island Traveler*.

Capt. and Mrs. Wells had by this time, buried all but two of their children in the Mattituck Parish Burying Ground, located near the Presbyterian Church Chapel in Long Island, N.Y. When daughter Sue (Wells) Teed died and was buried there in 1881, the same newspaper reported *A beautiful monument has been placed over the grave of Mrs. Isaac N. Teed. It is of a delicate grey marble, and is perhaps the most chaste and beautiful tribute to the dead to be found in our 'God's acre.'*

Chapter XVII—"Boy Spy" Returns to Town of 'Lost Love'

"As sure as I live, I will come again Geno."
Joseph Orton Kerbey to Sarah Eugenia "Geno" Wells

A year and a half before the war ended, Kerbey married a girl back in Pennsylvania while home on furlough. He was being attended by a private physician for a war-related wound to the groin. On September 17, 1863, Kerbey married sixteen-year old Mary Holmes Shaffer, daughter of Dr. Shaffer, an Elizabeth, Pennsylvania physician. By 1880, the couple had five children including a daughter named Mary, called "Mamie." Yet, the romantic Kerbey still carried the torch for Geno, reliving their *love and war story* in books he published and making frequent visits back to Fredericksburg.

During the summer of 1888, Kerbey was in Fredericksburg conducting tours of the battlefields and interviewing Confederate veterans. He detailed his trips in letters first printed in the <u>National Tribune</u>[266] . Kerbey wrote of his nostalgic sojourn in his book *On the War-Path: A Journey Over the Historic Grounds of the Late Civil War*, excerpted below.[267]

"Fredericksburg—what a cloud of war memories hangs over this old town! The mere mention of the name awakens the veteran's slumbering interests; like the pass-word, it clears the way, and raises the flood-gate through which rushes down upon us such a stream of reminiscences, that we are almost overwhelmed and in despair of being able to record them, lay down the pen, tempted to get into the swim and float down, like the other chips, through the whirlpools of time into the broad ocean of oblivion.

As long as life lasts there will never be effaced from the tablets of my heart and mind a single event connected with Fredericksburg during the war. To a majority of old soldiers of both armies this chapter, dated at Fredericksburg, may be like a letter from home, written by one of the 'boys.' I have estimated that every soldier of the Army of the Potomac, as well as that of Lee's Confederate Army of Northern Virginia, has at one time or other, been at Fredericksburg.

We were not here for three days only, as at Gettysburg, which has become the Mecca of American valor to which tourists throng daily, and neglect this more interesting field. We all <u>lived</u> here for a couple of years, every day of which was as a year of an ordinary lifetime. It was, indeed, an eventful period in the lives of all. Who will forget the first pleasant occupation of the country by McDowell in the summer of 1862...the return of Burnside in November, 1862, the shelling of the town on December 11th, the terrible battle on the 13th of December, our sad Christmas on the Rappahannock? How we all lived over the river on those Stafford Heights during the whole of that dreadful winter of 1862-63—the severe cavalry picket duty on the flanks, the mud march and its disappointments, then the Chancellorsville campaign during the leafy month of May, after which we moved off to Gettysburg.

General Grant again conducted the Army of the Potomac back to almost within gunshot at Spotsylvania, the Wilderness and Mine Run, so close that the wounded were brought to town. The ambulance procession is said to have been fifteen miles in length, reaching to Belle Plain. I mention all this in support of my statement that, at one time or another, all of both armies were here. The floating population, aggregated nearly half a million souls, and perhaps all of the survivors and their families and their friends may become members of our club and make this visit with us.

The most disastrous battles of the war, perhaps that the world ever saw, were fought here, and here repose the remains of 20,000 soldiers who died <u>at the front</u>, a majority of whom were slain in the battle, and are buried on the field, yet this Fredericksburg, a beautiful old town so rich in historical memories, and but an hour and a half from Washington City, is almost forgotten by the country, by the tourists who flock to Gettysburg, and Memorial day here is remembered only by a few Confederates of M. F. Maury's[268] camp who have quietly strewn the graves of Federal and Confederate alike with the flowers contributed by the ladies of the town.

...Probably there is not another ten miles square on the entire surface of the earth so replete with history—ancient, colonial, revolutionary as well as rebellion history—as this.

...St. George's Church,[269] the steeple of which our artillerymen used as a target when the Confederate signal officers were inside, looks as natural as ever, except that the three great holes we put through it have been patched over. In the almost heavy stillness of the nights, in these years of peace, when I hear the familiar old bell strike the hour, I think of the nights in years gone by when it tolled, in the same way, the hours to hundreds of thousands of sleeping soldiers bivouacing on their arms within sound of its tones; and looking now at the electric lights reflected upon its white surface, its tall spire pointing to the sky, it seems like a spectral reminder of the sure passing of time.

Relics are quite plentiful and genuine here. Perhaps the largest and most interesting collection of war relics to be found anywhere in the country may be seen here in the Museum of the Exchange Hotel. A courteous young gentleman, Mr. W. A. Hill[270] is the proprietor and owner. The tourist and visitor is referred to my friend, Mr. Hill as being a most competent guide, as well as an agreeable young man, whom everybody is glad to have met.

Post-war Exchange Hotel (first building on left), located at the corner of Main (Caroline) Street and Hanover Street, once housed a museum of Civil War relics.

(Postcard: "National Park Centennial Year 1872-1972")

War Relics.

Capt. Wells, who lived here during the war, has sent to Messrs. Cotton & Hills, proprietors of the Exchange Hotel, a twelve-pound cannon ball for their museum of war relics. The ball entered the second story window of Capt. Wells' residence, while himself and family were in the house, and passed through a partition, striking the opposite wall, and falling on the floor. The ball was fired from a Federal battery on Stafford heights during the fight here December 11, 1862.

State-Librarian Poindexter has secured from Boston a Confederate pike and guidon of the Ninth Virginia cavalry, which was captured by a company of Philadelphia cavalry in a battle against Burnside at Fredericksburg. The staff was cut in three places and sent home by the officer who captured it.

Mr. Poindexter has also received a Confederate States spur in a perfect state of preservation.

A 12-pound cannon ball fired into the Wells House on Dec. 11, 1862 was donated by Capt. Wells for display in the Exchange Hotel Museum.

(*Fredericksburg Star,* May 2, 1888)

The visitor to Fredericksburg will find listed among the many points of interest in addition to the battlefields, some of the residences of distinguished people. Among these, modestly claiming a share of *attention, is 'The Wells House,' the home of 'Geno,' the war heroine of the <u>Boy Spy</u>[271] narrative.*

Mr. Hill was induced to place this on his published list of attractions because of the number of tourists who stopped off to visit the battlefields and Mrs. Washington's home and grave, inquired of him 'if any one by the name of Wells lived here?' The object no doubt being to gratify curiosity as to the truthfulness of this love and war story. Not being familiar with it himself, he made some inquiries of the older citizens in regard to the Wells family; Mayor Slaughter[272] observing, 'Oh yes, I knew them very well—they were very sweet girls;' a number of others also knowing them; the interesting family of my friend Colonel Merchant,[273] lived neighboring them during the war.

I can only say briefly to those who have not been interested in the fortunes of <u>the Boy</u> and his war girl, that she was in the hands of the Rebels in the town, while he was out in the cold on the other side of the river and could only see the roof of the house—in which he could imagine they were all having a good time with the Rebel officers.

I am conducting the club around to the Wells House—we will stand together upon the same old porch from which I was so cruelly taken in the summer of 1862, to Old Capitol prison, this by special orders of the Secretary of War, E. M. Stanton; and I insist, for no other offense than that of having fallen in love with this pretty little black-eyed girl...

Though over a quarter of a century has elapsed, I recall every incident as freshly as if it had occurred last week. The scene on this little porch where I, in the custody of a staff officer, bade Mrs. Wells and Sue goodbye, while Geno, trembling with suppressed emotion, timid and blushing, almost afraid to trust herself to say farewell in the presence of the group, stood by the door. When I turned to her as the last to whom I should give a parting word, the dear little girl broke down completely, covered her face with her handkerchief to hide her tears and embarrassment.

I took the handkerchief from her face and put it in my pocket—and it is in my possession yet—boldly kissed her and said, tremblingly, sincerely and earnestly, 'As sure as I live, I will come again Geno.' It was the turning point in my life as well as that of Geno's and some others...Their terrible experiences during the shelling---Miss Sue's flirtations with the Confederate officers, Miss Mamie running the blockades to visit her father then a prisoner at Ft. McHenry, Baltimore, the attempts of a handsome staff officer of General Barksdale's Mississippi brigade[274] to capture the affections of Geno, the family's subsequent sufferings and privations, will indeed make a romance in real life that is truly stranger than fiction. As I have said, I shall never be able to do the subject justice until I write a book about it—and its name will be 'Geno.'

In looking up the whereabouts of some of the Confederate officers who were courting my girl in my absence, taking an unfair advantage of their military possession, I learned that Mr. Justice Lamar,[275] being a Mississippi Confederate, would be able to give me the desired information. I wrote him a brief note explaining my wishes and observed that I knew a gentleman of his standing had not much time or inclination to bother with love stories, to which he replied, in his courteous and kindly manner:

> *'It does not bother me to hear about a love story of the war, provided the <u>denouement</u> is a happy one. I find myself reading them whenever I have an opportunity or the labors and requirements of my duties will permit, and I fear that I sometimes play truant for this purpose. I am very much interested in 'Geno' already...'*

and he told me where I could catch the fellow in Mississippi that made love to Geno.

Front porch of Wells House. *On these steps were spent some of the happiest hours of my life, and by the way, some other fellows, North and South, will say the same thing...* (Major Kerbey)

(Photo courtesy University of Mary Washington, Fredericksburg, Virginia)

I have made a good photograph of the house...The porch is precisely as it was twenty-seven years ago. On these steps were spent some of the happiest hours of my life, and by the way, some other fellows, North and South, will say the same thing and be able to recognize the familiar, hospitable and once happy home of the truly happy Wells family.

...There seems to be a singular attraction still lingering about the old Wells house and vicinity aside from its delightful associations. There are three pretty young ladies living with their parents[276] in the house, not only pretty but accomplished and agreeable. The visitor who may be curious about the truthfulness of its history will be politely received and entertained by them. He will show the scars of the great battle, left in its walls. During the terrific shelling of the town by Burnside, while the Wells family lived there and took hasty refuge in

228

    the cellar, three cannon balls passed through the house, and one twelve pound shot lodged inside. This identical twelve-pounder may be seen at the Museum.[277]

    The sofa on which I had so often sat alongside of Geno while she charmed me with the guitar and 'them' eyes, was knocked all to pieces by a shell that tore through the parlor. Unfortunately the handsome Rebel officer was not at that moment sitting there. The battery that fired it was commanded by a Captain Kirby,[278] no relative or friend of mine, however.

Fredericksburg Trinity Church organist Juliet Annie Downs, who inherited the Wells' House, invited Major J. O. Kerbey to attend her wedding.

(Photo courtesy Judith (Hawkins) Barton of Fredericksburg, Va.)

    One of the ladies, who is a phenomenal player on the piano and the organist in the church of the town,[279] is always pleased to gratify the visitor by playing or accompanying her younger sisters,[280] who sing charmingly the old songs we used to sing in that parlor long, long years ago. Not only *'Juanita,'* but other old favorites: *'My Lost Evangeline,' 'In the Gloaming,' 'Ever of Thee,' 'Her Bright Smile Haunts Me Still,' 'Annie Laurie,'* and *'Tired, Oh Yes, So Tired, Dear,'* or *"Abide With Me.'* I am very fond of music, and to my old-fashioned taste the new is not so sweet as the old, especially when heard in this Wells House.

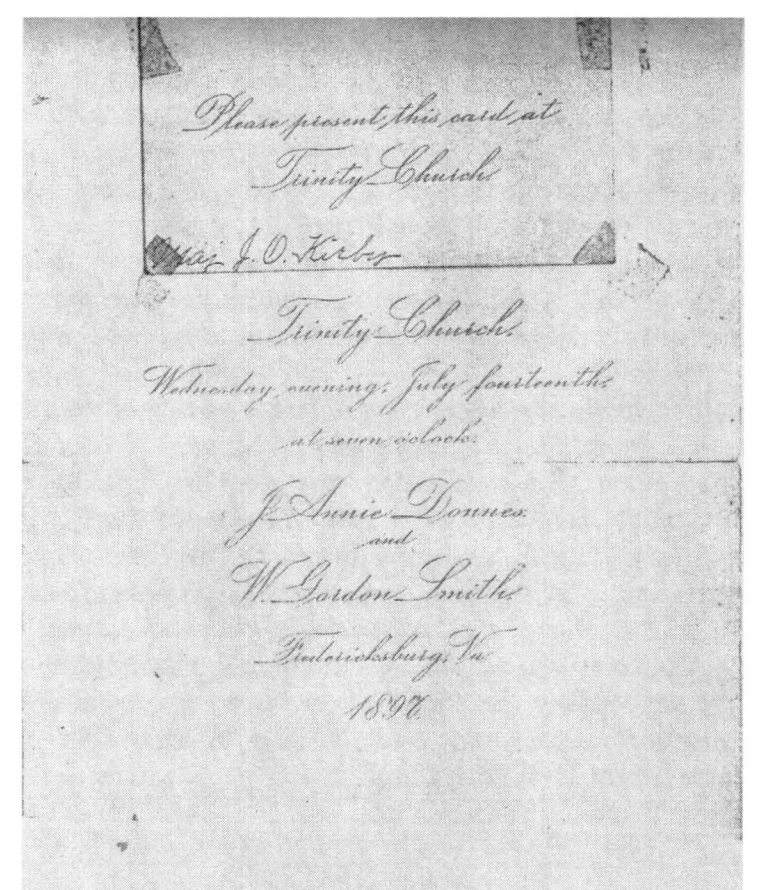

Above: Copy of Juliet Annie Downs' 1897 wedding invitation addressed to Major J. O. Kirby (sic).

(Courtesy Judith (Hawkins) Barton)

There are a number of pretty little female Rebels in Fredericksburg, which is famous for the beauty of its women and the hospitality of its men, and it preserves to a remarkable degree its distinctive old-time traditions. I love to listen to the mild voices and sweet accent of the Southern ladies—even if they have sometimes a mighty decidedly Southern inflection... I have visited Fredericksburg so often in recent years that I've become a rather familiar figure on the streets, being always pleasantly greeted as 'the Majah.' ...

...I love the <u>old</u> Army of the Potomac---its greatest battles were fought before Gen. Grant came out from the West to lead its recruited forces to the Wilderness, Cold Harbor and Appomattox. Not one of the old boys who survives will ever forget the frugal Thanksgiving dinner of hard-tack and coffee on those dreary plains, nor the sad Christmas on the Rappahannock—sad not only to them, but to the thousands of homes throughout the country that were placed in mourning and hearts of mothers made to bleed by the losses sustained here, December 13th.

It is interesting to note the different phases in veteran human nature that are exhibited by those who revisit these fields. They come from all sections but most numerously from New England and the Middle States, which were principally the homes of the Army of the Potomac, frequently in large excursion parties, their wives and families or friends accompanying them. Sometimes G.A.R. delegations, wearing the old blue uniform, the ladies and children decorated with the badges, headed by a band, will stir the colored inhabitants by a parade from the depot along the streets of the sleepy old town. Those who have come in contact with these visitors as guides or drivers of conveyances say they can always tell a <u>genuine</u> veteran. An old colored driver put it this way:

'Yaas, sah, dem real Yankees what war here in de wah don't want no guide buzzing in dar ears. Dey done tole me to talk to my hosses mor'n onct; and one old man said he'd give me a dollar extra if I'd button up my lips; so I jis keep my mouf shut and open my years, and I hear from them talkin' mongst *demselves all bout de wah, dat I can tell to others dat doant know nuffin bout it.'*

The gentlemen at the hotel say those whose names to their register are familiar are usually the least ostentatious guests. On the other hand, numerous old-<u>looking</u> men, wearing the uniform and badge of the G.A.R., are as aggressive and ready to fight their battles over again; in their casual intercourse with the ex-Confederates who may meet them, they insist upon injecting their political sentiments, mixed with war opinion.

...The old veteran who goes off alone, or accompanied perhaps by one or two old comrades, makes a bee-line for his old camp on Stafford Heights; but the chances are that he can not find the location. But few can realize what changes may be wrought in the surface or surroundings of a once-familiar spot by the growth of twenty-five years. The obliteration of the numerous military roads and fencing-in of the country entirely alters the topography of the old camp.

The old fellows go about in a dazed manner, as if they had lost something they were trying to find. They are all sure, however, of the railroad tracks and embankments, the ruins of the Phillips House and the Lacy House. The church steeples of the town, the old mill and the contour of the hills back of the town--once burned into their minds and hearts by a brand of fire and iron as Maryes Heights--is sadly familiar.

The old boys gaze long at this scene; perhaps their visions are not now so clear as when they were younger, and maybe their sight is dimmed by a tear-drop, as with a sigh they walk meditatively to the upper pontoon anchorage at the Lacy House. No one ever forgets a pontoon bridge. To how many thousands of brave hearts does it remain in memory as a bridge of sighs, a home on one side, and a prison or death on the other. Truly it was the crossing of the river of death to the many who never returned...

Fredericksburg is, I believe, the only place in which pontoons were extensively used during the war. I do not recall any other place where the armies were obliged to cross a navigable river under heavy fire to fight an enemy entrenched on the opposite shore, as was the case here...

Right here I will record another remarkable fact: Fredericksburg was the only town of importance bombarded at close range. Burnside's entire artillery shelled the old place for hours, yet <u>not a single death resulted from this hail of fire and shell.</u>

When it became apparent that the pontoons could not be laid in the face of the incessant fire from the houses along the riverbank, <u>the engineers volunteered to row their boats to the opposite shore</u> and assist in charging upon this Mississippi brigade. Volunteers were not called forth first as the official reports indicate, though as a reinforcement to those who had originally proposed it, others were called out. These brave boys...were ferried over and gallantly charged upon the hornet's nest and drove the Rebels out. Then the pontoons were laid and the army started to cross on a bridge, every plank of which represented a dead hero.

There is no monument to mark this spot at Fredericksburg, except the tree to which one side was anchored, where as much daring heroism was shown as at any of the many marked places at Gettysburg. But the boys will <u>never</u> forget that place...

Some of the purest and noblest blood of the Anglo-Saxon was spilled upon the plains before Marye's Heights as a free sacrifice upon the altar of liberty. At last, night came and ended the struggle; the great God of Battles and Commander-in-Chief of all gave the signal to cease firing by covering the Earth with darkness. The mantle of twilight, pinned by the evening star, was dropped upon the terrible scenes. An <u>aurora</u> <u>borealis</u> in the Northern sky soon lighted up the scene with its lurid gleams in a manner never to be forgotten. The horrors of that night, the scenes of despair and gradual death upon that bloody ground, in the bitter cold darkness, can not be described. There was no help for the dying. Oh, women of the South, reflect! There were brave men lying on your soil dying unattended...There were men *there whose wives trembled for them...There they lay on the frozen ground...Wearily, and with faint hope for the morrow, dying they must stay; their noble efforts idly wasted in a fruitless struggle; but they did not die in vain---in the end they were successful. Some of their bones rest in unknown graves today upon the crest of Marye's Heights they charged upon in vain, and they now sleep under the protecting folds of the flag that floats over the National cemetery there.*

...The Confederates occupying the Heights were of Longstreet's Corps, the troops principally from the extreme South, so that it is difficult to find an old resident who was in the lines then.

Captain S. Quinn, who is now superintendent of the city water works, was I believe, a member of Barksdale's Mississippi Brigade that assisted in preventing the building of the pontoons.

Colonel Rufus B. Merchant, the editor and proprietor of the bright little Fredericksburg Star, *though a native of this part of Virginia, was so eager to get into the war that he enlisted in Cobb's Georgia Legion before his State seceded. Being thoroughly familiar with the country, he was detailed as a scout, and as such served inside our lines during the greater part of the war. He was known as a fearless, daring little man, on whom Longstreet depended largely for reliable information.*

Probably there is not now a more popular resident of this old town than Mr. Merchant, and numerous Federal visitors in recent years have testified to his many courtesies and kindnesses. Through the columns of his Star, *many of the families of Federal soldiers have been able to look up matters of personal war history. The Rebel scout and the Yankee scout, though opposite in politics as well as in temperament, each holding tenaciously to the belief that he was right, are today the best of friends. Indeed, I do not know of anyone whose friendship I more esteem than that of my little Rebel.*

There is generally the best of feeling exhibited between the men of the Northern and Southern armies when they chance to meet.

Indeed, it may be safely asserted that the genuine old soldiers of both sides are always friendly in their intercourse. The men who carried guns and used them have now no enmity towards those that in turn fired back at them to kill...

As illustrating this feeling, I tell this true story of a recent experience: I happened to be in Fredericksburg on Memorial day of 1888...One evening, while seated on the hotel pavement, enjoying the delightful weather and eyeing the pretty Virginia girls that do their shopping in town on horseback, I was accosted by two gentlemen wearing the familiar old butternut gray, who quietly intimated that they had been sent to escort me up to their 'camp.' They declined to give any further information and looked as if they meant business. I saw that it was useless to resist, so nervously accompanied them up a back street...Into a large room of the Town Hall we were ushered, introduced to the High Mucky Muck who was sitting on a dais, wearing a Confederate officer's uniform from which dangled the Rebel battle-flag badge.

This gentleman's courteous manner, genial face and warm greeting rather assured me that I was in safe hands, as long as he held the baton. It was Captain Dan. Lee,[281] a brother of Governor Fitzhugh Lee[282] and a nephew of Gen. R. E. Lee. In a neat little talk, he explained that the members of the M. F. Maury Camp of Confederate Veterans, learning that four Federal soldiers were in town, of which I was one, desired to learn their wishes in the matter of the Confederate camp, offering their united services in assisting the four Federals in decorating the graves of the Federals in the National Cemetery on Marye's Heights, adding that their services were tendered gladly to this end... Major Birdsall,[283] an ex-Union soldier and the efficient superintendent of the cemetery, being present, accepted the serviced tendered.

On the morning of that Memorial Day[284] one never to be forgotten...the Fredericksburg Grays, a crack military organization composed of the young men of the town, fitly representing the New South, headed by the brass band of the town, escorted the four solitary

Federals to the rendezvous of the Confederates. Here we found eighty-one old Rebels in line to receive us; instead of the guns they used to carry, each had a bouquet of flowers in his hand. We were placed at the head of the little column; Captain Dan Lee, on behalf of some ladies then presented each Federal with a beautiful bouquet of flowers, stating that the ladies of the town had on this occasion divided their offerings between the Confederate and Federal cemeteries.

Under command of Captain Lee, we marched out the same old Hanover Street, or Telegraph road, the band playing patriotic airs, followed by the eighty-one Confederates in gray cloths, armed with bouquets. We followed precisely the same paths our army trod on their way to that terrible battle on that dreadful December day, twenty-five years ago.

Reaching the elevation known as Federal Hill, we pass the house Hooker occupied as his headquarters[285]; at this point our troops came in sight of the Confederates and received their baptism of fire; moving slowly down the little declivity, I point out to my companion the spot where Hancock, Humphreys and Couch held their brief consultation before the final charge. We cross the mill-race running through the low ground and go on beyond the depression under which our lines were formed.

The Martha Stephens' House on Sunken Road, c. 1865

Monument erected by the United Daughters of the Confederacy in 1917. Inscription: *Here Lived Mrs. Martha Stephens, Friend of the Confederate Soldier, 1861-1865. U.D.C.*

Passing the point usually designated as 'the farthest advance of the Union line,' we turn into the 'Sunken Road,' marching along it, behind and between the remains of the stone wall, past Mrs. Steven's house.[286] *Right here is erected a solitary stone, the only monument at*

Fredericksburg which marks the place where General Cobb of Georgia was killed. Almost involuntarily, we four Federals follow the example of Captain Lee and lift our caps as we pass it.

Reaching the gate of the Federal Cemetery which is located on the point farthest south...the band files to one side and plays a solemn dirge as we enter the sacred precincts of the dead. Every Confederate, as he moves in, reverently takes off his hat, uncovering to the light of a bright May sun eight-one gray-headed and gray-coated noblemen. Great God! What a scene was this. When I look back upon this picture and listen to the war talk of the croaker or politician, who, to get soldiers' votes, may appeal to his former prejudices, I recall this day and regret that all may not have witnessed it as I did...Inside the cemetery were assembled a number of ladies of the town. Addresses were made by both Federals and Confederates, and at the conclusion of the services at the rostrum, every grave was decorated—the Confederates and Federals—ladies and children assisting in this pleasant and beautiful task.

From this ground, once occupied as Lee's headquarters and bristling with Confederate glory, may be had a magnificent panoramic view of the section of country occupied by both armies.

I have previously stated that the number of interments almost equals Arlington. There are buried here 15,273 Union soldiers; of this number, <u>12,243 are unknown.</u> In every other respect it excels Arlington—it ought to excel Arlington in general interest to the old soldier of the Army of the Potomac. Those who sleep in this Marye's bivouac <u>died on the front;</u> a number of them in battle, or from wounds resulting there from, and are <u>buried in the battlefields.</u>

After the war the bones of a number were gathered from the surrounding fields and reinterred at this place. A great many could not be identified, and these sleep sometimes as many as six in one grave, being simply marked 'Unknown.' Probably every State in the Union is represented in this 'unknown army'...

...Reluctantly we are leaving Fredericksburg, the scene of so many bitter and sweet memories. To the old soldier there is a peculiar magnetism about the old town that attracts and holds him here like a loadstone. To the student or the tourist from any country it

The Gunnery Spring, Copyright R.A. Kishpaugh, Fredericksburg, VA

(Postcard postmarked 1941 courtesy Rebecca Campbell Light)

presents many very interesting features. There are a number of mineral springs inside the corporate limits, the most remarkable being that known as 'The Gunnery Spring,[287] *which is located on the battleground. A stream of pure cold water, sufficient to supply the entire town, bursts from the rocky hillside and flows in a never-diminishing volume into the neighboring Hazel Run...It is said of Gunnery Spring that any one who ever partakes of its water is fated to return again to the fountain head. A very sweet little girl with whom I walked down there one moonlight evening was the Eve who tempted me by proffering the cup from which I innocently accepted the fatal draught. She is now fully convinced of the truthfulness of the legend and the efficacy of this water.*

Perhaps the time may come when this old town, so close to the Capitol, may become a Mecca; such as has been made of Gettysburg, and maybe the blood-stained soil may yet produce a crop of monuments that will equal Gettysburg. If each separate deed of heroism done here were marked by a stone, the ground would be a forest of monuments. Who knows—perhaps the government will, in time, reserve more of this battle-ground as a National park; hotels may spring up around its numerous springs. Here might appropriately be commemorated alike in a commingling of monuments the heroism of both sides...

And now we have reached our journey's end, and your guide, with hat in hand and a cordial hand-shake...reluctantly says goodbye, with many thanks for your kind attention and forbearance. I hope we may all meet around the winter's fireside, and perhaps hear the wonderful story of 'Geno,' a romance of secret service and secret love during the war that is indeed stranger than fiction."

Epilogue- Part I: Final Goodbyes

Faithful and true to the end, Sarah Eugenia "Geno" Wells never married, living with her parents until her untimely death at age 30. She is buried by their side in the Mattituck Parish Burying Ground, Long Island, N.Y. (2009 photo courtesy Jeffery M. Walden, Mattituck, N.Y.

241

Mrs. Jane Teed Wells, wife of Captain B. F. Wells, died on July 9, 1889 at age 69. Her obituary was published in the *Fredericksburg Star* on July 13, 1889 (see below):

(Photo courtesy Jeffrey M. Walden, Mattituck, L.I., N.Y., 2009)

Death of an Estimable Woman.

Mrs. Wells, the beloved and aged wife of Capt. Wells, who resided here during the war, passed peacefully away at the residence of her daughter, in Baltimore, last Tuesday. Her remains were taken to her home, Mattituck, L. I., N. Y., for interment. She was truly one of God's noblest Christian women. The many friends here of Capt. Wells deeply sympathise with him in his great affliction.

On July 27, 1899, after *a long and eventful life,* Captain Wells, also passed away. His obituary was published in the Southold, N.Y. *Long Island Traveler,* on Friday, August 4, 1899:

Died
Mattituck, July 27, Benjamin Franklin Wells, aged 84y., 8m.

> Capt.
> Benjamin F. Wells
> BORN IN
> NEW SUFFOLK, L.I.
> NOVEMBER 27TH, 1814,
> DIED JULY 27TH, 1898.
> A LONG AND EVENTFUL LIFE

(Photo courtesy of Jeffrey M. Walden, Mattituck, L.I., N.Y., 2009)

Mattituck

In the passing away of Captain or "Uncle" B. Frank Wells last week by a stroke of paralysis, Mattituck lost an old resident and highly respected citizen. Mr. Wells will long be remembered here as one of the best hotel keepers we ever had. For many years the Mattituck House under the pleasing management of Mr. Wells, aided by his lovely wife and daughters, had a famous reputation and catered for a very fine class of guests. The Wickhams, Thomas A. Howell and Joseph P. Howell families, the Kellocks, Weirs, Parkers, Smiths, Vandenhoves, Clarkes, Schoonmakers, and others came in June and stayed till October waned, and the hotel was what it should be—a credit to the place.

Mr. Wells was born 84 years and six months ago, at New Suffolk. Early in life he was brought up among the Shakers and afterwards lived in the South. He married early in life Jane Teed, of Westchester County, a most estimable lady. To them were given twelve children, nine of whom lived to manhood and womanhood, but all had gone before Mr. Wells, except his eldest daughter, Harriet Crawford, of Baltimore, and his eldest son, Ben, whose care and devotion to his aged father have been wonderfully loving and kind. Mr. Wells was a man of deepest integrity and honor, though of quick, passionate temper; he was always ready to see and do the right thing by his fellow men, and he had hosts of warm, personal friends, who will feel his loss deeply.[288]

Epilogue – Part II: More Adventures for the "Boy Spy"

As for the wartime scout and "Boy Spy," Kerbey had more adventures in store with his appointment as U.S. Consul to Para, Brazil, of the Amazon region of South America.

"Major J. Orton Kerbey, Ex-Consul to Para, Brazil, author of "The Boy Spy," A Civil War Episode, "The Land of Tomorrow," and "An American Consul in Amazonia," late of the staff of the Pan-American Union Bureau."

(Photo courtesy Major J. Orton Kerbey. *An American Consul in Amazonia,* 288)

Kerbey was one of some 1,000 seekers for a consulate or diplomatic appointment in Brazil. He was endorsed by the Hon. James G. Blaine, Secretary of State, and on May 30, 1890 nominated by President Benjamin Harrison to the U.S. Senate, which confirmed unanimously his appointment as U.S. Consul to Para, Brazil. At the suggestion of Secretary Blaine, Kerbey was to explore the areas of the upper Amazon, to find new rubber territory and to make known to the world the natural resources of "Amazonia," the region of equatorial South America then wholly undeveloped and called by the natives *La Tierra de Manana* (The Land of To-morrow). Kerbey journeyed through the unexplored forests of India rubber trees and to the source of the Amazon River.[289]

Returning to Wilmore, Pa. in 1898, and seeking the "proper outfit" for another trip up the Amazon River, Kerbey wrote the following letter to "Outing," a late 19th century magazine covering a variety of sporting activities:

Dear Outing:
Thank you very much for the addresses of the several boat-builders...On a previous trip I suffered the loss of canoes, and, as Indians refused to go beyond their own limits or into a hostile country, and because of the difficulty of poling back up the turbulent streams, we had to foot or wade it for weeks, sometimes compelled to climb precipices or go for days through dense forests to get around a trifling point impassable by foot, that a boat would have done in five minutes. Having a good, strong, portable boat along will save a lot of trouble and render me independent of the Indian "kan-oahs."

I propose going again from the source to the Amazon, from a point in a ca'non of the Andes, some 15,000 feet in elevation, on the exact divide, where a very small pond or lakelet is formed from melted snows of adjacent Andes peaks. One outlet of this runs backward toward the Pacific, emptying into Lake Titicaca (the highest water); the other rivulet flows northwest, forming the Vilcanota, or the real source of the Amazon. I shall follow this Vilcanota stream on mules from the railroad to reach canoe navigation beyond Cuzco, on the Rio Urubama, which is a continuation of Vilcanota, or Yucay. This is precisely on the line of the Inca trail which Capac took with his golden wedge from Lake Titicaca to Cuzco, where he located the capital of that empire.

From beyond Cuzco we follow the historic and rich Ollantaytambo valley, or down the Urubama, five days on mules, to reach canoe navigation—so called.

This canoe trip is down the most romantically beautiful stream, full of large fish, and the forests abounding in large game, tigers or jaguars, tapirs, bears, and innumerable small game. The woods and rivers are full also of ducks, etc. In short, it's a rare country for sportsmen. Probably the most gamy animal is a wild boar or hog that lives in both river and forest. Maybe I think so because my four Indian paddlers would go for these things every day, running the canoes all over the rivers, in spite of my protests and demands to "go ahead."

It is about thirty days of exciting canoe journey over falls and cascades. Probably there is not another such canoe voyage to be enjoyed anywhere, not even in Africa, and I believe equatorial American is far more interesting than Stanley's Africa.

I am telling all this abruptly to you in answer to your kindly suggestion that "Outing" would do all possible to assist me in securing a proper outfit, and also congenial companions.

I don't care to appear as advertising for a companion, and I would have it understood that it's a desirable opportunity that only a few can enjoy. I imagine your magazine will reach the right sort. Of course, I want a gentleman who is willing to rough it…

I am, very sincerely,

Joseph Orton Kerbey

Wilmore, Pa.[290]

Back in the United States at the turn of the century, and in a further attempt to make a living off his Civil War past, Kerbey enlisted the help of Senator Boies Penrose of Pennsylvania to introduce the following legislation:

Under S. 3374[291] in the Senate of the United States, February 28, 1900, Mr. Penrose introduced the following bill; which was read twice and referred to the Committee on Claims: A BILL For The relief of Joseph Orton Kerbey...*That the sum of ten thousand dollars be paid...in recognition of his services in securing information which resulted in preventing the capture of Fort Pickens, Pensacola, Florida.*

249

56TH CONGRESS,
1ST SESSION.   S. 3374.

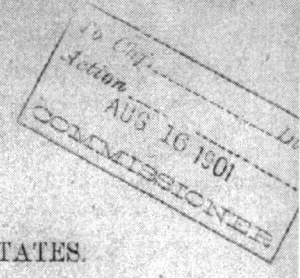

IN THE SENATE OF THE UNITED STATES.

FEBRUARY 28, 1900.

Mr. PENROSE introduced the following bill; which was read twice and referred to the Committee on Claims.

A BILL

For the relief of Joseph Orton Kerbey.

1 *Be it enacted by the Senate and House of Representa-*
2 *tives of the United States of America in Congress assembled,*
3 That the sum of ten thousand dollars be paid, out of any
4 money in the Treasury of the United States not otherwise
5 appropriated, to Joseph Orton Kerbey, of Wilmore, Cambria
6 County, Pennsylvania, in recognition of his services in secur-
7 ing information which resulted in preventing the capture of
8 Fort Pickens, Pensacola, Florida.

Senate Bill introduced Feb. 28, 1900 "For the relief of Joseph Orton Kerbey." for the sum of ten thousand dollars, read twice and referred to the Committee on Claims.

(National Archives)

In a 1905 interview, published in the Washington Post newspaper, entitled "Helped by Carnegie—Newspaper Man

Encouraged by a Former Fellow-workman," Kerbey related the following story about his old friend Andrew Carnegie:

I was an office boy associate with 'Andy' as a telegraph messenger when he was glad to be making $50 per month, out of which he saved $40, while I...spent $40 out of my $25. As a consequence, he has accumulated more money that I, but I have been very busy accumulating experience, which I am now anxious to unload, as a means of making a living off my past, as I have crossed the civil service limit, and am rapidly encroaching on Osler's age.

I am trying to inflict another book on an indiscriminate reading public...I appealed to my old friend 'Andy' for a subscription to the book for each of his libraries as a means of helping an old friend out...I received a letter... saying, 'He would guarantee the sum of $500 for the cost of printing an edition of my book 'Manana,'' of which in effect is equal to a free gift of 1,000 books.

The article continues: *Major Kerbey's book, 'La Tierra de Manana,' or 'The Land of To-morrow,' tells the story of rubber exploitation, and adds interest by detailing the actual adventure of a veteran cavalryman rough riding over the Andes on a mule, sometimes at an altitude of 17,000 feet, during a journey of eleven months from the Atlantic to the Pacific.*[292]

The Land of To-Morrow, published in 1906, describes Kerbey's exploration up the Peruvian Amazon and over the Andes to the 'California of South America.'[293]

Below: *Telegraph Age* book review of *The Land of To-Morrow* (New York, 1906 p. 238).

Book Notice.

"The Land of To-Morrow" is the title of a new volume by Major J. Orton Kerbey, the well-known old-time telegrapher. The book embraces over four hundred pages of text, has more than fifty illustrations, is printed on a finely finished paper, and is bound in cloth, with a decorative cover. Major Kerbey, who is a resident of Washington, a former newspaper man and ex-United States Consul at Para, Brazil, the great rubber shipping port of South America, who was instructed by his government to study and report on the india rubber industry in that part of the world, was a member of an exploring party to the headquarters of the Amazon, the trip being undertaken with a view of making a search for rubber. The newspaper training of the author is everywhere apparent throughout the pages of the book, for the story told by him is direct and lucid in style, giving information incident to the long journey, with its accompanying wealth of adventure, and finally of the object attained, in a manner calculated to hold the close attention of the reader from cover to cover.

The book has especial value, inasmuch as it throws so much light and information on the important industry of rubber gathering and of the need of conservation and cultivation of the product to insure a future supply. To the rubber importer, the rubber trade, as well as to the general reader, who loves a good story as well as an interesting book of travel, the volume possesses worth differing only in degree. Telegraphers who remember Major Kerbey as belonging to the fraternity, and who have read his previous books, "The Boy Spy" and "On the War Path," etc., will welcome this additional contribution of his to a literature which has found a wide and enjoyable reading.

The price of the book is $1.50. Address orders to J. B. Taltavall, TELEGRAPH AGE, 253 Broadway, New York.

The Land of To-morrow

A NEWSPAPER EXPLORATION UP THE
AMAZON AND OVER THE ANDES
TO THE CALIFORNIA OF
SOUTH AMERICA

By J. ORTON KERBEY

Author of "THE BOY SPY," "ON THE WAR PATH," etc.

NEW YORK
W. F. BRAINARD, PUBLISHER
EIGHTEEN EAST SEVENTEENTH STREET
1906

A TWENTIETH CENTURY TRAVELLER IN PERU
Frontispiece

Opposite: *The Land of To-morrow,* standing portrait of Kerbey

In a modern day critique of Kerbey's journey, he is described as *English Adventurer Major J. Orton Kerbey explored the Urubamba and followed the Inca trail from Lake Titicaca toward Cuzco. He considered that a pond in the mountains near the continental divide was the source of the Vilcanota, Urubama, Ucayali, and Amazon rivers. He was the first to go down the river.*[294]

The frontispiece of Kerbey's 1911 publication *An American Consul in Amazonia,*[295] is a portrait photograph of Andrew Carnegie, with the following inscription:

> *This volume is affectionately dedicated to ANDREW CARNEGIE, My Employer and Preceptor in early days and Constant Friend in later years. The Apostle of the World's Peace and the Special Friend of Pan-America.*

On the final page of his book, *The Boy Spy,* Kerbey wrote:

> *...I would, as a last word, again say that my efforts as a Spy during the Rebellion were prompted solely by a disinterested patriotism and a single desire to do some good for the country.*
>
> *When my time is up, and I am mustered out, I ask of my comrades of the Grand Army of the Republic, not a monument, but a simple head-stone to a grave, among the unknown at Arlington, marked—The Boy Spy.*[296]

When my time is up…I ask not a monument, but a simple head-stone to a grave… marked — 'The Boy Spy.' (J. O. Kerbey)

(Illustration on the final page of Kerbey's book *The Boy Spy*)

Having reached the age of seventy-two, Kerbey's life adventure ended on October 29, 1913 at the U.S. Soldiers' Home Hospital in Washington, D.C. He is buried at the Arlington National Cemetery, not with his wished for head-stone *The Boy Spy,* but a simple marker: *Joseph A. Kerbey.*[297]

Epilogue - Part III: Photo Gallery of the Wells House

The Wells House still stands. Built c.1812, the house passed through private ownership until May 20, 1966, when the Historic Fredericksburg Foundation, Inc. (HFFI), purchased the property to be preserved as a museum. Now returned to private ownership, HFFI maintains a historic easement on the interior of the property.

The Wells House

(2003 Photo by Robert A. Martin)

The Wells House

(1972 photo courtesy University of Mary Washington,
Fredericksburg, Virginia)

The Wells House

(1966 photo, courtesy *The Free Lance Star*)

The Wells House, southeast view

(1966 photo, *The Richmond Times Dispatch*)

The Wells House, February 18, 1937 photo

(Library of Virginia)

Bibliography

MANUSCRIPTS
National Archives, Washington, D.C. (NA)

    Joseph A. Kerbey Compiled Service Record

    B. Franklin Wells Court-Martial Files

    Petition of Mary Wells to Abraham Lincoln

    Petition of B. F. Wells to the Senate and House of Representatives in Congress

The Library of Congress Manuscript Division

    Betty Herndon Maury Diary, 1861-63, 1 v. (Robert A. Hodge typescript, transcribed from microfilm copy, 1980)

    Gen. Marsena Rudolph Patrick, USA, Diary, 1862-65. 3 v.

    John Sterling Swann Papers, Miscellaneous Manuscripts

Fredericksburg and Spotsylvania National Military Park, Fredericksburg, Virginia (FSNMP)

    James McClure Scott, Confederate War Reminiscences

Privately Held Civil War Collections
    Furr Family Papers, Private William Meek Furr Diary, 19th Mississippi Infantry (William Frazier Furr, descendant)

    Peel Family Papers, Peel Brothers of 19th Mississippi Infantry Papers (Kevin Hudson, Peel descendant)

Library of Virginia, Richmond, Virginia

Works Progress Administration of Virginia Historical Inventory for Spotsylvania, Virginia.

NEWSPAPERS AND PERIODICALS

Baltimore (Md.) Sun

Boston Traveller

Calendar of Virginia State Papers

Confederate Veteran (1894-1915)

DeBow's Review

Evening Star, Wash. D.C.

Fredericksburg (Va.) Christian Banner

Fredericksburg (Va.) City Directory

Fredericksburg Free-Lance

Fredericksburg (Va.) Herald

Fredericksburg Evening Star

Fredericksburg News

Fredericksburg (Va.) Star

Fredericksburg (Va.) Weekly Advertiser

Journal of the Military Service Institution of the U.S.

Long Island Traveler (Southold) N.Y.

Luzerne Union, Wilkes-Barre, Pa.

National Tribune Civil War Veterans Weekly

New York Times

Northern Neck of Virginia Historical Magazine

Outing Sports Magazine

Richmond Daily Dispatch

Richmond Times-Dispatch

Richmond Whig

Virginia Magazine of History and Biography

Weekly Advertiser, Fredericksburg, Va.

Washington Post

OTHER PUBLISHED PRIMARY SOURCES

Applegate, John S., Ed. *Reminiscences and Letters of George Arrowsmith of New Jersey, Late Lt. Col of the 157th Rgt., N.Y. State Vol.* New Jersey: 1893.

Baker, Lafayette C. *History of the U.S. Secret Service.* Philadelphia: Published by the Author 1867.

Beale, Jane Howison. *The Journal of Jane Howison Beale of Fredericksburg, Virginia.* Ed. Barbara P. Willis. Fredericksburg: Historic Fredericksburg Foundation, Inc., 1995.

Bosbyshell, Oliver Christian. *The Forty-eighth in the War.* Philadelphia: Avil Printing 1895.

Brown, J. Willard. *The Signal Corps, U.S.A. in the War of the Rebellion.* Boston: U.S. Veteran Signal Corps. Association, 1896.

Buel, Clarence C. and Robert U. Johnson. Eds. *Battles and Leaders of the Civil War.* 4 vols. New York: Century, 1887-1888.

Cummings, C. C. "The Bombardment of Fredericksburg." *Confederate Veteran*, XXIII.

Dowdey, Clifford, and Louis Manarin, Eds. *The Wartime Papers of R. E. Lee.* New York and Boston: Bramhall House, 1961.

Goolrick, Frances Bernard White. "The Shelling of Fredericksburg." *Confederate Veteran*, 1917.

Haupt, Herman. *Reminiscences of General Herman Haupt.* Milwaukee: Wright and Joys, 1901.

Johnson, Robert U. and Buel, Clarence C., eds. *Battles and Leaders of the Civil War*, 4 vols. New York: Castle Books, 1956.

Kerbey, Major J. O. *The Boy Spy.* Chicago: Belford, Clarke & Co., 1889.
_____. *On the Warpath: A Journey Over the Historic Grounds of the Late Civil War.* Chicago: Donohue, Henneberry, 1890.

_____. *A Boy Spy in Dixie.* Washington, D.C.: National Tribune, 1897.

_____. *Further Adventures of the Boy Spy in Dixie.* National Tribune: Washington, D.C., 1898.

_____. *The Land of Tomorrow: A Newspaper Exploration up the Amazon and Over the Andes to the California of South America.* New York: W. F. Brainard, 1906.

_____. *An American Consul in Amazonia.* New York: William Edwin Rudge, 1911.

Jones, Rev. J. William. *Christ in Camp: or Religion in Lee's Army.* Richmond: 1887

McLaws, Lafayette. "The Confederate Left at Fredericksburg." In vol. 3 of *Battles and Leaders of the Civil War*, ed. Clarence C. Buel and Robert U. Johnson, New York: Century Publishing, 1887.

Peel, Dr. Robert H., "The Last Roll." *Confederate Veteran*, v 10.

Robertson, James I. Ed. *Proceedings of the Advisory Council of the State of Virginia.* Richmond, Virginia: Library of Virginia Archives, 1977.

The War of the Rebellion: A Compilation of the Official Records of the Union and Confederate Armies. 128 vols. Washington, D.C.: U.S. Government Printing Office, 1880-1901.

U.S. Congress. *Congressional Serial Set Series of U.S. Publication Documents.* Washington, D.C.

Wells, Mamie L. *Reminiscences of the Late War.* Fredericksburg Star: Series, Fredericksburg, Va., 1888.

Wren, James. *From New Berne to Fredericksburg: Captain James Wren's Diary.* Ed. John M. Priest. Shippenburg, Pa: White Mane, 1990.

PUBLISHED SECONDARY SOURCES

Alvey, Edward, Jr. *History of the Presbyterian Church of Fredericksburg, Virginia 1808-1976.* Fredericksburg, Va.: Bookcrafters, 1976.

Angus, Colin, and Mulgrew, Ian. *Amazon Extreme.* New York, N.Y.: Broadway Books, 2002.

Bradsby, H. C., Ed. *History of Luzerne County Pennsylvania – City of Wilkes-Barre.* S. B. Nelson Publishers, 1893.

Bray, William J., Jr. *Rappahannock Dayboats: The Revolt Against Baltimore's Monopoly of Trade.* Northern Neck of Virginia Historical Magazine, Vol. XLI. Richmond, Va.: Dietz Press, 1991.

Brewer, James H. *The Confederate Negro.* Durham, N.C., 1969.

Craven, Rev. Charles E. *A History of Mattituck, Long Island, New York.* Published by the author, 1906.

Dudley, William S. *Going South: U.S. Navy Officer Resignations & Dismissals on the Eve of the Civil War.* Washington, D.C.: Naval Historical Foundation, 1981.

Dryer, Frederick H. *A Compendium of the War of the Rebellion.* National Historical Press Society, 1979.

Harrison, Noel G. *Fredericksburg Civil War Sites.* Two Vols. Lynchburg, Va: H. E. Howard, 1995.

Hayes, Rev. Charles Wells. *William Wells of Southold and His Descendants, A.D. 1638 to 1878.* Buffalo, N.Y.: Baker, Jones, 1878.

Hewett, Janet B. *The Roster of Confederate Soldiers, 1861-1865.* Wilmington, N.C.: Broadfoot, 1996.

Holly, David C. *Chesapeake Steamboats: Vanished Fleet.* Centreville, Md.: Tidewater Publishers, 1994.
_____. *Tidewater by Steamboat, A Saga of the Chesapeake.* Baltimore, Md.: John Hopkins University Press, 1991.

Fitzgerald, Ruth Coder. *A Different Story.* Unicorn, 1979.

Howison, Robert Reid. *Fredericksburg: Past, Present, and Future.* J. Willard Adams, 1898.

Krick, Robert K. *The Fredericksburg Artillery.* Lynchburg, Va.: H. E. Howard, 1986.
_____. *Lee's Colonels.* Dayton, Ohio: Morningside House, 1992.
_____. *9th Virginia Cavalry.* Lynchburg, Va.: H. E. Howard, 1982.

Long, E. B. and Long, Barbara. *The Civil War Day by Day: An Almanac, 1861-1865.* New York, N.Y.: DeCapo, 1971.

Manakee, Harold R. *Maryland in the Civil War.* Baltimore, Md.: Maryland Historical Society, 1961.

Miller, Francis Trevelyan, Ed. *The Photographic History of the Civil War: The Armies and the Leaders.* New York: Castle Books, 1957.

Musselman, Homer D. *Stafford County in the Civil War.* Lynchburg, Va.: H.E. Howard, 1995.

Quenzel, Carroll H. *The History and Background of St. George's Episcopal Church, Fredericksburg, Virginia.* Richmond, Va., 1951.

_____. Ed. *Preliminary Check List for Fredericksburg, 1778-1876.* Richmond, 1947.

Quinn, Mary Faber *The Influence of the North Branch Canal on the Pattern of Urban Land Use in Wilkes-Barre, Pa.* (M.A. dissertation) Catholic University of America, 1959.

Quinn, S. J. *The History of the City of Fredericksburg.* Richmond, Va. 1908.

Raus, Edmund J. Jr. *Banners South: A Northern Community at War.* Kent, Ohio: The Kent State University Press, 2005.

Scharf, J. Thomas. *History of the Confederate States Navy.* New York, N.Y.: Rogers & Sherwood, 1887.

Sigaud, Louis A. *Belle Boyd: Confederate Spy.* Dietz Press, 1943.

Tidwell, William A. *April '65: Confederate Covert Action in the American Civil War.* Kent State University Press, 1995.

_____. *Come Retribution: The Confederate Secret Service and the Assassination of Lincoln.* Jackson: University Press of Mississippi, 1988.

Toomey, Daniel Carroll. *The Civil War in Maryland.* Baltimore, Md.: Toomey Press, 1983.

Endnotes

---

[1] The steamer *Virginia* was chartered out of the Norfolk, Virginia based Old Dominion Steamship Company.

[2] *The Weekly Advertiser.* (Fredericksburg: July 9, 1859) 2.

[3] George Fitzhugh, a passionate and articulate defender of slavery during the antebellum period, was a major figure in the social commentary of Virginia.

[4] James D. B. DeBow, *DeBow's Review III* (June 1860), extract as published in the *Fredericksburg News* (July 20, 1860) 2.

[5] *Fredericksburg News,* 22 Sept. 1853; Fredericksburg *Weekly Advertiser,* 27 Sept. 1853.

[6] William J. Bray, Jr. *Rappahannock Dayboats: The Revolt Against Baltimore's Monopoly of Trade,* Northern Neck of Virginia Historical Magazine, Vol. XLI, (Richmond, Dietz Press, 1991) 4734.

[7] *Fredericksburg News,* 22 Sept. 1853; Fredericksburg *Weekly Advertiser,* 27 Sept. 1853.

[8] *Virginia Herald,* 27 July 1854, 8 Aug. 1854; *Weekly Advertiser,* 5 Aug. 1854; *Fredericksburg News,* 3 Aug. 1854.

[9] Rev. Charles Wells Hayes, *William Wells of Southold and His Descendants, A.D. 1638 to 1878* (Buffalo, N.Y. 1878) Baker, Jones & Co., 277.

[10] Rev, Charles E. Craven, *A History of Mattituck, Long Island, N.Y.* (Pub. By the Author 1906).

[11] H.C. Bradbury, Ed. *History of Luzerne County, Pa.,* Chapter XIX, "City of Wilkes-Barre. (S.B. Nelson Publishers 1893).

[12] Captain Gilbert Golding Teed (1825-1858) was Jane Teed's youngest brother. From Wilkes-Barre, Pa., Capt. Teed was drawn to Enterprise, Florida (now a suburb of Orlando) as a steamboat captain on the yet wild St. John's River.

[13] Mary Faber Quinn, "The Influence of the North Branch Canal on the Pattern of Urban Land Use in Wilkes-Bare, Pa." (M.A. diss., Catholic University of American, 1959) 47-48.

[14] *The Evening Star,* (Wash. D.C., June 16, 1858) 3.

[15] *Offers and Contracts, Maryland,* Route No. 3302, Contract made with Benjamin F. Wells dated April 1860 at $800 per annum, accepted April 24, 1860. (U.S. Congress, Congressional Serial Set Series of U.S. Pub. Docs. p. 205.)

[16] Dec. 9, 1887 Petition of B. F. Wells of Mattituck, Suffolk Co., State of New York to the Senate and House of Representatives in Congress Assembled Dec. 9, 1887, Items 6 and 8. (National Archives, Records of the U.S. House of

Representatives, Record Group 233, Accompanying Papers File, Benjamin Wells, 51st Congress.).

[17] *Fredericksburg Star,* (June 16, 1889).

[18] 1887 Petition of B. F. Wells to Congress; Spotsylvania County voted on Feb. 4, 1861 to elect "conditional Unionist" John Lawrence Marye Sr. as delegate to the Virginia State Convention, *Fredericksburg News,* (Feb. 5, 1861); *Richmond Daily Dispatch,* (Feb. 6, 1861). Only 30 of the 152 State Convention delegates were not "Unionists" or conservatives of some form.

[19] Permanent Enrollment (PE) #4 for 1861, 28 Feb. 1861, Port of Georgetown, D.C. National Archives Record Group 41-Bureau of Marine Inspection-Vessel Papers/Enrollments.

[20] Wells' pilot on the *Eureka* was Peter B. Robinson who was born in Virginia c.1798. He was listed in the 1860 Federal Census as living in Washington Ward 2, Washington, District of Columbia, giving his occupation as "Sailor." The 1870 census shows him as living in Washington, D.C.

[21] B. F. Wells letter Oct. 23, 1887, Mattituck, L.I., N.Y. to Mr. J. O. Kerbey (National Archives).

[22] *The Weekly Advertiser,* March 3, 1860.

[23] Fredericksburg Deed Book "T," p. 213, Deed of Trust to secure personal property of Mary J. Benson, recorded Jan. 17, 1861.

[24] Account of the *Fredericksburg Recorder* as reported in the April 15, 1861 *Richmond Daily Dispatch; Fredericksburg Herald.*

[25] *Fredericksburg News,* (April 16, 1861, p. 2, col. 1).

[26] The table for Virginia cited three regiments of 2,340 men to rendezvous at Staunton, Wheeling and Gordonsville, Virginia.

[27] John Lawrence Marye Sr., a Fredericksburg widower, was master of *Brompton,* situated on Marye's Heights of Civil War fame. Marye was married for the second time in July 1862 to Jane Hamilton of *Forest Hill* at Hamilton's Crossing.

[28] George H. Reese, editor, *Proceedings of the Virginia State Convention of 1861,* Richmond, 1965, Vol. IV, 83-4.

[29] The Provisional Confederate Congress, Session II, held May 7, 1861, contingent on the referendum vote, admitted Virginia into the Confederate States of America. The May 23, 1861 referendum on the Ordinance of Secession of Virginia was 132,201 for and 37,451 against.

[30] Minutes of the Common Council of the Town of Fredericksburg, April 19, 1861.

[31] Rev. Hodge's mother was a great-granddaughter of Benjamin Franklin of Philadelphia. His wife, Elizabeth Bent (Holliday) Hodge however was a

native of Winchester, Virginia. From 1861 to 1864, Hodge pastored at the Wilkes-Barre, Pa. First Presbyterian Church, later succeeding his father as professor at the Princeton Theological Seminary in New Jersey.

[32] *Richmond Daily Dispatch.* The church was damaged extensively during the Civil War. "...Part of the roof had caved in, pews had been torn out and, during 1864, used as coffins for the dead soldiers." Edward Alvey, Jr., *History of the Presbyterian Church of Fredericksburg, Virginia 1808-1976* (Fredericksburg 1976) 35, 53.

[33] Library of Virginia, WPA "The Wells House," p. 394. Alice (Hurkamp) Warren, a daughter of John G. Hurkamp (1818-1887) who owned a leather-working shop, a Tan Yard and a sumac mill in town. They were members of the Presbyterian Church.

[34] Major J. O. Kerbey, *On the War Path: A Journey over the Historic Grounds of the Late Civil War* (Chicago 1890) 125. During the Dec. 11, 1862 bombardment of Fredericksburg Mayor Slaughter and his 15-year old son made their escape in a buggy to Mannsfield, home of Arthur Bernard. There they remained with John L. Marye Sr. until near sunset when the bombardment ceased. Moncure D. Conway, "Fredericksburg First and Last," pt. 2. *Magazine of American History, XVII,* 461.

[35] The Ruggles' house at 1204 Charles Street is next to the Mary Washington house, mother of President George Washington. The house still stands.

[36] Executive Papers, Library of Virginia; Richmond *Whig,* April 22, 1861, 3; Fredericksburg *News,* April 23, 1861, 2.

[37] *O.R.* ser. 1, II, 775; Meriwether Stuart Ed. "The Military Orders of Daniel Ruggles, Dept. of Fredericksburg, April 22 – June 5, 1861." *The Virginia Magazine of History and Biography,* V.69: 1961, 149-180.

[38] As a former member of the U.S. Congress (from 1851 to 1859), Governor Letcher was well connected in Washington, D.C. society, and among Virginia's early recruits as a secret agent was Washington D.C. socialite Rose O'Neal Greenhow. From the war's outset, Letcher and his council devoted a good amount of time to clandestine operations. William A. Tidwell, *Come Retribution.* (Jackson, Miss: 1988) 10.

[39] Gov. Letcher Executive Files, Library of VA; Tidwell. *Come Retribution,* 10, 62; Ruggles' General Order No. 16 of May 28, 1861, assigned Maj. W. S. Barton as his Acting Assistant Adjutant General at Fredericksburg headquarters.

[40] Gov. Letcher Executive Files, LofVa.

[41] *Richmond Daily Dispatch,* Thur., April 25, 1861.

[42] James McClure Scott. "Confederate War Reminiscences of..." (FSNMP)

[43] Brig. Gen. Daniel Ruggles, commander of Va. State Forces on the Rappahannock.
[44] Henry H. Lewis, Naval officer in charge of the Rappahannock River. Born in Kentucky c.1838, Lewis resigned his USN commission effective April 20, 1861 and was appointed 1st Lieutenant CSN on June 10, 1861. Lewis was the son of Virginia-born Dr. Alfred L. Lewis and wife Caroline, who migrated to Kentucky. William S. Dudley. *Going South: U.S. Navy Officer Dismissals on the Eve of the Civil War.* Washington, D.C.: Naval Historical Foundation, 1981.
[45] B. F. Wells letter, Nov. 6th 1887, Mattituck, L.I., N.Y. to Mr. J. O. Kerbey (National Archives).
[46] On April 30, 1861, river steamer, *Joseph E. Coffee* of Norfolk along with steamer *Adelaide* from Baltimore and steamer *Belvidere* from Richmond were taken into custody by the U.S. Blockading Squadron at Old Point, Va. *Richmond Daily Dispatch.* May 3, 1861.
[47] Major J. Orton Kerbey wrote that Captain Wells had been engaged 'on the regular underground line between Richmond and Washington via the Potomac River' since the beginning of the war…and the general feeling among the citizens was that his sympathies were 'openly with the South.' Kerbey. *Further Adventures of the Boy Spy in Dixie* (The National Tribune, Washington, D.C. 1898) 5-79. Wells was eventually arrested for blockade running, charged with carrying Confederate supplies, and imprisoned.
[48] James H. Brewer. *The Confederate Negro.* (Durham, N.C., 1969) 192.
[49] William J. Bray, Jr., *Northern Neck of Virginia Historical Magazine,* Vol. XLI, No. 1, Dec. 1991, 4738.
[50] *Fredericksburg News,* April 26, 1861.
[51] Brig. Gen. Daniel Ruggles, Commander of Va. State Forces on the Rappahannock.
[52] B. F. Wells Petition (National Archives)
[53] Homer D. Musselman, *Stafford County in the Civil War,* (H.E. Howard, Lynchburg 1995), 8-10.
[54] O.R., ser I, II, 907.
[55] The Fredericksburg *Herald* ran a bitter editorial regarding the replacement of Ruggles that was reprinted in the Richmond *Whig* on June 8, 1861. The Ruggles house on Charles Street was sacked and pillaged during the Dec. 1862 Battle of Fredericksburg, the general's papers and books found there by Federal soldiers. Frances Bernard (White) Goolrick. "The Shelling of Fredericksburg." *Confederate Veteran* 1917, 564. The Ruggles/White house is still standing.

[56] William A. Tidwell *April '65: Confederate Covert Action in the American Civil War.* Kent, Ohio: Kent State University Press, 1995, 64.

[57] Holmes' picket line was along where the U.S. Marine Corps Base at Quantico now stands. William A. Tidwell. *April '65: Confederate Covert Action in the American Civil War.* (Kent State University Press: 1995) 64.

[58] Born in 1806 in Spotsylvania Co., Va., Maury served in the U.S. Navy and later became world famous as "Pathfinder of the Seas" and father of modern Oceanography. From 1834 to 1842, Maury and his family lived at 306-308 Charlotte Street (no longer standing) in Fredericksburg, where most of their children were born and where he wrote and published several important books on the study of ocean navigation. He was assigned to the USN in Washington in 1842, and when the Naval Observatory was completed, named its first Supt.

[59] The May 1861 letter published in the *Boston Traveller* also offered a *$5,000 reward for the Head of Jeff. Davis.*

[60] Betty Herndon Maury married her cousin William Arden Maury, a Washington, D.C. lawyer in 1857 with daughter Nannie Belle born the next year. A second daughter, Alice Woolfolk Maury, was born in June 1863.

[61] Letcher set up the Advisory Council on April 21, 1861. James I. Robertson, ed., *Proceedings of the Advisory Council of the State of Virginia* (Richmond: Library of Virginia Archives, 1977)1; William A. Tidwell. *Come Retribution* (Jackson: University Press of Mississippi, 1988) 52.

[62] Letcher to Lee, June 18, 1861, Box 18, Folder 14, Letcher Papers; Tidwell. *Come Retribution,* 61.

[63] Cousin John Minor's residence was located at 214 Caroline Street in Fredericksburg. The house stands today.

[64] Betty Herndon Maury Diary, (Courtesy Robert A. Hodge unabridged typescript) Library of Congress, Washington, D.C.

[65] Betty Herndon Maury's brother Lt. Richard Lancelot "Dick" Maury, then with the Virginia State Troops, Lt. Robert Dabney Minor, CSN, and a cousin, John "Jack" Maury.

[66] The impressed steamer *Virginia,* owned by the Old Dominion Steamship Company

[67] In early June 1861, Lt. Lewis proposed to Gen. Holmes that 300 men from a Tennessee regiment be used to seize the *St. Nicholas* at a landing downriver. Holmes deemed the plan too risky. An appeal to Maury, (further approved by Confederate War Secretary L. P. Walker), would not budge Holmes. Cdr. George N. Hollins, CSN, had an idea similar to Lt. Lewis. In a meeting with the Secretary of the Confederate Navy with Maury, Lewis and others, Hollins

learned that the Navy Secretary would not approve the plan but that Virginia Gov. Letcher would. Before finally approving the plan, Letcher had Maury join in a discussion where the plan was unfolded. Letcher, according to Hollins, then provided him with a draft for $1,000 and introduced him to Col. Thomas, a.k.a. *Zarvona,* (who had organized a Maryland zouave unit at Tappahannock, Virginia), to procure necessary arms and arrange details. Letcher had Secretary Walker order Gen. Holmes at Fredericksburg to send the Tennessee force to the Coan River, on the Virginia side of the Potomac, to support the operation. Returning to Fredericksburg, Lewis found in readiness the Tennesseans and some maritime officers. Embarking aboard the *Virginia* from Fredericksburg to Monaskon Landing, the party then marched overland to the Coan River to await the arrival of the *St. Nicholas.* David C. Holly, *Chesapeake Steamboats Vanished Fleet* (Maryland 1994) 106-130; ...Holly, *Tidewater by Steamboat, A Saga of the Chesapeake* (Maryland 1991), 69-71.

[68] *Richmond Daily Dispatch,* Tue., July 2, 1861.

[69] In the raid they seized the schooner *Margaret,* carrying a cargo of coal, the brig. *Monticello,* laden with coffee, and the schooner *Mary Pierce,* loaded with ice.

[70] Condemned as a prize of war, the *St. Nicholas* was purchased by the Confederate States Navy and rechristened the *CSS Rappahannock.* Commanded by Capt. Henry H. Lewis, CSN, she operated in the Potomac and Rappahannock Rivers until April 1862, only to be burned by departing Confederate forces as the Union army advanced toward Fredericksburg in April 1862.

[71] J. Thomas Scharf, *History of the Confederate States Navy* (New York 1887), Chap. 6; OR, Series 1, Vol. 4; Harold R. Manakee, *Maryland in the Civil War* (Baltimore 1961), 63-65; Daniel Carroll Toomey, *The Civil War in Maryland* (Baltimore 1961), 17-36; David C. Holly, *Tidewater by Steamboat: A Saga of the Chesapeake* (Baltimore 1991), 69-71; ...Holly, *Chesapeake Steamboats: Vanished Fleet.* Centreville, Md.: Tidewater Pub. 1994, 106-130. The *CSS Rappahannock* was burned in the April 18, 1862 evacuation of Fredericksburg.

[72] Joseph Orton Kerbey reported the rumor to Washington, D.C. and, under threat of arrest, Wells fled by rail to the home of his eldest daughter, Mrs. Harriet Crawford, in Baltimore, Md. Harriet Louisa Wells in 1857 married James B. Crawford, a Baltimore spice merchant.

[73] B. F. Wells, in his petition ...Dec. 9, 1887, Item 9, Nat. Archives & Records Admin.

[74] "Brave as a lion, 6'3" " and noted for his gentle temperament, Brig. Gen. Charles W. Field, CSA, had in 1857 married local belle Monimia "Nimmie" Mason, a sister of Wiley Roy Mason Jr. of *the Sentry Box* on lower Caroline Street. Gen. Edward P. Alexander, Gen. Dabney H. Maury, and Major Charles R. Collins, Aide-de-Camp of Gen. Field, were among five other Confederate officers that married Mason sisters and cousins.
[75] Naval Historical Center, Dept. of the Navy.
[76] *The New York Times,* April 18, 1862.
[77] *Richmond Daily Dispatch,* Thur., April 17, 1862.
[78] *Richmond Daily Dispatch,* Sat., April 19, 1862.
[79] Betty Maury Diary entries for April 13 and April 18, 1862. (LC)
[80] *Richmond Daily Dispatch*, April 21, 1862.
[81] B.F. Wells Petition, Dec. 9, 1887, Items 10-14.(NA)
[82] 1887 Letter of Benjamin F. Wells Jr., B. F. Wells Petition to Congress, Accompanying Papers File.
[83] Report of Lt. Samuel Magaw, April 29, 1862, ORN, Series I, Vol. V., 45, statistical data of USS Eureka, ORN, Series II, Vol. I, 81.
[84] *Fredericksburg Star,* Jan. 16, 1889, 3, col. 5.
[85] Report of Cdr. Foxhall A. Parker, April 22, 1864, ORN, Series I, Vol. V, p. 411.
[86] Mrs. Beale lived at 307 Lewis Street and kept a school for girls in a building in her yard. The house still stands.
[87] Jane Howison Beale. *The Journal of Jane Howison Beale, Fredericksburg, Virginia 1850-1862* (Historic Fredericksburg Foundation, Inc., 1995), 62
[88] Jane Howison Beale Journal, Ibid., 62.
[89] Betty Maury Diary, entry for April 30, 1862.
[90] Marsena R. Patrick Diary (entry for May 2, 1862).
[91] Col. Hoffman, an old friend of Captain Wells from New York, became a boarder at the Wells House.
[92] The town's railroad depot was located along the south side of Prussia Street (today's Lafayette Boulevard) between Caroline and Charles Streets.
[93] Herman Haupt, *Reminiscences of General Herman Haupt* (Milwaukee 1901) 49.
[94] Betty Maury Diary, entry for May 25, 1862 stated that the cars have been running between Aquia Creek and "here" (Fredericksburg) for more than a week.
[95] Haupt, Ibid. 49. The railroad bridge was completed and in operation on May 19, 1862.
[96] Marsena Patrick Diary, entry for May 23, 1862.

[97] Betty Maury Diary, entries for May 22 and May 25, 1862. Gen. Patrick recorded on May 18, 1862 that Haupt's *cars are running today from Acquia (sic) Creek to this place—I do not know whether they will cross the Creek (Rappahannock) or not, tonight...*

[98] An imposing structure that stands today at the southwest side of Princess Anne and Fauquier Streets, the Gordon House was the home of the wealthy Douglas Hamilton Gordon Esq., a Delegate to the Confederate Congress. The *Southern Ladies* in the home at the time of Patrick's halt in town were Gordon's wife, Anne Eliza (Pleasants) Gordon and his elderly mother Anna Campbell (Knox) Gordon, widow of Bazil Gordon of Falmouth.

[99] Marsena Patrick, Diary.

[100] Col. Haupt would have set up headquarters in one of the Richmond, Fredericksburg & Potomac Railroad's Fredericksburg Station buildings which had a brick freight depot, a ticket office and another "old office." The station complex ran along Prussia Street (now Lafayette Blvd.) between Caroline and Charles Streets. Noel G. Harrison, *Fredericksburg Civil War Sites April 1861-November 1862* (H. E. Howard, Lynchburg, 1995), 25. Joseph O. Kerbey, a civilian employee working under Haupt, referred to their workplace in town as *the railroad office*.

[101] Haupt, *Reminiscences*, 49, 54, 55.

[102] Photo out of J. Willard. Brown. *The Signal Corps U.S.A. in the War of the Rebellion.* (Boston, Mass: U.S. Veteran Signal Corps Association, 1896.) 652

[103] Senator Penrose of Pa. on Feb. 28, 1900 introduced A BILL, S.3374, *for the relief of Joseph Orton Kerbey...for the sum of $10,000 to be paid...in recognition of his services in securing information which resulted in preventing the capture of Fort Pickens, Pensacola, Florida.* (56th Congress, 1st Session, S. 3374—Read twice and referred to the Committee on Claims.)

[104] Janet B. Hewett, Ed., *The Roster of Confederate Soldiers 1861-1865, Vol. IX,* (Broadfoot Pub. Co., Wilmington, NC 1996), 134.

[105] On April 22, 1862, John Covode telegrammed Haupt to report "immediately" to War Secretary Stanton, who had him proceed directly to the Headquarters of Gen. McDowell on the Rappahannock. In 1861, Covode had invited Haupt to go with him to see President Lincoln. Haupt wrote: "Covode was not a man who paid any attention to the rules of etiquette. He took me to the White House, and without sending a card, walked up stairs, then along the hall to a room, opened the door without knocking, and ushered me into the august presence of Abraham Lincoln...Covode was greeted very cordially, and then I was introduced..." Haupt, *Reminiscences*, 43-44, 297.

[106] Brig. Gen. T. F. Rodenbough, USA Ret., *Cavalry Editor, Journal of the Military Service Institution of the U.S.* (New York, Jan. 1890); Major J. O. (Joseph Orton) Kerbey, *On the War Path: a journey over the historic grounds of the late Civil War* (Chicago 1890). 9-12; ---Kerbey, *The Boy Spy* (Chicago-New York-San Francisco 1889) 377.

[107] Joseph A. Kerbey letter dated Oct. 16, 1899 to Commissioner of Pensions, Wash., D.C. (Joseph A. Kerbey Federal pension file, National Archives)

[109] ---Kerbey, *The Boy Spy,* 377.

[110] ---Kerbey, *Further Adventures of the Boy Spy in Dixie* (The National Tribune, Washington, D.C., 1898), 5-79

[111] The Exchange Hotel burned in 1857 and was reopened after the war. The "Planters' Hotel" building still stands at the northeast intersection of Commerce (now William) and Charles Street.

[112] The Planters' Hotel was managed by Counsellor Cole and his wife Sarah (Carpenter) Cole during the war years. Married in Fredericksburg in 1837, the Coles had five daughters before sons Benjamin (b.1853) and Charles (b.1856). Their hotel clerk before the war was John C. Conway who enlisted in the Fredericksburg Artillery in 1861 and was killed at Gettysburg. Of the Planters' Hotel, a Union officer guest wrote back home: "The proprietor...is a very quiet man, who never seems to meddle with either politics or victuals, and the guest is annoyed very little with either. Here you may get some bacon, bread and butter, and tea, facetiously called a dinner, for fifty cents...", John S. Applegate, *Reminiscences and Letters of George Arrowsmith* (N.J. 1893), 129-130.

[113] Kerbey passed through Fredericksburg enroute to Richmond where in Jan. 1862 he enlisted in the Confederate Army to spy.

[114] Designated McDowell's Military Governor, on 7 May 1862 Gen. Marsena R. Patrick, USA, took possession of the Farmers' Bank Building, located at the northwest corner of Princess Anne and George Streets. The building that housed the Farmers' Bank is still standing.

[115] While in the U.S. Senate, Pennsylvania native Simon Cameron built up the Republican machine in his state, giving Lincoln his support only after he was promised a Cabinet post. Lincoln reluctantly appointed him Secretary of War, and when Cameron was censured for corruption, Lincoln appointed him Minister to Russia in Jan. 1862.

[116] Unknowingly, the paths of Kerbey and the Wells' daughters had recently crossed. In Washington, D.C. on March 8, 1861, (just prior to the family's move to Fredericksburg) both attended President and Mrs. Lincoln's first

public Levee at the White House. (Kerbey, "On the War Path," 18; Mamie Wells, "Reminiscences.")

[117] Among the furniture listed in Miss Benson's 1861 property inventory was "...one small sofa and two lounges." Fredericksburg Deed Book T, p. 213.

[118] John W. Forney (1817-1881) owner/editor of various Pennsylvania newspapers, was Secretary of the U.S. Senate 1861-1868.

[119] "Capitola" was a brief love interest of Kerbey while in Richmond, Va. the previous year.

[120] Possibly Peleg Clarke, Jr., the most notorious Unionist in Fredericksburg. Immediately announcing his loyalty to Union troops upon the town's takeover in April 1862, Clarke proceeded to identify local civilians who were allegedly smuggling supplies and military information out of the town. Harrison, *Fredericksburg Civil War Sites,* 52. The general population showed their disgust when a cavalcade of Union officers rode through town on May 2, 1862, while Peleg Clarke's two daughters waved their white handkerchiefs to welcome them. Patrick. *Diary,* entry for May 2, 1862.

[121] This incident was reported in the *Christian Banner,* the town's Unionist newspaper. Under the heading "Union Flag," and without giving names, the article stated that "Some of the fastidious female population of our town leave the side-walks and circle around into the streets to avoid passing under the Union flag..." *Fredericksburg Christian Banner,* June 14, 1862.

[122] Not only was the *Eureka* lost. With Capt. Wells in prison, Mrs. Wells and the children, in the fall of 1863, packed up only what they could carry in a pontoon boat and canoe to head down the Rappahannock River to "Monaskon." They left behind *...the remainder of our worldly goods until some favorable opportunity occurred for removing them.* It is unknown whether that opportunity ever presented itself.

[123] The Federals occupying Fredericksburg during the summer of 1862 were still smarting from the daring raid pulled off by Captains Hollins, Lewis and "Zarvona" the previous June 1861.

[124] The 23rd New York Volunteer Regiment, commanded by Col. Henry C. "Barney" Hoffman, USA, occupied the town beginning on 7 May 1862. Their headquarters were opposite the railroad depot in the lower part of town. Col. Hoffman, an old friend of Captain Wells, was then a boarder in the Wells' home.

[125] McDowell's troops filed into Stafford Heights opposite Fredericksburg on 18 April 1862, and entered the town on 2 May 1862 after the temporary pontoon bridge was completed. The Federals evacuated Fredericksburg on 31 August 1862.

[126] Capt. Wells descended from William Wells I of Southold, Long Island, N.Y., who died on Nov. 13, 1671 at age 63. His tombstone states that he was a *Gent., Justice of Ye Peace & First Sheriffe of New Yorke Shire...He livd in Love and Sweetly dyd in peace.* Hayes, *William Wells of Southold,* 28.

[127] Gaining little recognition by Gen. Irvin McDowell and the other commanders for naming civilians engaged in smuggling, Peleg Clarke, Jr. testified against McDowell during a court of inquiry. In reply, McDowell stated that the smuggling conspiracies unmasked by Clarke had been primarily *connected with his personal matters and animosities.* While in Fredericksburg, McDowell's quartermaster had seized 2,000 bushels of corn, in bags marked "Confederate States," from one of Clarke's own storerooms. By January 1864, Clarke was at a Union camp near Brandy Station, occasionally acting as an informant to Lafayette Baker, Secretary of War Stanton's Chief of Detectives. Harrison, *Fredericksburg Civil War Sites,* 52; Patrick. entry for Jan. 24, 1864.

[128] As McDowell's troops arrived in the area, Capt. Wells ran his small steamer, the *Eureka,* into a safe harbor below Port Royal to prevent her destruction by the evacuating Confederates. She was soon discovered by the crew of the Federals Rappahannock Flotilla and seized as a prize of war. Just prior to the December 1862 Battle of Fredericksburg, the Federals were using the *Eureka* on the Potomac River near Aquia Creek. She was subsequently used as a tender in an attack on the Confederate battery in the Piankatank River, where she was riddled with shot and almost wrecked. After repairs, armed with a light 12-pounder artillery piece, she was placed in the Potomac Flotilla, where, because of her speed and light draft, she was put to use as a naval scout, being able to nose into shallow water and creeks that were inaccessible to the larger boats. B. F. Wells, 1887 Petition to Senate and House; James Wren. *New Bern to Fredericksburg: Captain James Wren's Diary.* John M. Priest, Ed.. (White Mane Pub., Shippensburg, Pa. 1990) 95; *Fredericksburg Star,* Jan. 16, 1889.

[129] Mrs. Mary Ball Washington lived at the northwest corner of Charles and Lewis Streets. Still standing, the house is owned and maintained by the Association for the Preservation of Virginia Antiquities (Now Preservation Virginia) and open to the public.

[130] Located off Washington Avenue, the Mary Ball Washington monument erected over her grave in 1894 replaced an earlier monument begun in 1833 but never finished.

[131] As part of Gen. Ambrose Burnside's advance army of 6,000 men, the 9th New York Vol. Infantry "Hawkins Zouaves" commanded by Col. Rush C.

Hawkins rolled into Fredericksburg on the cars from Aquia Creek on 4-5 August 1862, remaining until 30 August 1862. Dressed similar to the original French Zouave uniform, the 9th N.Y. Infantry wore fezzes, proper jackets and vests and dark blue slightly baggy trousers. (Patrick, diary entry for 4 August 1862; Frederick H. Dyer, *A Compendium of the War of the Rebellion* (National Historical Press Society, 1978)

[132] Gen. Marsena Patrick wrote in his diary on July 31, 1862: *"The 'Chief of Police' as he styles himself, has been here from Washington since yesterday. He has been making himself generally busy about our affairs & has telegraphed to Washington that all things are in very bad condition here— nobody here is doing his duty."* Patrick continued in this line on August 1, 1862: *I have given the 'detectives' and 'Chief of Police' a lesson in military usage today.* Patrick was referring to Col. Lafayette C. Baker, USA, War Secretary Stanton's Provost Marshal and Chief of Detectives, who thought of himself as head of the 'Secret Service' of the U. S. Stanton and Patrick had a long and bitter controversy over Baker's role. At the beginning of the war, Baker, under the direction of Gen. Winfield Scott, and using the alias "Sam Munson," infiltrated Confederate lines as a traveling photographer to spy on Confederate forces in Virginia. One version of Baker's adventures in Virginia was: that he was captured as a spy, and escaped while being held for trial in Richmond; that he was picked up in Fredericksburg, first on charges of vagrancy and later as a spy; and that he again escaped from jail with the help of a town prostitute he had been staying with and managed to reach Union lines. Arriving in Washington, Gen. Winfield Scott made him a captain and put him in charge of his intelligence service. Patrick, Diary, July 31, 1862, August 1, 1862, January 1863; *Lafayette Baker AKA: Sam Munson, Union Spymaster and Chief of U.S. Intelligence During American Civil War.* The Signal Corps Association (Glen Burnie, Md.); Lafayette C. Baker. *History of the United States Secret Service.* (Philadelphia: published by the author, 1867.)

[133] Accused of being a Confederate spy and mail courier, Isabelle "Belle" Boyd was captured by the Federals on 29 July 1862 near Warrenton, Virginia and sent by train to Washington, D.C. Chief of detectives Lafayette C. Baker met her train and accompanied her to Old Capitol Prison. Kerbey and Boyd were fellow inmates until her release at the end of August 1862 due to a lack of evidence. Louis A. Sigaud, *Belle Boyd: Confederate Spy* (Dietz Press 1943) 67-73.

[134] Geno had celebrated her 15th birthday in Fredericksburg on Jan. 8, 1862. Kerbey turned 21 on Feb. 4, 1862.

[135] The Seven Days' Battles around Richmond, Va. 25 June-1 July, 1862.

[136] Kerbey used the term *love making* as courtship, in the sense of the romantic Victorian period.

[137] Beautiful dark eyes seemed to be a characteristic of Captain Wells' daughters. In a letter to his future wife, a 19th Mississippi Rgt. surgeon described Geno's older sister Sue as a *black eyed beauty*. Dr. Robert Hunter Peel letter date-lined *Field Hospital – Posey's Brigade Near Fredericksburg – June the 10th/63*. Peel Family Papers, letter in possession of Peel descendant Kevin Hudson, courtesy of Jack Durham.

[138] Henry Wadsworth Longfellow, *Evangeline*, a narrative poem published in 1847, tells a sentimental tale of two lovers separated by war.

[139] *Il Bacio*, translated from the Italian: "The Kiss." Kerbey married Mary Holmes Shaffer on Sept. 27, 1863 in Elizabeth, Pa. The daughter of Dr. John Eckert Shaffer and Elizabeth Stillman Holmes Shaffer of Washington and Elizabeth, Pa., Mary H. Shaffer was born in 1847, the same year as Geno Wells. Apparently she was not only wise but understanding.

[140] Never marrying, Sarah Eugenia "Geno" Wells died in her 30th year at the home of her parents on Long Island, N.Y.

[141] Geno's brother George T. Wells was then age 13 and Emma Jane "Jennie" Wells 11.

[142] The consequence of his own betrayal, Kerbey admitted that he acted to prevent the arrest of Capt. Wells and was responsible for his escape by providing him with a pass to board a northbound train heading to Baltimore, Maryland.

[143] The notion that Kerbey was a covert spy, or his romantic notions concerning Geno Wells, were apparently not lost on Capt. Wells.

[144] Col. Daniel Craig McCallum, USA, a native of Scotland, was appointed by War Secretary Stanton on Feb. 11, 1862 as Military Director and Superintendent of U. S. Military Railroads. He was made Brig. Gen. on Sept. 24, 1864. McCallum was a popular poet, and in 1870 published *The Water-Mill and Other Poems*.

[145] Col. Thomas A. Scott, USA, supervised agencies responsible for military telegraphs and railroads after June 1862.

[146] In Richmond, Virginia on Jan. 14, 1862, *Joseph A. Kerbey* took the Confederate oath of allegiance, mustering in as a private with the 3rd Maryland Artillery Company, CSA. Hewett. *The Roster of Confederate Soldiers*, 134.

[147] In 1862, War Secretary Stanton appointed Thomas T. Eckert as chief of the War Department Telegraph Office. President Lincoln was a regular visitor to Eckert's office to read telegrams from the war front.

[148] Away for two months, Patrick was back in town on July 28, 1862 with headquarters at the old Farmer's Bank building, remaining until August 9, 1862 when he was relieved by Gen. Isaac I. Stevens. Patrick Diary.

[149] Gen. Patrick's office was two blocks up George Street, west of the Wells' home.

[150] The "private mansion," a two-story brick structure located at the northwest corner of the intersection of Princess Anne and George Streets, had housed both the Fredericksburg branch of the Farmers' Bank of Virginia and the Taliaferro-Ware family. The private entrance on George Street led to the then-vacated living quarters of 70-year old widow Catharine Taliaferro, and her son William Ware. William, the bank's cashier, had taken the bank records and specie to Danville, Virginia. The building stands today.

[151] *Joseph A. Kerbey* was commissioned a 2nd Lt., Signal Corps, U.S. Volunteers, on July 15, 1864 to rank from March 3, 1863, and accepted the commission on Sept. 1, 1864. He mustered out May 1, 1865. He was incarcerated at Old Capitol Prison in August 1862 and held for two months.

[152] On Patrick's staff in Fredericksburg were Asst. Adjutant Generals Capt. James P. Kimball, Capt. William W. Beckwith and Capt. Edward A. Springsteed, all of New York State.

[153] While military governor of the area, the kindly Patrick gained the respect of local families by the posting of guards at the homes of unprotected civilians and attempts at suppressing Union soldiers' raids on domestic food supplies. Kerbey was arrested just prior to Gen. Marsena R. Patrick's second departure from Fredericksburg. On Aug. 9, 1862, Gen. Patrick turned over the duties to Gen. Isaac Stevens, USA, Commander of First Div., Ninth Army Corps, Burnside's Army. By Aug. 13, 1862, Stevens had delegated duties to Lt. Col. Henry Walter Kingsbury and Lt. Col. Griffin A. Stedman, of the 11th Conn. Vol. The Union army occupation of Fredericksburg ended on August 31,1862. Patrick Diary entry for Aug. 7, 1862; Lucille Griffith, *Fredericksburg's Political Hostages: The Old Capitol Journal of George Henry Clay Rowe*, (*The Virginia Magazine of History and Biography*, Vol. 71, No. 4, Oct. 1964) 399-499.

[154] In addition to Confederate spy Belle Boyd as a fellow inmate (she was arrested on July 29, 1862 and interviewed by Lafayette Baker at Old Capitol Prison), Kerbey was soon joined by nineteen of the "oldest and most esteemed" citizens of Fredericksburg, including Mayor Montgomery

Slaughter, Rev. W. F. Broaddus, the town's Baptist Minister, and George Henry "Clay" Rowe, a 30-year old Fredericksburg lawyer who kept a prison journal. Arrested on August 13, 1862 and held the first night in the same Provost Marshal quarters in Fredericksburg as Kerbey, the men arrived at Old Capitol the next day. They were to be held prisoners there for two months. Rowe recorded that he was *...startled to see...a richly dressed and handsome young lady; that he unconsciously stopped, she bowed, and I returned the salutation.* On August 22, 1862, the evening before Belle Boyd's release, she told Rowe and several others her life history, *"...it was near 1:00 o'clock when she finished, relating that the immediate cause of her arrest was her being detected bearing dispatches to General Jackson in the Shenandoah Valley.* Griffith, *Fredericksburg Political Hostages,* 419-420.

[155] Arrested for *disloyalty,* Kerbey was held at Old Capitol Prison for two months and released under a *parole of honor,* whereby he agreed *...not to go south of a certain point until authorized or released from parole.* On October 30, 1862, *Joseph A. Kerbey* enlisted as a private in Co. B, 2nd U.S. Cavalry, joining the troop on its organization at Carlisle Barracks, Pennsylvania. He reenlisted in the Signal Corps in July 15, 1864 to rank from March 1863.

[156] Kerbey's arrest occurred sometime around the first week of August 1862: after Lafayette Baker's visit to Fredericksburg (July 30-August 1st); and after Hawkins' Zouaves paraded in town (Aug. 4-5); but prior to Gen. Patrick's departure on August 9, 1862.

[157] Kerbey, *Further Adventures of the Boy Spy,* 5-79.

[158] Mamie L. Wells (1842-1875) *Reminiscences of the Late War,* published (posthumously) in ten weekly installments in *The Fredericksburg Star* newspaper (July 11, 1888 through August 11, 1888).

[159] Potomac Creek.

[160] Belle Plain, in Stafford County, Virginia. Approximately nine miles northeast of Fredericksburg on Potomac Creek, Belle Plain was later used as a Union supply depot and hospital staging area.

[161] The Fredericksburg town clock is located in the tower of St. George's Episcopal Church. In 1851, Fredericksburg Common Council accepted the responsibility of maintaining the clock. Still standing, St. George's Church is located at the northeast corner of Princess Anne and George Streets. Carrol H.Quenzel, *The History and Background of St. George's Episcopal Church, Fredericksburg, Virginia* (Richmond 1951), 35.

[162] Home of Alexander Keene Phillips, which was accidentally burned by Union soldiers.

[163] Chatham, the home of the Major J. Horace Lacy family (still stands).

[164] Rappahannock River.

[165] Col. Ball's cavalry was quartered at Citizen's Hall (the old theatre), then located on the west side of Princess Anne Street between Charlotte and Hanover Streets, not now standing.

[166] Several shells were reported to have passed through "White Plains," the home of Mr. Sidney H. Owens, near Princess Anne Street and Virginia Avenue. One shot fell in the garden of Mr. Joseph Alsop, fronting Main Street (Princess Anne St. at Lewis St., still standing), in addition to a shot through the Paper Mill factory. The only injury sustained on the part of citizens was George Timberlake, son of John Timberlake, a looker on at the upper end of town, who lost a foot, lacerated by a passing shot.

[167] Jane Beale, entry for Nov. 17, 1862.

[168] Patrick, Diary entry for Nov. 18, 1862.

[169] Beale Diary entry for Nov. 18th, 1862.

[170] Beale Diary entry, Nov. 19, 1862. In one of two letters to Col. Ball dated Nov. 15, 1862 Lee wrote: *It is reported that the enemy is moving from Warrenton to-day, and it is probable that he is marching upon Fredericksburg. I desire you to be on the alert, and give me notice of any movement you may discover...* In Lee's second letter, he refers to a telegraph sent Ball the previous day. *O.R.,*1014.

[171] Accompanying the Mayor to "Snowden" was Douglas H. Gordon, a member of Town Council and William A. Little, Recorder. Robert R. Howison, *Fredericksburg: Past, Present and Future* (J. Willard Adams, 1880) 14, 15.

[172] *O.R.* Vol. XXI, 783.

[173] Gen. J.E.B. Stuart communicated Lee's response back to the Mayor, who then prepared a written reply to Gen. Sumner.

[174] Patrick Diary entry for Nov. 22, 1862. S. J. Quinn, *The History of the City of Fredericksburg* (Richmond, Va. 1908) 85-86; French John's wharf was named for resident ferry operator John DeBaptist (1740-1804), a native of the Caribbean island of St. Kitts. Ruth Coder Fitzgerald, *A Different Story* (Unicorn, 1979) 50-52.

[175] *O.R.*, 784-5

[176] Ibid. 785

[177] *O.R* Vol. XXI, 1026.

[178] Clifford Dowdey and Louis H. Manarin, Ed. *The Wartime Papers of R. E. Lee.* New York and Boston: Bramhall House, 1961, 343.

[179] Patrick Diary entry for Nov. 22, 1862.

[180] Ibid.

[181] Diary of Pvt. William Meek Furr, Co. E, 19th Miss., Featherston's Brigade, Anderson's Division. (Furr Family Papers, LOC).
[182] The 17th Miss. Regiment, Barksdales Brigade, commanded by Col. John C. Fiser.
[183] 18th Miss., Barksdale's Brigade, commanded by Col. W. H. Luce.
[184] 13th Miss., Barksdale's Brigade, commanded by Col. J. W. Carter.
[185] *Battles and Leaders of the Civil War,* Vol. III, Maj. Gen. LaFayette McLaws, *The Confederate Left at Fredericksburg,* (New York: Century, 1887-1888) 86.
[186] Artist Alfred R. Waud, *Harper's Weekly.* Dec. 13, 1862, 794 (LC)
[187] Capt. B. F. Wells's letter dated Nov. 6, 1887 to Mr. J. O. Kerbey. LC
[188] Major John S. Hard, 7th S.C. Inf., Co. F., Kershaw's Brigade, McLaws' Div., was killed on Sept. 20, 1863 in Battle of Chickamauga, GA.
[189] Capt. Andrew Robinson Govan, 17th Miss. Infantry, Barksdale's Brigade, McLaws Div., mortally wounded in Battle of Chickamauga.
[190] Lt. James M. Crump, 17th Miss. Infantry, Co. B, Barksdale's Brigade, McLaws Div., wounded in Battle of Chickamauga.
[191] Capt. Bowling J. Martin, Acting Commissary of Subsistence to Gen. McLaws, may have been filling in for Gen. Barksdale's ACS, Capt. Thomas F. Leonard, who was reportedly "drunk more than half the time and does not attend to his duty." Robert E. L. Krick, *Staff Officers in Gray* (University of North Carolina Press 2003) 201, 215.
[192] Dr. Peel had five brothers and four cousins fighting for the Confederacy, of whom six were killed or wounded, and another imprisoned. When his brother Lt. Albert L. Peel was killed in action at the Battle of Spotsylvania Court House, Dr. Peel found his body and buried it on the battlefield. He likewise buried the body of his friend, Colonel Thomas Joseph Hardin. Peel wrote that after the war "...these noble women of Spotsylvania wrote to me that the graves of Col. Hardin and Adjutant Peel had been found and the remains removed to the Confederate cemetery. God bless those noble Southern women, and the grand old State of Virginia." Dr. Robert H. Peel, "The Last Roll" *Confederate Veteran,* Vol. 10, 367.
[193] Assigned to Longstreet's First Corp., Gen. Richard H. Anderson's Division, Gen. W. S. Featherston's Brigade, which included the 12th, 16th, 19th and 48th Mississippi Infantry.
[194] Peel Family Papers. Photocopy of Dr. Peel's letter by permission of Kevin Hudson, Peel descendant, courtesy of Jack Durham.
[195] Dr. Robert Hunter Peel letter datelined *Field Hospital – Posey's Brigade, Near Fredericksburg – June the 10th/63* to his sister-in-law, Alice Maud

Matthews, Holly Springs, Miss. Dr. Peel was courting Alice after the death of his first wife, Virginia. Peel Family Papers. Copy of letter courtesy of Peel descendant Kevin Hudson, courtesy Jack Durham.

[196] Rev. J. William Jones, *Christ in the Camp: or Religion in Lee's Army* (Richmond 1887) 267-268.

[197] Ibid., 295.

[198] Quinn, *The History of Fredericksburg*.

[199] *The Richmond Daily Dispatch,* Wed., March 18, 1863.

[200] Ibid.

[201] Rufus B. Merchant Obituary, *Fredericksburg Star,* Oct. 7, 1905, 3. col. 2; Library of Virginia, Carrol H. Quenzel, Ed., *Preliminary Check List for Fredericksburg, 1778-1876* (Richmond 1947) 146-147.

[202] Mamie L. Wells, *Reminiscences.* Published as a series in 1888, the *Star's* editor and proprietor was Rufus B. Merchant.

[203] The Capitol in Richmond, Virginia.

[204] Gen. William Barksdale's brigade of Gen. Lafayette McLaws' division, picketed the town and along the river, extending from the dam above Falmouth to below Deep Run to the south. These Mississippi sharpshooters were positioned in rifle pits dug in close to the riverbank, at cellar doors and windows of the houses near the river. Buel and Johnson, Ed., *Battles and Leaders,* Vol. III, Maj. Gen. Lafayette McLaws, *The Confederate Left at Fredericksburg,* 86.

[205] Mamie Wells' mother, Mrs. Jane (Teed) Wells. At 4:30 a.m. on 11 Dec., 1862, from his headquarters at the Market House/Town Hall, Barksdale reported to McLaws that the Union pontoon bridge being constructed was nearly half done, and that he was about to open fire on them. McLaws then ordered the firing of the two signal guns posted on Marye's Heights. A member of Barksdale's brigade stationed near the middle pontoon crossing in the early morning hours of 11 Dec. wrote: *"When they glided in...the first pontoon...I withdrew with my comrades and reported it to my captain, Andrew Govan, of Company B, 17th Mississippi. He sent me to General Barksdale, at the city [sic] hall, who was up with lights expecting it. My orders were to tell Captain Govan to open fire on the pontoons...and so was opened the bombardment of Fredericksburg.* C. C. Cummings. "The Bombardment of Fredericksburg." *Confederate Veteran,* XXIII, 253.

[206] McLaws wrote that nine separate and desperate attempts were made to complete the bridge, each *"attended with such heavy loss from our fire that the efforts were abandoned until about 10:00 a.m., when suddenly the tremendous array of the Federal artillery opened fire from the heights above*

the city. The roar of the cannon, the bursting shells, the falling of walls and chimneys, and the flying bricks and other material dislodged from the houses by the iron balls and shells, added to the fire of the infantry from both sides and the smoke from the guns and from the burning houses, made a scene of indescribable confusion, enough to appall the stoutest hearts!" Buel and Johnson, Ed. *Battles and Leaders, Vol. III,* Gen. Lafayette McLaws, 87.

[207] Captain Andrew R. Govan, 17th Mississippi Regiment, Barksdale's Brigade (a beau of Mamie Wells).

[208] Colonel John C. Fiser, Commander, 17th Mississippi Rgt., Barksdale's Brigade.

[209] Down Sophia Street (Water Street), paralleling the river.

[210] In a letter to a refugee friend, published in the Richmond paper, Mamie identified the officer as Lt. Col. Robert Thomas Cook of McLaws' Cobb Brigade, Phillips Georgia Legion, as being killed at this corner on the evening of 11 December. In his report of the battle, Colonel Benjamin G. Humphreys reported the death of an officer of the 21st Miss. Infantry at this corner. From his staging area at the Market House/Town Hall, Captain R. C. Green, CSA, with his company of 21st Mississippians, was detached to the foot of George Street, at its intersection with Sophia. Troops of the 2nd (Philadelphia) Brigade, advancing in force down the riverbank, immediately opened fire on him. Stubbornly resisting, Green was finally struck down by a minie bullet. His company then fell back, bearing his body with them. With the enemy in pursuit, the 17th opened a galling fire and drove them off the streets up toward the pontoon bridge. They held them in check until about 7:00 p.m., at which time the Mississippians were ordered to withdraw from the town. *O.R.* 605-607

[211] Possibly their neighbor Pamelia (Perry) Mills, age 45, wife of tailor Walter M. Mills, who had five children ranging from 7 to 15 years. The Mills' family lived across the street on the river side of Sophia Street south of the Wells' House. During the shelling Capt. Wells also came to the aid of Alice (Jett) Honey, wife of bridge keeper Harrison Honey, who with her three infant children and some neighbors, had taken refuge in the basement of John Hooe Wallace's home and store at the southeast corner of Caroline and William streets. When the Wallace chimneys were struck with balls, Wells led them to a place of safety. Library of VA, WPA: *'The Wells House,* (testimony of Maggie Honey, daughter of Alice (Jett) Honey), Feb. 18, 1937.

[212] *Harper's Weekly* Jan. 3, 1863 edition, p. 6 comment on Waud's sketch: *Mr. Waud's picture is well described in the following extract from the* [N.Y.] *Herald correspondence: 'Some of the houses on the river-front are completely*

torn to pieces...How could anything remain here and live? And yet, strange to say, people did remain, and I have yet to learn of any casualty to those who did so. Quite a number...took their families into the cellars of their houses, and there remained in safety.. In an enclosure on a corner...the bodies of about a dozen men...all our own men with one exception, and he was an aged man, to all appearance fully sixty years old. His dress was that of a civilian and he had been shot while in the act of aiming his piece: for even in death his arms retained their position and in his face was the mark of hate.

Probably the old man, carried away by his passion, volunteered. But clearly he paid for his mistaken zeal.'

[213] "A Federal Colonel from Philadelphia" was probably Colonel (later Gen.) Joshua T. Owen, USA, Commander of the 2nd (Philadelphia) Brigade, 2nd Div., 69th Pennsylvania Infantry, Sumner's Right Grand Div. Owen wrote in his report of the battle of the 11th: *"After dislodging most of the sharpshooters, and advancing as far as Caroline Street, I established my pickets and directed the regiment to sleep on their arms."* Report of Col. Joshua T. Owen, USA, *O.R.*, 277. Owens horse was killed under him in the battle. Regarding the night of the 11th, Mamie Wells, in a letter to a neighbor, wrote: *"...They are breaking into houses like so many demons. With terrible force they throw themselves against our doors, back and front, but an officer (Yankee, though he was,) saved us."*

[214] In extracts of a letter published in the *Richmond Daily Dispatch* on Jan 2, 1863, Mamie Wells described much of the same scene the family experienced on the night of the 11th.

[215] Brig. Gen. James Nagle, USA, Cdr. 9th Army Corps, 2nd Div., 1st Brigade, along with officers of the 48th Pa. Infantry commanded by Col. Joshua K. Sigfried, USA, may have used the Wells House as their headquarters. Captain James Wren, USA, Co. B, 48th Pa., who had known Capt. Wells in Pennsylvania, wrote in his diary on the 12th: *"I slept tonight in the Building of Mr. Wells who used to run the packet boat from Wilkes-Barre to the tunnel. He said he carried Machinery for us when we war building & erecting our Colliery at Wilkes-Barre. He knew me by some of the men of our regiment calling me by Name, 'Major Wren.' He then Came up & said he knew me & I told him that my Brother, Thomas Wren, was the one he knew as 'Tom,' [who] attended to the Colliery. I did not want to have much to say to him as he was a rebel & we had Just Confiscated his boat & our government was using it on the river down near Aquia Crick* [Creek].*"* (James Wren. *From New Bern to Fredericksburg: Captain James Wren's Diary.* 1990) 95.

[216] Dec. 14th. In his diary of this date, Capt. Wren wrote: ...*We Camped in Captain Wells' house last night.*
[217] Although an effort had been made by Col. John C. Fiser of the 17th Miss. Rgt. to alert the civilians yet in town of their mortal danger, some homes were overlooked, including that of Jane Beale. Beale, Nov. 11, 1862 entry, 129. Capt. and Mrs. Wells elected to remain in their home because of the illness of a child too sick to travel.
[218] Possibly Brig. Gen. James Nagle, USA, Cdr., 9th Army Corps, 2nd Div., lst Brigade.
[219] Confederate forces across town and in the hills above Fredericksburg were unaware of the Union army's night withdrawal to the other side of the Rappahannock River until the following morning.
[220] Possibly Col. Joshua Owen, the Union officer that had earlier befriended the Wells family. His brigade commander, Gen. Oliver Howard, had taken the Gordon home as his headquarters. During the looting, Owen had a 3' tall bronze equestrian statue that had been taken by a soldier from the Gordon home crated, addressed to his home, and carried across the upper pontoon bridge. The crate was seized as "illegal plunder," and transported to the War Department. In Nov. 1863, the Secretary of War declared the statue was indeed "unlawfully taken," and over the objections of Owen, by then a General, returned to Gordon's family. Harrison, *Fredericksburg Civil War Sites, Vol. II,* 61-62.
[221] Mary Price (or Pryor) was the casualty. Mamie Wells' wrote: "...*Mary Price, a black woman, was killed by a shell—cut quite in two. She had gotten, for protection, under a bed in a room through which a shell passed. I saw her on Wednesday. She had been killed the previous Thursday, but there was no one to bury her...every house not inhabited has been sacked and ruined inside. They committed every species of outrage...*" Rev. James Power Smith reported that Mary Pryor, a Negro woman, was killed in the December 1862 shelling. *Fredericksburg Star,* Dec. 25, 1886.
[222] Col. Joshua T. Owen established his pickets in the neighborhood on the evening of 11 December 1862. *O.R.,* 277.
[223] Extracts from Mamie Wells' letter published on page 1 of the *Richmond Daily Dispatch,* January 2, 1863. The letter describes their family of ten confined to the cellar of their home for five days; the temporary arrest of their father during the battle; a Federal officer saving them from soldiers at the front and back doors, and other events also recalled in Mamie Wells' *Reminiscences.*

[224] "Aunt Clara" may have been Clara Beckley, the only black female by the name of "Clara" listed in the 1860 Federal census as a 50-year old black "Washwoman" in Fredericksburg.

[225] Eighteen year-old Benjamin Franklin Wells Jr.

[226] Robert Thomas Cook, Co. B, Infantry Battalion of Phillips' Georgia Legion was appointed Major on July 1st and Lt. Col. on July 6, 1862. As part of Cobb's brigade, the 18th and 24th Georgia Regiments and Phillips' Legion were sent by Gen. Cobb to relieve Gen. Barksdale's Mississippians on the evening of 11 December. The Legion took position along the line of battle, on the left; the men lay on their arms during the night, with pickets and scouts taking 15 prisoners. It was during this time, *before the engagement was fairly commenced,"* that Cook was killed. His body was recovered and he is buried in the Presbyterian Cemetery, Dalton, Georgia. *O.R.,* 607; Robert K. Krick, *Lee's Colonels.* Dayton, Ohio: Morningside House, 1992, 98.

[227] Mamie Wells, in her *Reminiscences,* wrote"...*our own merciful escape is due to a Federal Colonel from Philadelphia—I think his name is Ormes.."* Mamie may have confused "Ormes" with "Owen" -- Probably Colonel (later General) Joshua T. Owen, USA.

[228] According to Fredericksburg native, the late Anne Wilson Rowe, her mother said that her great-grandmother, Ella McCarty Martin, when asked how they managed to survive in the hard times in Fredericksburg right after the war, always replied: *Well, the fields were full of turnip salad and the rivers were full of fish.* (Anne Wilson Rowe in speech delivered in December 2005 on the 143rd anniversary of the 1862 Battle of Fredericksburg.)

[229] When Capt. John Sterling Swann, Co. A, 26th Battalion, Va. Inf. was being held a prisoner at Fort Delaware in 1864, he said ...*There were many rats in the prison grounds...the more needy prisoners...would eat them with avidity.* (LC, Manuscript Div., Misc. Manuscripts)

[230] The Battle of Chancellorsville, 1-4 May 1863.

[231] On 18 August 1863, Captain Wells was captured by the gunboat *U.S.S. Currituck* while foraging for food on Totusky Creek in Richmond County, Virginia. Charged with running the blockade and carrying supplies to the Confederate Government, he was taken to Old Capitol Prison. After receiving word that his family had removed from Fredericksburg to Monaskon, and being convinced that his family would be safe there, he signed the Oath of Allegiance and was released on December 3, 1863 into the care of his married daughter living in Baltimore.

[232] Benjamin Wells Jr., then age 19 and George T. Wells, age 14.

[233] Lancaster County, in the Northern Neck of Virginia.

[234] Nelson T. Wells was born on 22 May 1857 and died 4 March 1877.
[235] "Monaskon" plantation, Lancaster County, Virginia, was beautifully situated on the Rappahannock River with a steamboat landing. The oldest part of this still-standing two-story house with brick ends and large chimneys, dates to 1690. By deed dated 1852, John Chewning deeded the 205-acre plantation, then called "Smithfield," to Justice Addison Lombard Carter (c1820-c1871). Son of Joseph Addison Carter and Eliza Chinn Nutt, Carter married Mary Duval Jones in 1841. Justice Carter's estate sold the 205-acre plantation called Monaskon in 1871. In 1900, it was known for its garden seed farm and the community later became a resort. Capt. Wells was familiar with Monaskon as a steamboat landing for the *Eureka*, and had made previous plans to make Monaskon a place of refuge for the family.
[236] Corotoman plantation, Lancaster County, Va., was the home of the Carter family, descendants of Robert "King" Carter.
[237] Federal gunboats.
[238] "Monaskon," their refuge home in Lancaster County, Virginia.
[239] Captain Wells was charged with running the blockade and carrying supplies to the Confederate Government in August 1863 and held in the Old Capitol Prison in Washington, D.C. until his release on December 3, 1863.
[240] Capt. Foxhall A. Parker, Commander of the Potomac Flotilla.
[241] Mrs. Harriet (Wells) Crawford, wife of James B. Crawford of Baltimore, Md.
[242] *Baltimore Sun*, Baltimore, Md. "Political prisoner," Franklin Wells, "citizen," was registered into Fort McHenry on Oct. 10, 1864 and released on February 16, 1865. (Ft. McHenry Prison Records)
[243] Harriet (Wells) Crawford.
[244] Gen. Lewis Wallace, USA, then in charge of the State of Maryland.
[245] Cong. Charles Denison (1818-1867) a Democrat, represented the Wyoming Valley of Pennsylvania and died in Wilkes-Barre in 1867.
[246] Major John Hay, President Lincoln's Assistant Private Secretary.
[247] President Abraham Lincoln.
[248] This first public levee, an evening reception of President and Mrs. Lincoln, was held at the White House on Friday, March 8, 1861. The then-smiling President ...*was dressed in black, with white gloves, turn down collar, and with his luxuriant black hair parted down the middle. Mrs. Lincoln wore a rich bright crimson watered silk, with point lace cape, white and red camelias in her hair, pearl band and necklace, and other ornaments of pearl.* (*The Evening Star, Washington, D.C.; The Richmond Daily Dispatch,* March 11,

1861.) This was one of the last social events attended by Mamie Wells and her sisters prior to the family's move to Fredericksburg.

[249] Secretary of War, Edwin M. Stanton.

[250] James B. Crawford, a Baltimore merchant and husband of Harriet (Wells) Crawford.

[251] Henry J. Raymond, editor of *The New York Times*.

[252] Capt. Foxhall A. Parker, Commodore, USN.

[253] 19 November, 1864.

[254] Morris Montgomery, b. c.1809, a native of Maryland, was living in Fredericksburg near the town wharf in 1861 and testified by letter that Wells... *remained strictly neutral pursuing his business...that he refused to raise the rebel flag upon his boat...that at the time Gen. McDowell made his attack in Fredericksburg, the Rebels burned all the vessels they could get hold of in the River, Captain Wells was lying with his Boat at the wharf, and escaped with her to the Federal lines down the River, the Boat layed near my house and I had plenty of opportunity to watch her, which I did and never saw a Rebel Flag on her. I saw her daily, other vessels had the Rebel Flag flying upon them. I always believed him to be loyal.* (Morris Montgomery letter dated Jan. 19, 1865, Baltimore, Md., contained in 1865 Petition of Mary Wells to Abraham Lincoln.

[255] J. L. McPhail, Provost-Marshal General, State of Maryland.

[256] 8 February 1865, a Wednesday.

[257] Holograph Petition of Mary Wells to Abraham Lincoln, National Archives Record Group 153-Court Martial Files, Adjutant Generals Office, Court-Martial File on Franklin Wells #LL2498, Old Military and Civil Records, File NWCTB2310246-KAT

[258] Judge Joseph Holt, Union Judge Advocate General.

[259] On this date, 8 February 1865, the Federal House of Representatives passed a joint resolution declaring that the Southern states were not entitled to representation in the Electoral College. Lincoln signed the resolution but disclaimed he had thus expressed any opinion as he also disclaimed any right to interfere in the counting of votes. E.B. Long, *The Civil War Day by Day* (Garden City, 1971), 636.

[260] Capt. B. F. Wells' letter datelined Mattituck, Nov. 21, 1887 to J. O. Kerbey. Petition of B. F. Wells, Accompanying Papers. (NA)

[261] Petition of B. F. Wells (NA)

[262] Major John S. Hard, 7th S.C. Infantry, Co. F., Kershaw's Brigade, was born in 1832 in Charleston S.C. He was killed on Sept. 20, 1863 in the Battle of Chickamauga.

[263] Capt. Andrew Robinson Govan, 17th Rgt., Miss. Vol. Infantry, Barksdale's Brigade, was born in 1836 in Tenn. He was mortally wounded in the Sept. 19-20, 1863 Chickamauga battle.

[264] Later promoted to Captain, James M. Crump, 17th Rgt., Miss. Vol. Infantry, Co. B., Barksdale's Brigade survived the war. Crump married Caroline H. Smith on Nov. 29, 1865 in Marshall County, Miss.

[265] Capt. B. F. Wells' letter datelined Mattituck, Sun., Nov. 6th [1887] to J. O. Kerbey. Petition of B. F. Wells, Accompanying Papers (NA)

[266] *The National Tribune* was a Civil War Veterans' weekly newspaper established in 1877 in Washington, D.C.

[267] Kerbey, *On the War Path,* 117-142, 153-164, 167-168, 301.

[268] A Confederate veteran's camp named for Naval Commander Matthew Fontaine Maury, CSN.

[269] Completed in 1849 and the third to stand on the site since 1735, St. George's Church faces Princess Anne Street at George Street.

[270] William A. Hill and Leander Cotton were proprietors of the Exchange Hotel (the building still stands). Hill died in 1890 and Cotton sold the business the next year. The Museum of the Exchange Hotel included a 12-pound cannon ball fired into the Wells House on Dec. 11, 1862, which was donated by Capt. Wells. The relics were sold to a Massachusetts firm in 1891. *Fredericksburg Virginia Star,* October 31, 1891.

[271] Kerbey, *The Boy Spy.*

[272] Mayor Montgomery Slaughter, Civil War Mayor of Fredericksburg, served from April 4, 1860 until removed by the military on July 15, 1868. The next Mayor elected by the people was not until July 1870. Quinn, *The History of the City of Fredericksburg,* 337.

[273] Enlisting in Cobbs' Georgia Legion at the beginning of the war, Merchant was detailed as a scout with Hampton's 2nd S.C. Cavalry. Merchant married the Wells' neighbor, young Henrietta Mills, in 1866.

[274] According to Captain Wells, Captain Martin of General Barksdale's staff was fond of Geno Wells but the feeling was not mutual.

[275] A Supreme Court Justice after the war, Lucius Q. C. Lamar first served as a Colonel in the 19th Mississippi. Suffering the effects of vertigo after action as regimental commander at Williamsburg, he resigned his commission. After serving abroad as a Special Commissioner, he returned home and reentered the military as a judge on the court of the 3rd Corps, receiving a parole at Appomattox.

[276] Juliet Annie, Ella and Maggie Downs, daughters of Virginia (Perry) Downs and William F. Downs. Isabella Benson, the wartime owner of the

Wells House, sold the property in September 1863 to Juliet A. Perry and it was passed down to her granddaughter Juliet Annie, remaining in the Downs family until 1917.

[277] Donated by Capt. Wells to the Exchange Hotel Museum in April 1888, this 12-lb. Shot was evidently part of the collection which was sold in October 1891 to a Massachusetts firm.

[278] Then First Lt. Edmund Kirby, USA, of the First U.S. Artillery. He reported that he *"had instructions to fire into the buildings on the opposite bank, where the enemy's sharpshooters were posted...we fired solid shot most of the day..."* O.R., 225.

[279] Juliet Annie Downs, daughter of William and Virginia Downs, was a music teacher. In 1897, she married William Gordon Smith at Fredericksburg's Trinity Church, and Major Kerbey was invited to attend the wedding. The invitation to Major J. O. Kirby (sic) is preserved today by Downs' descendant Judith (Hawkins) Barton. Juliet Annie (Downs) Smith inherited the Wells House, passed down from her grandmother, Juliet Anne (Jenkins) Perry (1814-1898). Perry had purchased the house from Isabella J. Benson on Sept. 28, 1863 (Deed Book "U" p. 22, recorded Dec. 29, 1864). Widowed in 1902, Annie remarried in 1904 to Henry D. Armstrong. The house was kept in the Downs family until 19 March, 1917 when Juliet Annie (Downs Smith) Armstrong and Henry D. Armstrong sold it to E. R. Purks (DB "KK" p. 557.

[280] The 1888-1889 *Fredericksburg City Directory* lists owner Juliet Ann Perry residing in the Wells House at Sophia Street, corner of George, which she purchased from Isabella Benson in 1863. Her 24-year old granddaughter Juliet Annie Downs, was a music teacher and church organist at the Fredericksburg Trinity Church, and sisters 21-year old M. Ella Downs and 20-year old Margaret "Maggie" Downs, both sang in the Trinity Church choir.

[281] Captain Daniel Murray. Lee, CSN, a grandson of Gen. Robert E. Lee.

[282] Gen. Fitzhugh Lee, CSA.

[283] Major Andrew J. Birdsall, USA.

[284] Wed., May 30, 1888.

[285] Under heavy Confederate fire, Hooker remained at Federal Hill long enough to scan the scene with his field glasses and issue orders to Couch, Howard and others.

[286] Fredericksburg resident Maj. W. Roy Mason of the *Sentry Box* wrote that he witnessed the death of Gen. Thomas R. R. Cobb of Georgia, who *fell at the door of Mrs. Martha Stevens... the Molly Pitcher of the war* [who] *refused to leave her house... Mrs. Stevens still lives in her old home at the foot of*

Marye's Heights, honored by every Confederate soldier... "Notes of a Confederate Staff-Officer," BLCW Vol III, 100.

[287] The Gunnery Spring was at Gunnery Green at the corner of Ferdinand Street and Gunnery Road. Long a Fredericksburg landmark, the marker and tablet are gone, and the spring covered over.

[288] The *Long Island Traveler*, Friday, August 4, 1899. Copy of Capt. Wells obituary courtesy of Southold Library and Mattituck-Laurel Library, Long Island, N.Y.

[289] Major J. Orton Kerbey. *An American Consul in Amazonia*. New York: William Edward Rudge, N.Y. 1911.

[290] Joseph Orton Kerbey letter dated July 28, 1898, published in *Outing Magazine*, , Sept. 1898, Vol. XXXII, No. 6

[291] A copy of Senate Bill S.3374 was found in Joseph A. Kerbey's Federal Pension File (NA).

[292] The Washington Post, Friday, Dec. 15, 1905, p. 2.

[293] J. Orton Kerbey, *The Land of To-morrow: A Newspaper Exploration up the Amazon and Over the Andes to the California of South America.* New York: W. F. Brainard, Publisher, 1906; (frontispiece portrait of Kerbey with the caption *A Twentieth Century Traveller in Peru.*)

[294] Colin Angus and Ian Mulgrew, *Amazon Extreme: Three Guys, One Rubber Raft, and the Most Dangerous River on Earth.* New York: Broadway Books, 2002.

[295] Kerbey, *An American Consul in Amazonia,* frontispiece portrait.

[296] Kerbey, *The Boy Spy,* 556.

[297] Joseph A. Kerbey is buried at Section Ns So Site 2328, Arlington National Cemetery, Arlington, Virginia.

Index

Aurora Borealis, appears after the battle, 232
Baker, Lafayette C., Chief of Detectives, 88, 132n
Ball, Wm. B., Col, CSA, 114, 115
Baltimore City Jail, political prisoner of, 183-185
Barksdale, William, B/G, CSA, 119-124, 129, 139, 159, 226
Battle of Fredericksburg, description, 148-159
Beale, Jane Howison, 55, 114-115
Belle Plain, Stafford County, 108, 109
Benson, Isabella and Mary Jane, owners of Wells House, 13-15, 276n, 279n
Birdsall, Andrew J., Supt. of Union Cemetery. 234-238. 183n
Black Jack, Capt., USA, Fort McHenry Provost, 195
Blockade running, 108-113, 169-181
Bombardment of Fredericksburg, description, 133-147
Boyd, Belle, 92
Braxton, Carter M., Lt., CSA, 26-27
Burnside, Ambrose, Gen., USA, defeat at Fredericksburg (mentioned) 153
Cameron, Simon, Union Secretary of War, 74, 115n
Camp M.F.Maury, Confederate Veterans, 222, 234
Carter, Addison Lombard, Judge, owner of *Monaskon*, 166, 235n

Chatham, 16, 57, 62, 110-111, 121, 133, 231, 163n
Chewning, John, sold *Monaskon* to Judge Carter, 166, 235n
Cobb Monument, 237
Congress, House Bill for relief of Capt. Wells, 217-218
Cook, Robert Thomas, Lt. Col, Phillips GA Legion, 158, 226n
Corotoman, 166, 236n
Cotton, Leander, owner of *Exchange Hotel*, 222-224, 270n
Covode, John, PA Congressman, friend of Kerbey, 71, 77, 80, 84-86, 88-89, 91, 101
Crawford, Harriet Wells, of Baltimore, MD, 108, 184, 203, 216, 243n
Crawford, James B. Baltimore spice merchant, 192, 250n
Crump, James M., Lt., 17th Miss. Inf., CSA 124, 190n
Denison, Charles, PA Congressman for Wyoming Valley, 187, 245n
Downs, Juliet Annie, inherited Wells House, invited Kerbey to wedding, 228-229, 279n
Eureka steam boat, xvii-xx, 6-7, 11-13, 16-18, 16-29, 47, 49, 52-55, 216, 19n
Exchange Hotel & Museum, 73, 222-224, 228, 111n, 270n, 277n
Farmers Bank, 58
Federal Hill, Gen. Hooker's temporary headquarters, 235, 285n
Fiser, John C., Capt., CSA, Comm. 17th Miss. Inf. 141, 208n.

Florence Nightengale, (Mamie Wells), 95
Free Blacks, 28, 48n
French John's wharf, 117
French Lady, (*Zarvona*), 41
Freshet, Rappahannock River great flood of April 1861, 16, 24n
Gentry, Mr., of Kentucky, union telegrapher, 101-103
Gordon, Ann Eliza Pleasants, 64, 99n
Gordon, Douglas Hamilton, Esq., 65, 98n
Govan, Andrew Robinson, Capt., CSA, 17th Miss. Inf., 124, 141, 189n
Greenlaw, Rose O'Neal, Confederate spy, 32
Gunnery Spring, 238, 287n
Hard, John S., Major, CSA, (Kershaw's Brigade) S.C. Inf. 123, 188n
Haupt, Herman, Colonel, Chief of U.S. Military Railroad, 59-62, 68, 72
Hawkins' Zouaves, 9th N.Y. Inf., parading in town, 86, 131n
Hay, John, Major, Pres. Lincoln's Private Secretary, 187-188, 209, 246n
Hill, William A., owner of *Exchange Hotel & Museum*, 222-225, 270n
Hodge, Rev. Archibald Alexander, 20-21, 31n
Hoffman, Henry C. "Barney," Col., USA, 23rd N.Y., xxii, 58-59, 73, 81-84

Hollins, George N., CSN Commodore, 37, 39, 43-44
Holt, Joseph, Union Judge Advocate General, 208-209, 258n
Hurkamp, Alice (later Mrs. Warren), 21, 33n
Hurkamp, John G., 21
Il Bacio, "The Kiss," 94, 139n
Kerbey, Joseph Andrew (Orton), Major, USA, xvi-xxii, 18, 67-73, 107, 147, 216-237, 245-254
Kirby, Edmund, Lt., USA, First U.S. Artillery, 228, 278n
Lamar, Lucius Q. C., Col., CSA, 19th Miss. Inf., Supreme Court Justice, 226, 275n
Lancaster Co. VA, Northern Neck, refuge at, 164-165, 170, 233n
Lee, Daniel Murray, Capt., CSN, grandson of R. E. Lee, 124, 230, 234-237, 281n
Lee, Fitzhugh, Gen., CSA, VA Governor, nephew of R.E. Lee, 234, 282n
Lee, Robert E., Gen, Cdr., CSA, xxi, 29, 36, 49, 114-121, 161-162,
Lee, William Henry Fitzhugh "Rooney," Gen., CSA, son of R.E.Lee, 49
Leonardtown, MD, Union held, 172, 176.
Letcher, John, Gov. of VA, 19, 25-26, 35-37.
Lewis, Henry H., 1st Lt., CSN, master-mind of St. Nicholas caper, 27, 29, 35, 37, 39, 42, 44n

Lincoln, Abraham, President, xvii, xx, 2, 7, 18, 20, 27, 46, 62-63, 105, 188-202, 206-210, 213, 147n

Lockwood, Henry Hays, Gen., USA, CG of Dept. of MD, 203, 205

Longstreet, James, Gen., CSA, 115-117, 121

Lorigan, George, marries Mamie Wells, 215

Lucerne Co. Historical Society, Wilkes-Barre, PA, staff, 123, 191n

Martindale, John Henry, Gen., USA, 203

Marye, John L. Jr., "Jack," 60

Marye, John L. Sr., 16, 19-20, 60, 73-74, 153, 231-232, 234, 237, 18n

Mattituck, Long Island, N.Y., 214-215, 219, 240-244

Maury, Betty Herndon (Maury), 35-37, 46-48, 56, 63

Maury, Matthew Fontaine, Commander, CSN, 34-36, 41, 55

McCallum, Daniel C., Col., USA, Dir. of U.S. Military RR, 98-101

McLaws, Lafayette, Gen., CSA, 120-122, 131, 136, 206n

McPhail, J. L., MD Provost-Marshal General, 199, 200, 255n

Memorial Day, in Fredericksburg 1888, 233-237, 284n

Merchant, Rufus Bainbridge, Cobbs Brigade, CSA, 131-132, 225, 233

Mills Family, daughter Henrietta, 131

Mississippi 13th Infantry, CSA, 122, 130

Mississippi 17th Infantry, CSA, 121, 129

Mississippi Brigade, pickets guard town, 140, 232

Mississippi, 18th Infantry, CSA, 121

Monaskon plantation, Lancaster Co., VA, 166-169, 203, 235n, 238n

Monaskon, "old Aunt Bettie," taught how to card, spin cotton, 164-167

Monaskon, "old Negroes on the place," 164-167

Monaskon, "old Uncle Jesse," a storyteller, had oyster roasts, 166-168

Montgomery, Morris, of Maryland, resided near town wharf in 1861, 199, 254n

Morris, William W., Gen., USA, Fort Henry Cdr. 192, 193, 195, 211-212

Nagle, James, Gen., USA, 149, 151, 281n

Oath of Allegiance, Federal, 175-176, 179

Old Capitol Prison, 169-171, 184, 202, 225, 239n

Owen, Joshua T., Col., USA, Cdr. Phila..Brigade, 146, 158, 313n, 227n

Parker, Foxhall A., Capt., Commodore, USN, 193-194, 206, 252n

Patrick, Marsena, Gen., USA, Provost Marshal, 57-65, 103-106, 115-121

Peel, Addison, Adjutant, 19th Miss. Inf., Co. I, 125

Peel, Albert L., 19th Miss. Inf., 125, 128

Peel, Dr. Robert Hunter, Surgeon, 19th Miss. Inf. Rgt., 125-128, 194n

Peel, Thomas Jefferson, 19th Miss. Inf., Col. J, 125

Peel, Volney, 3d Miss. Cavalry, 125

Peel, William Hunter, 11th Miss. Inf., Co. C, 125

Perry, Juliet Ann Jenkins, owner of Wells' House, 279n
Phillips House, 57, 111, 131, 162n
Phillips, Alexander Keene, 4-5, 57, 111, 173, 231
Pinkerton Spy, 87-91
Planter's Hotel, 73, 112n
Point Lookout, 171-175, 178, 180
Pontoon boat, towed by canoe down Rappahannock River, 164
Presbyterian Church, 20-21, 28, 128n
Presidential pardon, Capt. Wells, 210, 213
Quinn, Silvanus J., Capt., CSA, 13th Miss. Rgt., Co. A, Barksdale's Brigade, 130, 233
Rats, for food, selling to soldiers, 161, 229n
Raymond, Henry J., Editor, the N.Y. Times, 192, 197-200, 251n
Relay House, 194
Religious Revival of soldiers in town, 129
Robinson, Peter B., *Eureka* pilot, 53-54, 20n
Rodenbough, Theophilus, Gen., USA, endorser of Kerbey book, 68-71, 106n
Ruggles, Mortimer B., Major, CSA, 34
Ruggles, Richardetta Hooe, Mrs. Gen. Daniel Ruggles, 24-25, 34
Russell, Robert S., married Jennie Wells, 215
Scott, James McClure, Jr., Pvt. CSA, Braxton's Artillery, 27, 42n
Shaffer, Mary Holmes, of PA, married Kerbey, 220, 139n
Sigfried, Joshua K., Col, USA, Cdr. 48th Pa Inf. (Capt. Wren's C.O.), 149

Slaughter, Montgomery, wartime mayor, xx, 22-23, 55, 60, 115-119, 130, 225
Snowden, home of John S. Stansbury, 115
Sorrel, G. Moxley, Major, CSA, Gen. Longstreet's staff, 117
Stanton, Edwin M., Union Sec. of War, succeeded Cameron in '62, 66, 88, 92, 98, 101-103, 105, 192-193, 225
Stephens, Martha, house on Sunken Road, 235-236
St. George's Church, steeple, town clock, 111, 222, 269n
Stiles, Joseph C., Rev., Chaplain of 17th Miss. Inf. 129
Sumner, E. V., Maj. Gen., letter to Mayor Slaughter, 116, 119
Teed, Isaac N., marries Sue Wells, 215, 219
Thomas, Richard H., Col., CSA, aka *Zarvona,* 36, 38-40, 42-44, 71n
Trinity Church, in town, Juliet Downs organist, 228, 279n
U.S.S. Currituck, Federal gunboat, 162, 184, 202, 231n
U.S.S. Louisiana, "peeping Tom" at porthole, 180-181
Wallace, Lewis, Gen., USA, State of MD, 187, 208, 211, 244n
War of 1812, Redcoats, 167
Wells House, photo gallery 255-259
Wells House, post-war tourist attraction, 224-226
Wells, Benjamin Franklin, Jr. 18, 51, 53, 157, 162, 225n, 232n

Wells, Benjamin Franklin, Sr., xvi-xxii, 5, 7-12, 15, 17, 21, 27, 44, 51-52, 54, 75, 79, 88-89, 91, 107, 121, 162, 169, 183, 202-205, 239n
Wells, Jane Teed, Mrs. Capt. Wells, 17, 216, 241, 244
Wells, Mary A. "Mamie," xvii, sxiii, xx, 13, 17-18, 75-76, 95, 108, 112, 121, 124, 134-135, 148-149, 156, 161, 169, 183, 195, 202, 207-208, 215, 217, 220, 226
Wells, Sarah Eugenia "Geno," xvii-xxii, 18, 75-101, 105-106, 124, 215-228, 239-240
Wells, Susan Frances, "Sue," 17, 75-78, 81, 95-97, 101, 219, 226
Wells, William of Southold, L.I., N.Y., 8, 83
White House, Mamie Wells at, 187-192, 200-208, 209-210
Willard Hotel, Wash., D.C., 197
Wren, James, Capt., 48th PA Inf., knew Capt. Wells from PA, 150, 215, 216n

CPSIA information can be obtained at www.ICGtesting.com
Printed in the USA
267191BV00005B/3/P